America
the Raped

THE ENGINEERING MENTALITY
AND THE DEVASTATION OF A CONTINENT

BY
GENE MARINE

 SIMON AND SCHUSTER · NEW YORK

For my mother

CONTENTS

FOREWORD

BELIEVE IT OR NOT, I wrote this book because I finished early with Isaac Deutscher.

Early in 1967, *Ramparts* was about to publish a part of his important work on the Russian revolution, and I took it home to trim a couple of lines so it would fit into the allotted space. I finished early, got to bed early, got up early, got to work early—and in the hallway encountered Warren Hinckle, who was and is my boss.

"Why don't you," he said casually, "do an article on conservation?"

I reminded him, of course, that I grew up in San Francisco's Mission District, that the absence of concrete makes me nervous, and that the effect of fresh air on my lungs after all these years might be disastrous. He said something blithe about a "fresh approach." I tried saying things in dire tones about the expense account, and he only said, "Well, of course you have to go look at the Great Swamp and everything." "What," I asked quite seriously, "is a Great Swamp?"

It seems, now, a long way from there to here. The article turned out to be two long articles, not really on "conservation" at all, and—after some important conceptual instruction from my agent, Cyrilly Abels, and a lot of help from Richard Kluger of Simon and Schuster (which included stocking my library with related books and materials)—the articles turned into this book.

Along the way, there were some second thoughts, some new discoveries, some decisions that seem easier in retrospect than they were at the time.

Putting the material into book form seemed to make it necessary to look more carefully at its historical and social significance, to probe more deeply into the meanings of the subject. The "en-

gineering mentality" is more than a glibly chosen target, more than
a handy gimmick on which to string a collection of Luddite complaints. It is a serious threat to other values, values which seem to
me more truly human and therefore—anthropocentrically, no
doubt—more valuable.

But to change the concept, to attempt a serious and abstract
discussion of trends in American (or worldwide) values, would
be to write another book entirely; and to be honest, I am a reporter and uncomfortable in the role of sociologist, political
theorist or scholar. Happily, the book I would have wanted to
write (and could not have written) has already been done, and for
those who are not fazed by a serious and sometimes difficult
work, it is the intellectual tree on which this book is a twig. It is
Jacques Ellul's *The Technological Society* (New York: Alfred A.
Knopf, Inc., 1964; originally published in French in 1954). Few
will agree with all of an abstract and complex discussion by a
French Catholic sociologist; but he has put the problem and its
dimensions so that its immediate applications in this book are, I
hope, apparent.

As a reporter, then—albeit a concerned one—I have decided to
stay with my "story," to try to be clear at the expense of scholarly
apparatus, rather than meticulous at the expense of readability.
In practice this has turned out to mean a lot of notes at the end
of the book—because the seriousness of my intent must imply the
full identification of sources and, indeed, biases—but no little
numbers on the pages, because they are temptations to distrac-
tion. A glance at the notes will show the method I have chosen;
it has its drawbacks, but so has any other compromise. I hope it
works.

In the text and especially in the notes, I have tried to express
some of my thanks to a number of people, and inevitably I'll
leave someone out—for which my apology in advance. A few people deserve special mention.

In a first book, there is always the temptation to offer gratitude to anyone who has ever been of help over a professional lifetime. I'll resist the temptation here with but one exception: I am
compelled to mention the enormous debt I owe to Carey Mc-

Williams, editor of *The Nation,* of whom I can truly say that he made a friend and a writer of me at the same time.

Of course my gratitude to Warren Hinckle and to *Ramparts* is great, and not only for what amounted to a weeks-long paid vacation in virtually every beauty spot in America. In the articles that led to this book, as in everything else I've written for *Ramparts,* I was completely free to select my own approach and to develop my own material. That's as much as any reporter can ask, and much more than most ever get.

To the rest of the *Ramparts* staff, my thanks not only for encouragement but for filling in so that the book could get written at all; and a special note of thanks to Anna Willis-Betts, who came up with an unending stream of clippings and other useful information during all of 1967.

On my search for information itself, I must have been helped importantly by several dozen people, but I have to single out a few for acknowledgment: Rod Vandivert of the Scenic Hudson Preservation Conference; Ron Dagon, the Croton-on-Hudson city ecologist; Stewart Ogilvy of the Sierra Club and *Fortune;* Gary Soucie of the Sierra Club in New York City; photographer Pat Caulfield; Assistant Secretary of the Interior Stanley A. Cain; Senator Gaylord Nelson of Wisconsin; Representative John Saylor of Pennsylvania; Frank Kieliger, of the staff of Representative Phillip Burton of California; John Milton of the Conservation Foundation; Stewart Brandborg of the Wilderness Society; Bill Odum of the University of Miami Marine Institute (who provided a quick cram course on the ecology of southern Florida); Superintendent Roger Allin of Everglades National Park; Rod Pegues of the Sierra Club in Seattle; and Hugh Nash of the Sierra Club in San Francisco. None of them, of course, is to be blamed for anything you don't like about what you read; some of them don't like some of it either.

Finally, there are three people whose contribution has been very special indeed:

In my beginning research, I came across Dr. Eugene P. Odum's *Ecology*—a superb little book published in 1963 for the college-freshman level in Holt, Rinehart and Winston's Modern Biology series. It's available in paperback for $2.25, and I cannot urge the reading of another book more strongly. Later I was to meet Dr. Odum. His knowledge, his wisdom and his insight were of major importance to my writing, which is not to say that any of my errors or omissions should be blamed on him or that my ideas are necessarily at all like his.

Attorney David Sive, who has represented the Sierra Club, forced my mind to consideration of the deeper implications of the data I was gathering, and thus changed both the tone and the meaning of both my *Ramparts* articles and this book.

And then there is Judith Van Allen Marine. I cannot, as so many writers do, thank her for her meticulous reading of the manuscript, for her superb typing, for her devoted preparation of the index. She is too busy and too valuable a person to waste her time with such secretarial nonsense. But I can, and do, thank her for being alive and for having been where I was while the articles, and then the book, were being written. No nourishing plant was ever more necessary to an ecosystem than she is to mine.

G.M.

1 · WHO NEEDS A SWAMP?

FIFTY YEARS AGO, more or less, Americans rose up in anger against the rape of their country.

The fight of a few dozen men, led by giants—Theodore Roosevelt, Gifford Pinchot, John Muir, John Wesley Powell—was against the uncaring lumbermen, who despoiled hill and valley and left eroding soil and sick rivers in their wake; against the unthinking farmers and stockmen, who replaced precious and fertile grasslands with thorn scrubs and dust bowls; against the mindless hunters who wiped out a hundred species and endangered a hundred more. The spoils of their victory are the national parks and forests, the wildlife refuges and wilderness areas, the national seashores and monuments, the soil conservation services, the hundreds of state parks and forests and preserved areas that followed them into existence.

Left when the battle had ended was a mushy purr-word—"conservation"—and a vague, persisting conviction that except for a few renegade lumber companies and mining firms, the rapine had ended. In fact, it has hardly begun.

The old rapists have learned technique. The Georgia-Pacific Company still strips virgin redwood and Douglas fir from the slopes of California's northern coast and pine from the Passamaquoddy Indian Township in Maine. But the company has learned to donate a few thousand dollars to a study of the habits and habitats of the American eagle; and when conservationists protested a proposed gypsum plant on the Hudson River at Little Stony Point, New York, Georgia-Pacific gracefully withdrew, murmuring, "We don't want to spoil the gorge." Pacific Gas and Electric, Kennecott Copper, Consolidated Edison, the assorted lumbermen looking covetously at the Adirondack Forest Preserve and the watershed region of Idaho's upper Selway River—they are all still with us, substituting seduction for rape wherever possible but no less determined to have their way with the land.

Their younger brothers, too—the pulp mills, the manufacturing chemists, the steelmakers, the myriad industrialists who pump garbage into our streams and sulfur dioxide into our skies —have learned the techniques of seduction. Detergent manufacturers, who for years assured us that their products weren't hurting the water—but who were forced to change the products anyway—now brag about the change, as if it were their own idea, in a periodical devoted to "water conservation" and carefully distributed to conservation-minded groups across the country.

But while a dozen groups have arisen to keep the old rapists in check—or at least to try to—the new rapists are loose upon the land. Theirs, still, are the vicious, violent, *laissez-faire* techniques of the turn of the century. They are not necessarily employed by lumber companies or mining companies or railroads; a lot of them work for you and me. They are the public servants who work for the Port of New York Authority or for the state highway commissions. They work for the United States Forest Service or the National Park Service. They are in the Army's Corps of Engineers and the Bureau of Reclamation and the Bureau of Public Roads. They are dedicated, single-minded men. And when they talk—which is as rarely as they can manage—theirs is the language of fanatics.

They are called Engineers.

They build bridges and dams and highways and causeways and flood-control projects. They *manage* things. They commit rape with bulldozers.

They are hard to fight off, because they must be fought off with words, and the weapons we have are inadequate. In New Jersey there is a fantastic land of wonders, still substantially as it was when the glaciers retreated three thousand years ago. It is called the Great Swamp. The Engineers of the Port of New York Authority want to put a jetport on it—an absurd and irreversible crime. But who needs a "swamp"?

The salt marshes of the Georgia coast have become an outstanding laboratory for the study of the bases of life; there, the University of Georgia Marine Station has learned much of how shrimp and other seafood depend on the unusual—and diminishing—estuarine conditions for their life. Yet Dr. Eugene Odum, the leading researcher in the field, reports that "we are often asked, 'Of what value is the salt marsh?' or 'What can be done with all that wasted land?'"

The Engineers know: build a dam, build a levee, build a wall, dredge, fill, *change*. The marsh grass will die, the phytoplankton will die, the algae will die—and thus the shrimp and the bass will die, but the Engineers don't care. What good is a salt marsh? Who needs a swamp?

The question itself hides an assumption. It implies, says Professor Ian Cowan of the University of British Columbia, "that the biological world can be divided into the useful and the useless with obvious corollaries of attitude and action." Even the land is divided into "the useful and the useless" by the Engineers, including those in my home state of California who recently set out guidelines "for evaluating recreation activity and resources in connection with water resources development." Along with some "excellent quality" areas and some "fair quality" lands, the California Engineers made another classification:

Poor Quality: Recreation activity not prohibited but limited by lack of facilities or resource. Uncontrolled environment.

So much for hiking in the untouched woods, fishing in the unspoiled river, getting away from a jammed crowd of fellow vacationers.

When some of these remarks appeared in article form in *Ramparts*, I heard from a number of engineers, some of whom accused me of issuing a blanket condemnation of all engineers for sins of which only a few are guilty—several of them pointed out that the Army Engineers get the men who are left over after the good jobs are gone—and others of whom argued that after all, we have to have engineers, and it's up to the rest of society to decide what they ought to be doing. "Or in other words," one of them added, "if one wishes both to keep goats and grow flowers, the goats must be kept out of the garden."

Of course there are "good engineers." A couple of them are quoted elsewhere in this book. And in a sense, the book is *about* keeping the goats out of the garden. But that analogy is not so good as it looks; it assumes that we want to keep goats *over there* and raise flowers *over here*. A human society does not divide so neatly. The question is, whose yard is it and who's planting it?

So not all engineers are the Engineers of whom I write, and for that matter not all the Engineers are engineers (it's no accident, for example, that public relations, as a profession, has been spoken of as "the engineering of consent"). But neither is the word chosen, nor the attack directed, arbitrarily. For there is, in America, such a thing as an "engineering mentality." There is an engineers' way of looking at problems, an engineering approach to public questions, to planning, even to correcting the malfunctions that were introduced by Engineers in the first place. It is the simple, supposedly pragmatic approach of taking the problem as given, ignoring or ruthlessly excluding questions of side effects, working out "solutions" that meet only the simplest definitions of the problem. It is an approach that never seeks out a larger context, that resents the raising of issues it regards as extraneous to the engineering problem involved.

See a river as a fisherman, and you see it as something from which to extract fish. Left alone by the rest of us, you might overfish it, even kill off the game fish or some other life form that is in balance with it. See the river as a lumberman, and it is something that will carry logs; in its upper reaches you see the riverbed as a potential roadbed for dragging logs out of the wilderness. Left alone, you might destroy the life of the river. See the river as an industrialist, and you see it as a cheap and convenient carrier for your industrial wastes. See it as a city official, and it is a handy place to dump garbage and sewage.

Of some of these problems the rest of us are becoming aware. Fishermen themselves are aware of the dangers inherent in their own activity. But we do not understand that to see the river as an engineer is to build a bridge across it—and that building that bridge may have consequences just as disastrous, though somewhat more remote, as overfishing or garbage dumping. The point is not that we ought not to build bridges; the point is that the Engineers—all of those who take the engineering approach, build the bridge and get the people and the cars from one side of the river to the other and to hell with the side effects—are shaping the nation unchecked, molding the land and murdering thousands of its inhabitants, raping America while the rest of us look the other way.

For these reasons, the phrase "engineering mentality" is not lightly or whimsically chosen. It describes a way of looking at things, even a way of defining words, that is typical of an engineer's approach, even though there are individual engineers who are exceptions and even though many, possibly even most, Engineers are not technically engineers. Engineers, devotees of the engineering mentality, are people who see the world as engineers, as a class, are taught to see it; to try to talk to an Engineer is precisely like the experience of landscape architect Lawrence Halprin when he tries to talk to engineers:

. . . when you talk about values, they think you are talking about esthetics. And when you talk about esthetics, they think you're talking about beauty. And when you talk about beauty, they think you are talking about decorative additions. It's very difficult to get across that when we talk about environmental planning and value judgments, it has very little to do with the detailing of a bridge railing or improving the appearance of something an engineer has already done.

The Engineers are indeed dividing the biological world "into the useful and the useless with obvious corollaries of attitude and action." And our own attitudes and actions don't help much in checking them.

Everybody wants to save deer. Deer are lovely, gentle things with soft brown eyes, and we are reared on the legend of Bambi. But who wants to save a menacing wolf or a skulking coyote? In some areas we still pay $50 apiece for cougar—and scream to high heaven (or, more importantly, to Washington) about crop damage by runaway populations of deer. No matter that a renowned wildlife ecologist can insist that "biologically, the wolf can only help to preserve deer range . . . in a naturally productive condition." In northern Minnesota, America's only breeding ground of gray wolves, killing a wolf will still earn you a bounty.

Everybody is for "conservation"—but what is it?

Does it mean more campsites in Yosemite National Park? Does it mean the absolute preservation, untouched by campsites or roads or anything else, of the Great Smokies or the Cascades—to be enjoyed only by the strong and hardy with packs on their backs? Does it mean careful, controlled "harvesting" of timber (as in national forests) or its being left entirely alone? Does it mean "conserving" the energy of a river by damming it for hydroelectric power and flood control, or leaving it alone in freedom to be beautiful and unproductive—and occasionally to destroy?

In the Wilderness Society, or the Sierra Club, or the Conservation Foundation, nobody knows. Each has its ideas about a particular location at a particular time, but on the general question each will murmur platitudes about something for everybody. Some even have specific plans along those lines, but they don't know what "conservation" means, and they admit it under pressure.

But the Engineers know. They can quote what they think is Pinchot: Conservation is the wise use of natural resources. And the wise use of any natural resource is to change it for the better, use it, divert its course if it's a river, change its shape if it's a mountain, improve its growth if it's a forest—even if it's a forest that has been doing quite well, thank you, for several thousand years before the Engineers came.

Conservation is clean air and clean water and clean soil—but what is "clean"? Free of pollutants? Or free of nutrients? Free of *some* pollutants and less dirtied with others? What new interactions will result? And who draws the lines?

Conservation is open space—but what is "open"? A place to drive through, to see green and lovely areas instead of roadside signs? A place to camp overnight? A place that must be reached by horse or mule or on foot?

Conservation is saving redwoods—but do they have to be the same redwoods that were there a hundred or three hundred years ago? Why?

Two generations ago, John Muir and Gifford Pinchot fought for different versions of what "conservation" might mean, and the fight is still going on—debilitating the fight against the Engineers, who hold the concepts of both men in contempt. The descendants of Pinchot, who want to manage for use, to build access roads and campsites, quibble with the descendants of Muir, who want untouched wilderness—and the Engineers calmly build freeways across the middle of the argument.

When someone notices the Engineers, it is usually in one place at one time. A fight is mounted against a road here, a dam there, a utility plant in another place.

But we can watch a road built across the Great Cascades, and there will still be ample space. We can sacrifice a bass spawning ground and a treasured forest to allow Con Ed to dig its hole in Storm King and flood the trees behind with its reservoir. We will survive, and so will the Great Cascades and the Hudson River. The Engineers, however, are not only straining to fill in the Grand Canyon and to dam the last wild stretch of the Missouri, to wall off the rich estuaries of Long Island and to cover the Great Swamp with asphalt. They are in every section of every state, ripping, tearing, building, changing.

Theirs is a rape from which America can never, never recover.

II · THE BUG OF BERMUDA

IN 1944, a retired American industrialist, who owned a handsome home in Paget Parish, Bermuda, decided that the place would look nicer with a few decorative shrubs around the house.

He looked around, but he didn't see anything he liked. The landscape was dominated then—as it had been 332 years earlier when the first British colonists settled—by groves of Bermuda cedars, many of them fifty feet tall. Their reddish-brown, knotty wood was a Bermuda staple, not only as firewood and lumber but as a raw material for souvenirs, as coffin material, and—in cross section, so tough were its fibers—as flagstones. Most important to the island, rows of these tall, aromatic evergreens gave Bermuda its tropical flavor, served as windbreaks for crops, and were anchors for the soil to keep it from being washed into the ever-precious rainwater on which the island colony depends.

There were 2,000,000 Bermuda cedars.

They are too big for decorative shrubs, however, and the prosperous American decided to import a few shrubs from a mainland nursery. They were carefully inspected at both ends of their trip, of course, but the inspectors overlooked at least one pregnant *Carulaspis visci*. The *Carulaspis visci* is a scale insect that reproduces (without need for a mate) throughout most of the year. Distributed by wind, it attaches itself to a plant, drills into a twig, and grows a protective "scale." After reproduction, the tiny young emerge to ride the wind again and repeat the process.

One year after the American imported his shrubs, the Bermuda legislature appropriated £14,000 to exterminate the insects before the insects exterminated the Bermuda cedar. The powerful insecticides that might have reached the *Carulaspis visci* under their protective scales could not be used, lest they get into the water (on the mainland at about the same time, we were happily pouring DDT all over everything). Imported ladybird beetles, which control the scale insect in Ontario, were not successful—there are beetle-eating lizards in Bermuda which don't exist in Ontario.

Four years later—five years after the prosperous American decided to decorate his grounds—the Bermuda legislature gave up. The appropriations now are for removing dead cedars to where you can't see them from the road. There are no windbreaks now to protect the banana plants, whose leaves are shredded and dried by wind; Bermuda now imports bananas.

In Africa, it seemed fairly obvious that somebody ought to kill some crocodiles. Most people believe that they keep the valuable fish population down, and occasionally they eat a domestic animal or even a small child. With a little prodding from traders who know the value of crocodile hides, thousands have been killed since World War II.

Today, the *Tilapia*—an important fish that provides protein to African diets—is in danger of disappearing, its eggs being eaten by dragonfly young, by carnivorous water beetles and by crabs, all of which used to be held down by the crocs. Bigger *Tilapias,* in greater numbers, are eaten by the widespread Mozambique catfish, once themselves the prey of adolescent crocodiles.

Around Lake Victoria, Africans once treasured the rare lungfish *Protopterus* as a delicacy and cursed the abundant crocodiles that ate them. Today, plentiful lungfish attack more valuable fish, even in fishermen's nets; they have become a pest.

In the Malagasy Republic, stray dogs and wild pigs, whose young were once crocodile prey, now raid cultivated land and threaten farmers with financial ruin—and the dogs have brought several outbreaks of rabies as well.

Throughout Africa, governments are being called upon to solve the problem of villages flooded when plant growth chokes a river; nobody remembers that the crocodile used to keep the channels open.

For a time, governments were also called on to protect the crops of villages from raids by suddenly abundant hippopotami. Today, the hippo-hunting—itself originally an unforeseen result of crocodile-hunting—has nearly wiped out the hippos. The destruction of hippos, in turn, has led to the growth of papyrus—through which the hippos once maintained broad trails—to the point at which the papyrus dams rainwater and floods crops. Small children are not so often eaten by crocodiles any more: they starve.

It all seemed so simple, at first.

Ecology is the study of how things fit together, or, if you prefer, the study of interactions between life forms and their environments. We know very little about it, but Engineers know—or act as if they knew—absolutely nothing.

Most of us have had to learn a little ecology in the past few years in order to deal with the political problems of radioactive fallout and air and water pollution. Some of us learned that, while the Engineers in the Atomic Energy Commission were telling us that the strontium-90 on some area or other contained less radioactivity than a watch dial, the soil and then the grass and then the cows were gradually concentrating it into meaningful amounts. Others of us learned that a harmless scattering of DDT (0.02 parts per million) in the water of Clear Lake, California, was concentrated by plankton (to 5 parts per million), concentrated again by fish (to several hundred parts per million), and ultimately killed the grebes that ate the fish. In the tissues of the birds, DDT concentration was 1,600 parts per million.

This phenomenon of "concentration"—the ability of some life form or other to pick a particular element or substance out of its environment and, so to speak, to collect it all in one place—is common enough, but still little understood by a lot of people. It means that the killer clam of the Pacific Ocean, for example, has what we might call a special mechanism for getting all the cobalt it can out of the water it lives in; when nuclear tests in the Pacific released into the water an amount of radioactive cobalt so small that instruments could barely detect it, the clams nevertheless "found" it all, and did so with such efficiency that Navy radiologists were later alarmed that someone might have eaten one and ingested more radioactive material than is good for the human body.

The process works so well that some species will concentrate other elements related to the one they're really after. The best-known example is the concentration of strontium-90 by cattle in the United States: Sr^{90} is related to calcium, and if the cows were getting enough calcium their systems wouldn't make use of the strontium-90 they found sprinkled around their pastures. But if the calcium was a little short, into the bones and into the cows' milk went the deadly and long-lived radiostrontium. From cows it went, too often, to babies.

But to know how it works is not to say that we know *when* it will work. As an example of how little we know, four Italian scientists spent five years—from 1960 to 1964—studying Sr^{90} concentrations in the Adriatic and the Ligurian Seas. They found that the concentration was higher in Adriatic water than in Ligurian water. But they also found that plankton in the Ligurian water concentrated twelve times as much strontium-90 as plankton in the Adriatic water. They don't know why; they think it has something to do with the presence of protozoa called *Acantharia* in the Ligurian Sea, but they aren't sure.

There are a hundred examples of this concentration factor. On the Columbia River, the Engineers managing nuclear reactors release phosphorus into the water in very small, nonpollutant amounts, but in radioactive form. Not long ago somebody discovered that wild geese, which get their food from the river, concentrate radiophosphorus in their eggs. A gram of egg yolk turned out to have several thousand times the amount of phosphorus found in a gram of river water.

The Engineers never count on this sort of thing.

The government builds dams and highways, levees and reactors, and every one rips into an ecological system far more complex than anyone yet understands. "No one," says Dr. Eugene P. Odum, who is one of the world's leading ecologists, "has yet identified and catalogued all the species of plants, animals and microbes to be found in any large area, as for example, a square mile of forest." But science in government is dominated by the Engineers, and the government is doing almost no work in ecology, giving almost no grants, encouraging almost no one. Instead, as could be expected of Engineers, they study things that somebody wants to manage.

The Office of Science and Technology, for instance, reported in

1966 that almost all government research related to "conservation" is

concerned with economically valuable species, such as those used by man for food or fiber, foods of domestic and game animals, and pests and disease organisms. Considerable attention is being devoted to recreational facilities and game species of birds and mammals and a large part of the expenditures is utilized for studies of soil stability and hydrologic processes.

Just so you'll know the jargon, that's called "mission-oriented" research. Dr. Sidney Galler, assistant secretary for science of the Smithsonian Institution, was asked for his own estimate, and said that "less than $5 million in 1965 were invested in the acquisition of basic knowledge and the discovery of new ecological principles" as opposed to "well over $200 million" for mission-oriented research.

What are we talking about? When most people think of ecology —if they have ever heard of it at all—they tend to think of food chains: minnows eat mosquitoes, bream eat minnows, bass eat bream. Odum calls it the grass-rabbit-fox chain, and it is, of course, an important factor in ecology. Dr. F. Raymond Fosberg told a symposium not long ago: "I remember when I was a kid being tremendously impressed by a statement that was made, and I have no reason to doubt this statement, that the progeny of a single gravid rose aphid for a year, if unchecked by all environmental factors, would equal the bulk of the earth."

A pair of writers on this same general subject have noted that "without hawks, owls and other predatory birds who feed on the rodent population, the United States would be covered with 2½ inches of mice from coast to coast." And famed conservation writer Peter Farb, noting the folly with which wolves, coyotes and bears have been wiped out or decimated in the West, writes: "The reduction of these natural predators has reverberated throughout Yellowstone. As just one example, elk have increased phenomenally and have chewed through their habitat in such numbers that they have ruined it. The result is that in one of the continent's havens for a dwindling wildlife, some elk have had to be shot almost every year (5,000 were killed in 1962 alone)."

Pretty silly, isn't it?

Even that much understanding of ecology is enough to warrant a second, harder look at the Engineers. Consolidated Edison's operation at Storm King would probably suck up the eggs of the bass that go up the Hudson to spawn—and thereby affect bass fishing, and God knows what other kinds of life, as far away as South Carolina. The fantastic Corps of Engineers plan for walling up the Long Island estuaries (as "hurricane protection") would probably finish off a hundred species, as the growing of ducks on Long Island Sound has finished off the once-thriving oyster beds (the additional nutrients provided by duck manure made it possible for a different variety of plankton to become dominant —but it happened to be a kind that oysters can't digest).

There is more to ecology, though, than food chains and gross changes in the environment. Nobody cares much about the mussels of the Georgia salt marshes except a few raccoons who make an occasional meal of them; there aren't very many of them and they don't grow very fast. But the mussels, as it happens, play an important part in recycling the phosphorus in the whole system, making it available for use and reuse by the marsh grasses and other forms of life in the marsh—and on these depend the shrimp, which are a major economic factor in the area and, not incidentally, feed a number of human beings.

Ecologists, by the way, are a little worried about phosphorus. It seems that man-made erosion has overtaken the natural mechanisms by which phosphorus is used and then returned to availability. As any farmer who uses fertilizer knows, we make up for this, at the moment, by mining phosphate rock. But there will come a day.

Ecologists use the word "niche" to make clear that every life form and every element in an ecosystem plays its role—even though the actors in similar dramas may not look at all alike. It's a young science, and not everybody is agreed on the use of terms, but most people go along with Dr. Odum, who, in what is probably the best elementary book on ecology, puts it this way:

. . . the grazing kangaroos of the Australian grasslands are ecological equivalents of the grazing bison (or the cattle that have replaced them) on North American grasslands since they have a similar functional position in the ecosystem in a similar habitat. Ecologists use the term *habitat* to mean the place where an organism lives, and the term *ecological niche* to mean the role that the organism plays in the eco-system; the habitat is the "address," so to speak, and the niche is the "profession." Thus, we can say that the kangaroo, bison and cow, although not closely related taxonomically, occupy the same niche when present in grassland ecosystems.

It isn't *hawks* that are important if you want to keep from walk-ing around with mice up to your ankles; it's the filling of the niche now filled by hawks—a niche that also relates to dozens of other life forms and substances as well as to mice. It's difficult to overstress the importance of some of these concepts; they turn up no matter what the "environment," or ecosystem, you're talk-ing about, as Dr. Stanley Cain recently noted:

I have been fascinated to note that some leaders in medical research have recently arrived independently at the sound ecological conclusion that it might be more desirable to replace harmful viruses and bacteria with innocuous types than to leave niches open by trying to keep our bodies free of those forms. By the same principle, the broad-spectrum antibiotic or pesticide is likely to empty not just one niche but several. Ever since antibiotics came into use, physicians have been plagued by secondary infections resulting from the destruction of an innocuous intestinal flora thus leaving ecological niches available for drug-resistant and pathogenic staphylococci.

Thanks to Rachel Carson and others, most of us know about what broad-spectrum pesticides can do to various ecological niches; widespread, ignorant use of DDT has polluted water all over the world (it has been found, for example, in the fat of Antarctic penguins). But even worse than the pollution—worse to think about, anyway—is the ignorance that accompanied it.

Proteins—the "building blocks" of everything alive, including you and me—are nitrogen compounds. But nitrogen is a scarce element—90 percent of all the nitrogen there is can be found in the air, and plants cannot use it directly. They depend on certain bacteria, and on blue-green algae, to convert the nitrogen to am-monia, which they can use. On top of that, there are a couple of other kinds of bacteria that change the ammonia into nitrate, which is the way most plants actually do use it. You and I get our nitrogen mostly from the plants. Even then it would all disappear except for still other bacteria, which recover the nitrogen from dead plants and animals and turn it back into ammonia. Finally, all the nitrogen in the world would have turned into ammonia a long time ago except for still other types of bacteria that can regenerate molecular nitrogen from nitrate.

Each of these bacteria, each of these algae, fills a niche. DDT kills bacteria (and empties niches), and nobody has ever known exactly *what* bacteria. If DDT had proved to be toxic to any of the types of bacteria mentioned above, man—in his unthinking attempt to kill a few plant pests—would have wiped himself and every other form of life off the face of the earth.

More will be said about the "population explosion" in later chapters, but merely to mention it is to make clear the importance of another ecological term we would do well to keep in mind: the *limiting factor*. It's fairly obvious that food supplies and space are limiting factors on human population growth, and that the hawk population is a limiting factor on the mouse population. But other things can limit as well. Temperature, for instance; trout are known to be "stenothermal," meaning that they cannot tolerate a wide range of temperatures (bass are "eurythermal," the opposite word). Cut down the trees along a river—thus letting more sunlight in—and the trout may well disappear. Too much or not enough of anything—even light, under some circumstances—can be a limiting factor. And while the importance of a particular limiting factor in a particular case may be obvious, the concept itself can be equally important. Listen to forester-ecologist J. D. Ovington:

For example, we are being asked questions about what numbers of people the earth can support in different areas. But we don't yet know what is the basic, primary production of these areas, the total production of the earth, and how this varies. We don't know where there is gross underproduction due to some critical limiting factor. In parts of Australia, if you put down zinc or boron, you can increase production enormously.

I think ecologists must be perfectly honest in this, and have to make their needs felt, because man's future depends upon this ecological knowledge. We are now beginning to look at the functioning of ecosystems and this is the sort of material which will give the answers that are required.

If the Engineers don't ruin everything first. For this is not the kind of thinking that concerns them. It is not only that actions like pushing a freeway through a wildlife refuge or flooding the Grand Canyon with a dam mean nothing to them. It is that they do not care whether they wipe out our only chance to understand the ecology of vast regions of the earth and thus, perhaps, keep from killing ourselves. It is the Engineers who pollute our air and our water—and they may yet do worse than that. They may drown most of us.

Dr. Syukoro Manabe of the Environmental Science Services Administration has tossed together a little mathematical salad, blended in a high-speed computer, and come up with some discoveries about atmospheric motion. It seems that, what with industrialization and its attendant burning of carboniferous fuels, we have managed since 1900 to raise the amount of carbon dioxide in the atmosphere by at least 10, and possibly 15, percent. Normally, of course, carbon dioxide is always being released, but we seem to be releasing it faster than the plants can use it. The research director for a large insurance company dispassionately told a Congressional committee in 1966 that the effect of this additional carbon dioxide

has been to increase the temperature in the lower atmosphere—that is, the troposphere—by about 0.2° C. and to decrease the temperature in the upper atmosphere—that is, the stratosphere—by about 2° C.

. . . The implication of this situation is related to the volume of water contained in the masses of ice in polar regions. If the earth is warmed, the ice melts and the sea level would be raised so high that, were it to happen, we would probably have to swim home from this building this morning.

The buildup of CO_2, to put it simply, lets the sun's heat in, but it does not let the heat back out again when the earth radiates it. This is called, cutely enough, the "greenhouse effect." Sunday supplement stuff, of course—except that the testimony goes on to say that the danger "is something we must resolve in a matter of decades. The situation could become serious by the end of the century." That's thirty-one years from now.

Possibly the best and most dramatic example of the failure of the Engineers to understand what they are doing is demonstrated in our most ambitious attempt to create a completely artificial, if temporary, ecosystem—which is the ecologist's word for the whole life-plus-environment complex. A nuclear submarine, intended to stay under water for a long time, is of course a self-contained ecosystem, at least for a while, and so is a missile launch control station; but the best-known artificial ecosystem is a space capsule.

The Russian manned satellite contains air—plain, simple old air, like the stuff you and I used to breathe before we moved to the city. When we Americans set out to build a capsule, however, we found out that it leaked—and in order to keep it from leaking, we would have had to make the capsule much heavier. This was something of a problem, since our rocket engines did not have the thrust that the Russian engines had.

Leave it to us, said the Engineers. We'll make the ecosystem just that much more artificial, but we'll solve the problem. Pure oxygen can be used, at only one-fifth the pressure of air; you won't have to plug the leaks so tight, you can use rockets with less thrust, it'll all work out fine. And indeed it did—until the first astronauts for the first time confronted the fact that you can have a spark, or even light a match, in air—but not in oxygen. The Engineers improved on nature and killed three men.

To save Storm King, or the Grand Canyon, or the redwoods, or the Great Swamp because they are pretty—because they have an esthetic value that may become increasingly precious to urbanized man over the decades—is a worthy enough cause; but it bogs down in the arguments over what to save and why, and, worse, it meets the Engineers on their own ground. We need the power, they say. Or we need the lumber, or the jetport, or the copper, or whatever. And there are other pretty places—which, in fact, there are.

But worse than we need the power or the copper or the jet-port, we need the ecosystems on which we depend for life. And worse than we need a respect for wildlife or for beauty, we need an ecological understanding of the world around us. We need to understand the nature of the rape before we can fight the rapist.

Although this book concentrates on the United States, a look elsewhere may dramatize the importance of an ecological approach. An ecologist who has taken such a look is Dr. Gerardo Budowski of the Inter-American Institute in Costa Rica, an authority on the ecology of Central America. He notes that in that area, for the past thirty years, "technological advances and increases in population have resulted in land-use patterns that have taken a tremendous toll in the use and abuse of natural resources," and that those patterns, combined with other factors, have "resulted in poverty for a large sector of the population." But with the poverty has come information about the rest of the world—including information about how the rest of the world, and its affluent minority, lives:

The result is what many have called a revolution of expectations, of which we are witnessing violent outbreaks in the forms of revolutions, general discontent, and other manifestations of disconformity. What is worse, it appears that what many believe to be a violent upset due to present conditions is possibly very mild in comparison with what may come.

It is doubtful whether Fulgencio Batista ever thought of Fidel Castro as a "manifestation of disconformity," but the point is clear. And if you don't think it has anything to do with you, then you just haven't counted the people in the world who want what you've got—and who are probably entitled to some of it. And yet —the crushing poverty aside—what is happening to the people of Central America, as described by Dr. Budowski, sounds very much like what is happening to you:

. . . the most destructive effects have been the tremendous impact on soils, natural vegetations, water regime, and wild animals. Productive areas are being depleted at fast rates and converted to sterile lands. Water resources are being mismanaged so as to make them unusable for the future. Immense genetic reservoirs of valuable plants and animals have been or are being destroyed. Even worse, this loss of biologically indispensable material is often irreparable, since it involves an irreversible trend.

The destructive impact is apparently geometric in its progression. . . .

We will come back to the destruction of genetic reservoirs later. For the moment, it is enough to notice that all this is happening because not only plants and animals but the native Indians have been driven out of their adjusted ecological niches—without planning, without understanding, a blind technological trend in the uncaring hands of Engineers and those who share the engineering mentality. And *because* it's happening, we have learned the names of places like Santo Domingo and the Bay of Pigs.

Budowski believes that behind this destructive trend is more than simply population pressure—although that is, as we will see later on, a much more important problem *right now* in Middle America than in the United States—and that something can be done; he describes, as an example, a Mexican government project called Colonia Yucatán in which an ecological approach to forestry is combined with a compassionate approach to human beings. But we are so far behind having such an approach as a part of our national understanding—much less our national planning—that our survival is in serious question.

As recently as January, 1967, the Interior Department held a Water Resources Research Seminar, at which Assistant Secretary Stanley Cain, a noted ecologist and a past president of the Ecological Society of America, delivered a paper. "This paper proposes to show," he began, "that our historic unconcern for ecological side effects in water resources developments has resulted in great damage to the environment, including economic and other losses."

It is absolutely ridiculous that a high official of the Interior Department should have to present a paper, in 1967, to make that point within his own department. The Department's own Bureau of Sport Fisheries and Wildlife was able to say two years earlier that there are more than 200 forms of vertebrate animals in the United States and Puerto Rico whose existence is at least threatened (the number of endangered invertebrates and plants must of course be much larger). And anyway, strontium-90 and thalidomide and DDT should surely have taught us by now that we ought to know something about "ecological side effects" before we go barging around changing everything in sight.

The Department of Agriculture knows perfectly well, for instance, that we have been so successful in developing and growing hybrid corn that we have almost lost hundreds of corn varieties that can't compete economically and aren't grown by farmers any more—thereby making it impossible to experiment with new hybrids, discover possible new disease-resistant strains, or make any other use of the genetic information stored in those varieties.

This is one of the most difficult concepts of conservation to communicate—and the one least understood by conservation groups. From wanting to save the redwoods because they are pretty, some organizations have progressed to wanting to save a particular group of redwoods because of their ecological value. But few people have yet reached the idea of the conservation of genetic information—the idea that we ought to keep every species of animal or plant alive, and in its own ecosystem, because we have no way of knowing what characteristics of what animal or plant or microbe may some day prove to be in some way valuable.

This is not a simple idea, and it does not mean just keeping animals and plants alive in zoos and greenhouses. Even a natural-seeming habitat won't necessarily do it: Maintaining the few remaining bison herds, for example, requires that the herds be "thinned" regularly to keep their numbers within the capacity of the range. But there is no way to know that the same bison are being "thinned" as they would be "thinned" by a herd of predatory wolves on the prairie. As a result, you may wind up with a different bison in a few hundred years. Ecologist A. Starker Leopold has suggested that the ring-necked pheasant in North America (introduced from the Orient about forty years ago) has already become two genetically different birds—in the Imperial Valley of California and on the Saskatchewan prairie—despite the fact that they have evolved from the same stock.

But simple or not, it has to be done, because—as another scientist, Dr. Rezneat Darnell of Marquette University, told the United States Senate—"our most valuable national resource" is "the native species of plants, animals and microbes which are of enormous potential use to civilization."

These forms [Dr. Darnell went on] represent untapped sources of antibiotics, medicines, drugs, natural pesticides, industrial raw materials, foodstuffs and ornamentals. They include our hopes for successful biological warfare against crop pests. Since these species are already adapted to the American environments they are potential sources of hereditary material for improvement of production and disease resistance in our crop species. In the future our native fauna and flora will undoubtedly be put to uses wholly undreamed of today. In aggregate these species represent the total hope for environmental stabilization of oxygen for human respiration, clean water for human consumption, and indirectly, perhaps even such factors as planetary temperature.

Even the Engineers should be able to make sense out of that. But you can't use what you haven't got. The variety of corn that is not grown today, because it is uneconomical to do so in competition with today's hybrids, may prove to be the variety that will turn out, tomorrow, to be resistant to an as yet unforeseen disease. Some by-product of the whooping crane or the California condor may be tomorrow's wonder drug. The ecology of the Long Island estuary may provide the clue that will enable us to project a far more viable ecosystem for a space station.

Everything fits together. Everything. And nobody seems to care, least of all the Engineers.

III · ALGAE AND AEROJET

NANCY MAYNARD is a graduate biologist at the Marine Institute of the University of Miami. She looks rather as though her life should be dedicated to dinners and dancing at The Beefster, with a Clos Veugeot to accompany the *boeuf charolaise*. In fact, it is dedicated to wading hip-deep in the Florida Everglades, studying the ecology of epiphytic algae.

In her laboratory at the Institute, overlooking that part of Biscayne Bay which is south of the Rickenbacker Causeway and still excruciatingly beautiful, Miss Maynard explained to me that algae (or any other life forms) are "epiphytic" when they live on the surface of other life forms—in this case, on the saw grass that is the most common vegetation of the Everglades. Her studies are done in the southeastern part of Everglades National Park near Barnes Sound, where the water that covers the glades has almost reached an estuarine state—that is, where it is about ready to mix with the salt water of the sea. Nancy Maynard is one of the people who "need a salt marsh."

Why these particular algae? I asked her curiously. Her answer was disarmingly simple: "Because they won't be there very much longer."

By the time I talked with Nancy Maynard in Florida, I had already had drilled into me by ecologists—Ron Dagon in New York, John Milton and Stanley Cain in Washington, the great Eugene P. Odum in Georgia—the concept of the conservation of genetic information. But it is not all that easy to break old thinking habits, and I found that I had applied the idea mostly to the standard candidates for conservation: the whooping crane and the California condor, the alligator, the cougar. It is more difficult to remember that the same concept applies to the ebony spleenwort in the New Jersey Pine Barrens, or to ears of corn, or to epiphytic algae.

Cain made the same point in a recent paper, in which he described the concern expressed by a number of scientists over construction of a salt plant at Scammon Lagoon in Baja California. The lagoon is used every winter as a breeding place by 2,000 California gray whales—who travel 6,000 miles from their Arctic feeding grounds—and the scientists became concerned lest the disturbance, and possible accompanying pollution, destroy this vital habitat. Fortunately, because of the scientists' concern, the salt company and a special team of Mexican fishery experts are making an exhaustive study of Scammon Lagoon; but Cain's point was that California gray whales weigh 100 tons: "We might never even have heard of this case if the species involved had been a six- or eight-inch fish, rather than a 50-foot model."

I had a pretty good idea, too, why the epiphytic algae of the Everglades were expected to disappear, but I asked anyway. For reply, Nancy Maynard asked me, "Do you know about C-111?"

The only C-111 I had ever heard of was an armed forces cargo plane, but I had picked up enough Florida vocabulary to know that it had to be a Corps of Engineers canal. In fact, Nancy Maynard was the fourth person in three days to urge on me a flood-control map of central and southern Florida, showing in garish red and green the existing and proposed network of canals, levees, dams, pumping stations and control centers with which the Engineers are transforming all of the bottom of the state. To anyone who has ever so much as heard the word "ecology," the map is a horror. It is an uncaring and terrifying symbol of the triumph of the Engineers and the rape of America.

The key to the existence of southern Florida—not only its Miami Beach-Jackie Gleason economic existence, but its ecological existence—is the flow of water. From the central part of the state, water flows into Lake Okeechobee. From there it does not so much flow as seep southward and southwestward, across vast acres of saw grass dotted with higher areas (or "hammocks") that bear shrubs and trees (on these hammocks for centuries lived the Seminoles, feeding on some of the 150-odd species of fish, the dozens of species of birds, living in harmony with deer and alligator, moccasin and panther). Finally, the water flows into Florida Bay, mixing gradually with the salt water of the ocean to form one of the richest estuarine areas in the world. "This tremendous productivity," explains the National Park Service, "is in part dependent upon gradual salinity gradients from fresh to sea water across a broad estuarine belt. The major aquatic species to a degree are abundant because they have free access to whatever proportions of the salt gradient they need at different times in their life cycle."

The shrimp, for instance, which breed in those estuarine waters where fresh water mixes with salt, need an exact proportion of salt in the water—no more, no less—at any given moment in their lives, and it varies from one period in their lives to another. Of course they need other things as well, including the nutrients that come to them in the fresh water; and, as with most life forms, we cannot say with any certainty just what conditions, and in what combinations, are ultimately necessary to their survival. All we know is that it's complex—as is clear from the Service's description of the water cycle of the Everglades:

The key to the fertility of this area, as well as to the perpetuation of the ecosystems and life forms of the park, is the annual cycle of flooding and desiccation. The warm summer rains fall on the northward lands and a thin film of water spreads across the marshes; it picks up nutrient and slowly flows southward; enormous quantities of fresh water organisms come to life and flourish in these incubating shallows. These waters ultimately flow into and dilute and enrich Florida Bay and the brackish coastal bays.

The productivity of a fluctuating water system is, or should be, well known to anyone who has ever seen a rice paddy—the richest and most productive artificial agricultural ecosystem man has ever created. The fluctuation itself, in southern Florida, is of a kind that can barely be imagined in the rest of the country. As an example, at the Corkscrew Swamp Sanctuary (in Collier County, Florida, outside the Everglades National Park), M. Philip Kahl, Jr., who was studying the ecology of the wood stork, recorded that in one season, the surface of Saylor Pond grows to two hundred times its smallest area—but its depth increases by only 20 inches.

From the point of view of the casual visitor, this fluctuation makes February a fine time to visit the Everglades; when the water is low, the animals, birds and fish come together in the relatively few wet areas and are easily seen at places like Taylor Slough. From the point of view of some of the wildlife, the fluctuation is essential; some of the birds, for instance, are grope feeders: They simply light in or next to the water and plunge their bills in at random. In low water there is enough food compressed into a small area to last them through the difficult high-water months.

Kahl's scientific prose is not entirely devoted to the wood stork; he also notes in passing what the Engineers have done to the Everglades (only the southern portion of the Everglades in protected in the national park; the rest is open to travel, hunting, airboating—and management). The fertile system described just now is the natural system, but, writes Kahl, it is no more:

Originally, the Everglades were fed by water overflowing the south rim of Lake Okeechobee, but water-control measures by man, largely within this century, have altered the situation considerably. At present, the overflow from Lake Okeechobee is diverted down drainage controls to the Atlantic Ocean and to the Gulf of Mexico; as a result, the Everglades region now gets most of its water from local rains only.

You don't have to be an expert to know that that's going to foul up the whole Everglades ecosystem.

Actually, the Corps of Engineers is charged by Congress with the responsibility for providing water to the park, whatever else it does—and every year, as Congress pours more money into changing Florida into a sort of Kansas-with-a-seacoast, the legislators are nevertheless careful to keep that provision in the law.

But it works out better on paper than in fact. The water that the Engineers "control" from Lake Okeechobee south is stored under the actual control of something called the Central and Southern Florida Flood Control District ("C&SFFCD" for short), set up in 1949—two years after the national park was established. This means in practice that five unpaid men, meeting once a month, control a project they cannot possibly understand. Of the five men who ran the District in 1966, for instance, one managed his own investments at Kissimmee, one was a real estate operator at Melbourne, one was an agriculturalist at South Bay (much of the Corps operation involves draining the area south of Lake Okeechobee to open it up for agricultural development), one was an insurance man in Coral Gables, and one sold Chevrolets at Fort Pierce.

In 1965, this group and the Corps of Engineers brought down on themselves a little well-earned indignation by holding up water from the drought-ridden Everglades and from the national park until several species of wildlife were endangered and the breeding of others had declined to a point from which recovery is still uncertain. In the meantime, in the Everglades north of the park, deer which would normally have retreated slowly to high ground as the water rose were, instead, wandering all over the area. Finally, as indignation grew, the District agreed to release water to the park and to the glades—and released it in one great rush, drowning thousands of deer.

Obviously, to talk about "how much water the Everglades get" in terms of acre-feet per year is nonsense. The Everglades constitute one of the most delicately balanced ecological mechanisms found anywhere in the world. There are countless examples, some of them dramatic, to demonstrate the result of all this water management in southern and central Florida.

In May, 1961 (the national park counts its alligators, as best it can, in May), along the Shark Valley Loop Road and in that area, park officials counted 375 adult alligators and 75 young. Every year since, the numbers have declined, until in May, 1966, in the same area, they counted only 24 adults—and no young. "We still don't know," Assistant Park Superintendent Carroll Burroughs said in June, 1967, "how many animals were lost in 1965."

Burroughs was speaking after still more alligators and other animals and birds had been lost in a three-month drought in 1967, during which a state forester said, according to *The New York Times,* "that from the air it appeared the entire Everglades National Park had been burned over."

In 1966, ecologist Durward Allen listed eight vertebrates (never mind all those algae) as dependent for their existence on the Everglades water situation, all of which, he said, are "rare or declining": crocodile, manatee, panther, Everglades kite, bald eagle, Florida sandhill crane, white ibis and roseate spoonbill. That's not counting the alligator. Cain said at the same time that the Engineers are "rapidly eliminating the biotopes"—that is, the ecological living conditions—for flamingos, egrets and anhingas as well as some of the same vertebrates listed by Allen. And even these—as Park Superintendent Roger Allin points out—are only the birds and animals we know about for sure:

Simple life forms can recover, providing there is sufficient brood stock, in a period of a year or two; but many of the longer-lived forms such as alligators and some of our unique and rare birds may take years to recover to their former population densities. In fact, it may be several years before we are even able to determine the extent of impairment to some of our life systems.

Nor is the provision about "sufficient brood stock" just a phrase thrown in for scientific accuracy. Some birds—the royal and Sandwich terns and the American oyster catchers are examples—have disappeared from southern Florida as breeders. Taking all species of wading birds together, the Everglades area boasted a population of 1.5 million breeding adults in the 1930s. By the mid-1940s the total was down to fewer than 300,000, and during the period from 1950 to 1962 it was usually below 50,000. The same kinds of figures can be found for fish, crustaceans and amphibians, and there is simply no question that it is a direct result of the frenetic activity of the Engineers.

How delicately the Everglades life depends on the water situation is demonstrated by Kahl's study of the wood stork. When the water drops to a certain level every year, the wood stork lays eggs. It doesn't matter what day it is, or how long the days are, or what the temperature is, or how much light there is: When the water level hits that point, that's it. And it isn't just the *amount* of water, either; if rain made up the difference for all the water drained off by the Engineers, it still wouldn't help the wood stork. For one thing, there are nutrients in the natural flow water (and of course nobody knows what nutrients and nobody knows how they are used in the delicate ecosystem), and there are almost certainly other elements that affect the oxidation of organic soils, the trends in plant succession, and a number of other factors. To complicate matters, water used first for agriculture is likely to contain pesticide residues.

The wood stork knows whether the water is natural or not. North of the national park is an east-west highway, the Tamiami Trail, beneath which the Everglades water flows through a series of culverts; this is one of the places at which water flow is regularly measured. Park officials have discovered that whenever the water flow through the Tamiami Trail is 300,000 acre-feet or more per year, the wood stork successfully nests; whenever the water flow falls below 225,000 acre-feet, the nesting fails. Rain doesn't make up for it, no matter how much there is; the water has to flow in from the north in the normal fashion.

The park, then, is slowly dying, thanks to the Engineers. Outside the office window of Superintendent Allin, just inside the park boundary near Homestead, I saw woody brush dominating a landscape that should have been mostly saw grass and a few hammocks. It is what happens when year after year is dry, and it will take years—if, indeed, it can ever be done at all—to restore the area to its "natural" form.

In nature, of course, wildfire would be a major ecological factor acting toward restoration, and would serve also the function of decomposing much of the organic material for reuse. During the drought of 1967, nearly a million acres of brush and timberland burned in southern Florida, most of it outside the park. Although the natural role of fire is little understood by the general public, it is well understood by ecologists. Still, Park Service policy is against even controlled burning, and of course wildfire cannot be allowed to burn uncontrolled when there is always a minimum of three or four thousand visitors in the park.

"I'd like to burn it," Allin admitted to me, "but I'd like even more to see the park get the water it would naturally get."

On the garish Corps of Engineers map that Nancy Maynard pressed into my hand, I found a short red line, running a few miles northwest from Barnes Sound and crossing U.S. Highway 1. On that master plan for billion-dollar chaos, the one tiny line is inconspicuous enough, but it's the one she wanted me to see. It is labeled "C-111."

C-111 is a canal that already exists, although at the moment it has a "plug" in it. The plug was supposed to be pulled a few weeks after I was there, but the National Audubon Society managed to get a court order holding up the procedure. The situation is still unresolved. If it were pulled, it would mean serious enough damage if only Nancy Maynard's epiphytic algae are destroyed—the algae whose ecological role, possibly a crucial one, she and her co-workers are only now trying to determine. But the destruction is, in fact, likely to be far more dramatic.

C-111 has two avowed purposes. One of them is that ubiquitous excuse for anything the Engineers want to do: flood control. The canal will take the fresh water that flows "overland" in a southwesterly direction into the park and divert it into Barnes Sound—thus changing, when and if it works, the salinity of the sound and probably of whole sections of Florida Bay. When there isn't fresh water to divert, the salt water of the sound will come up the canal—and change salinity in the other direction.

In addition, if there is salt water in the canal, as there will be during times of drought, then a hurricane or even a high wind from the southeast is almost certain to blow a lot of that salt water over the canal's banks and into the Everglades, where it will flow south and southwest—salt and all—and damage the whole ecology of the area. In a way, this is the bitterest irony of all; the Corps of Engineers' first excuse for messing with southern Florida was that hurricane winds would sometimes blow water out of Lake Okeechobee, flooding surrounding lands.

The second purpose of C-111 is to provide a channel for barge transportation to a plant operated by the Aerojet-General Company. C-111 is openly called "the Aerojet canal," and true or not, it is widely believed that Aerojet's tremendous political influence as a prime defense contractor bolsters the Engineers' determination to ignore the protests of the Park Service and virtually everyone else about the opening of the canal.

The water that will not flow into the park, remember, carries nutrients on which much of the vegetation and wildlife in the park depends, and nobody yet knows who needs which nutrients.

One of the results of other changes in the past has been the disappearance of a single species of snail—which in turn resulted in the disappearance of the Everglades kite, a bird that lived on the snail (20 kite still struggle for survival in the Loxahatchee Wildlife Refuge). Completely dependent on the present aquatic environment, according to a study made in 1964, are all 47 species of amphibians in the park, 24 of the 42 species of reptiles (including the alligator, the crocodile, and 13 of the 15 kinds of turtles), at least 89 of the more than 200 species of birds (many of the others are marsh dwellers, partially dependent on aquatic food), almost all of the 12 species of mammals (including, surprisingly, the Everglades Park deer, whose most important single food item is the water lily), and, of course, the 150 species of fish and the hundreds of invertebrates. Virtually all of the vegetation in the Everglades is also dependent on maintenance of something like "natural" water flow ("In this ecological region," the study says, "an elevation of a foot or two is sufficient to produce marked ecological change due to change in duration of flooding").

This does not all depend, of course, simply on the loss of nutrients. Far more important, says the Park Service, is "the diluting effects of these waters which will be diverted to Barnes Sound. Without question, salinities in Florida Bay will be increased and circulation retarded. The eastern portion of this area could well become nothing more than a brine basin within a few years."

Just about all the fish in the Everglades require just the right depth and duration of water, and the right salt content, in order to feed and to reproduce. A lot of them go back and forth from fresh to estuarine water, staying where the salt gradient is just right. A lot more live in estuarine water all the time.

Even if conserving genetic information were not of overriding importance, Floridians will be cutting off not only their noses but their ears, hands and feet if they don't stop the Engineers pretty soon. As long ago as 1964, the scientists who made the study just mentioned reported that "Florida Bay . . . shows increasingly frequent and long-sustained periods of super-salinity," and added:

Salinities of 70 parts per thousand, twice that of seawater, are already frequently encountered. This can be serious biologically; salinities this high are lethal to the eggs and young of nearly all marine species, and the adults of only a few species can tolerate such salinity.

Think about that—especially if you live in, or like to visit, Florida. Because those "marine species" that will all die off if the Engineers are not stopped include, among a lot of others, the menhaden—which supports by far the greatest fishery of the United States; the black mullet, which supports the largest food-fish landings in Florida; the spotted sea trout, which Florida fishermen love so well; the snook; the tarpon; blue crabs; stone crabs; oysters; and the extremely valuable pink shrimp, worth millions of dollars a year commercially to Florida and vital as a food for many fish besides.

There is no way around this. It is possible, I suppose, that the citizens of Florida don't care any more than anybody else does about the conservation of genetic information. It is even possible that they are willing to let the Engineers destroy millions of dollars worth of industry and tourism. For any such determined Florida promoters, I offer one more long-range warning from Dr. Odum, who suggests that too much drainage "would not only ruin the area as a wildlife paradise but would also be risky in that salt water might then intrude into the underground water supply needed by the large coastal cities."

You can already get salt water out of the kitchen faucet, some days, in Atlantic City, New Jersey. Why not Miami?

But the Engineers intend to go on, and this year it's C-111. The "hydrologic change" caused by that one little canal, itself only about 7 miles long, will spread over at least 200 square miles. Within those 200 square miles are 60 percent of the park's roseate spoonbills, 25 percent of the great white herons, 15 percent of the American eagles and 95 percent of the dwindling numbers of crocodiles (not alligators)—among other species. All of these birds and animals are already in the "rare and endangered" classification.

Of course the Park Service has complained. The Engineers, however, have an answer. We'll pull the plug, the Corps has said, "to see what damages would occur and thereby justify the Service's claim that a plug is necessary"! If ever there was an Engineer's answer, that's it. The Park Service treats it with the contempt it deserves:

First, irreparable damage might well occur within a matter of hours; second, it may well be that many of the damages which could occur would not be obvious even with close surveillance. Very likely such changes could be subtle, long-term biological changes which in their ultimacy would be devastating, but not readily observable in the early stages of their unalterable course.

The Engineers couldn't care less about the roseate spoonbill, much less the epiphytic algae. In fact—just so they get to build something, and Aerojet gets its barge access to the sea—they couldn't care less about the Everglades, indescribably beautiful and unique as they are, and constituting as they do the only national park that was created specifically to preserve an ecosystem.

The Audubon Society's injunction is still in force, and happily, budget problems have forced the Engineers to refrain from pushing the operation. In the meantime, the publicity has forced them to come up with a plan for a series of "gated culverts" which they say will prevent salt water intrusion. The Park Service thinks they might work, and a consulting engineer recommended by the Audubon Society has approved the idea. Still, it isn't clear how the "gated culverts" will solve such problems as the increased salinity of Florida Bay, and there is as yet no assurance that the plan will be followed.

Even the wholesale havoc of C-111 isn't enough for the Engineers. Now they're talking about moving over to the other coast to dam the rivers, streams and sloughs of the Shark River and Whitewater Bay drainages, and about building a couple of hundred or thousand "low-head dams" throughout the interior of Everglades National Park itself.

There is no stopping the engineering mentality. We can only try to stop the Engineers.

IV · THE GOLDEN SAND DUNE

THE UNITED STATES Army Corps of Engineers, for peculiar historical and political reasons, has legal authority over "the execution, operation, maintenance and control of river and harbor and flood-control improvements authorized by law, and the administration of laws for the protection and preservation of navigation and navigable waters in the United States."

The Corps not only does its own dredging, filling, building, ripping, tearing, blocking and gouging, but it licenses that done by private firms. It makes quite clear what its criteria are for issuing such permits: ". . . the decision as to whether a permit will be issued must rest primarily upon the effect of the proposed work on navigation. . . ."

If this means digging up sludge and dumping it in the middle of Lake Erie to add to the colossal pollution of that once-lovely lake, so be it.

The law does require the Engineers of the Army to "coordinate applications for permits" with the fish and wildlife people of the Federal Government and the affected state, but it does not require the Engineers to pay any attention to those experts' recommendations, except to transmit them to the applicant. In the New York-Long Island area alone, the Federal Bureau of Sport Fisheries and Wildlife, from 1962 to 1965, recommended denial of twenty-four dredge-and-fill permits; sixteen of the permits were issued anyway. During the same period the Bureau recommended that thirty-five other projects be approved only with restrictions intended to protect fish and wildlife; 21 of *those* projects were authorized by the Engineers without restrictions.

Between 1954 and 1964, between Delaware and Maine, 45,000 acres of precious estuarine land were lost—one-third of them directly to harbor and channel dredging by the Corps of

Engineers and the rest of them to activity conducted with the Engineers' approval. Inevitably, the harbor and channel dredging is destructive to fisheries and wildlife—and the Engineers say it has to be that way, because they have to do their work as cheaply as possible.

As we shall see, they don't do it all that cheaply, although certainly, like any government agency, they *ought* to do what they do with a minimum of cost. The Engineers have gone beyond mutterings about their cost problems, however; they have grimly fought several attempts in Congress to make it necessary for permits to be approved not only by the Engineers but by the Interior Department. In a 1967 essay quoted earlier, Dr. Cain wrote that

it is not reasonable to expect the Corps of Engineers to bring to bear in estuarine situations the variety of technical skills and expert judgment necessary to reflect recreational, ecological, fish, wildlife and esthetic values, as well as the navigational values for which they have traditional responsibility. A growing body of opinion supports the conviction that permits to dredge or fill such waters should be required from the Department of the Interior as well as from the Corps of Engineers if natural resource values other than commercial and navigational ones are to be served.

That body of opinion is not growing any too fast, partly because a lot of Congressmen are very closely tied to the Corps of Engineers—especially the powerful Southern Congressmen who dominate much Congressional activity—and partly because a lot of Congressmen see it simply as a bureaucratic battle for power between two government agencies. A couple of Congressmen, Representative Herbert Tenzer of New York and Representative John Dingell of Michigan, have proposed legislation to accomplish this dual-responsibility goal, but so far it hasn't gotten anywhere.

Of course the depredations of the Engineers aren't confined to the Everglades and the northeastern estuaries. The Corps' Gathright Dam, on the Jackson River in Virginia, will flood the state-owned Gathright Wildlife Management Area. Citizens in the Mill Creek area, on the watershed of the upper Huron River in Michigan, are striving mightily to halt a ridiculous project there, and in St. Maries, Idaho, virtually the whole population of the area turned out to protest three proposed dams on the St. Joe River.

The last natural estuary area in the Puget Sound complex, near Tacoma, is threatened by a project to dredge out the bay and construct a railroad yard. In the upper part of Florida, the Corps' Cross-Florida Barge Canal—a virtually useless multimillion-dollar operation, of value only to a few businessmen in Ocala—not only rips apart the ecology of the northern part of the state but destroys priceless tropical riverways in the Oklawaha area. A proposed Corps of Engineers dam on Big Walnut Creek in Indiana will destroy an unusual gorge and some rare vegetation that is different from all the surrounding glacial till plain of the state.

On the west coast of Florida, commercial developments are hurt by occasional "red tides," caused by massive gatherings of a tiny organism, *Gymnodinium breve*. A bunch of Engineers have now proposed that the red tides be controlled by putting *G. breve* on a diet enforced by a series of dams; the idea is that the dams will block the flow of tannic acid, B_{12} and other substances which, to *G. breve,* are nutrients. It doesn't bother the Engineers that nobody knows the role played by tannic acid, B_{12} or *Gymnodinium breve* themselves in the ecology of the area—an ecology on which the commercial development of the area depends.

An outstanding example of the Engineers run wild is the Corps' project for a combination floodgate-seawall-sand dune project along and near Long Beach on Long Island, New York. The point of this magnificent dunedoggle, which will cost at least $60 million, is reputedly to protect Atlantic Beach, Long Beach, Lido and Point Lookout from wave damage in case of a hurricane, and to prevent flooding in some towns inside the dune. The Interior Department says it will be damaging to bass fishing, but not for long. Normal wave action will ruin the dune almost as soon as it is built. The Engineers reply simply that the local taxpayers will have to maintain the dune after the Engineers have built it. A local citizens' group, the Hempstead Town Lands Resources Council, has suggested wryly that, considering the cost of such maintenance, it might be cheaper to build the dune out of gold instead of sand.

The Corps claims that the project is necessary, and points to the fact that Long Island damage from Hurricane Donna, which killed 148 people in 1960, was about $90 million. What they don't point out, though, is that wave damage and flood damage aren't the same thing. The wave damage from Donna was more like *one* million dollars—which may call for protection, but hardly the $60 million worth that the Engineers are proposing.

To make up for sealing off much of the estuarial flow, the Engineers propose to put partially closed floodgates at East Rockaway inlet, Reynolds Channel, Swift Creek and Long Creek. In case of hurricane tides—even if their plan works—this will simply throw the full force of the tides against these gates, and against the bridges, nearby islands and the Meadowbrook Causeway.

During Hurricane Donna, the Meadowbrook Causeway was under water. During the Corps' projected hurricane—a model they invented to argue the need for the project—the Causeway would be under five feet of water. The Corps' "flood control" measure, it turns out, might delay a flood for a few minutes under hurricane tides, but that's all it would do.

The Engineers, in fact, don't do very well with shorelines anywhere in the country. They love to build jetties and breakwaters and other devices to change the nature of a beach, and they ignore things like littoral drift—the tide action that moves sand from one beach to another. When President Johnson appointed a distinguished advisory panel on oceanography to look into this and other matters, they came back with a blistering report on the whole thing:

The Panel was distressed to find a high failure rate of construction projects in the surf zone and on beaches. The destruction of beaches by breakwaters designed to extend them, the silting of harbors and marinas as a result of construction designed to provide shelter, and the intensification of wave action by the building of jetties supposed to lessen wave action are but a few examples of the inadequacy of our knowledge and practice in coastal construction.

Having completely ruined the beaches of San Diego—one of which has lost 11 million cubic *yards* of sand over the last twenty years—the Corps of Engineers now proposes to dredge out San Diego Bay to try to repair the damage. Aside from the fact that no one knows whether it will work, the Engineers are in a fight with the California State Resources Agency, which says that the dredging project will destroy marine life in the bay.

There is nothing obscure about the damage that the Engineers cause with their dredging projects. In 1966 testimony before Congress, Assistant Secretary Cain described one of the areas that the Engineers most love to mess with:

The Long Island wetlands . . . teem with life. Over 55 species of shorebirds, rails and herons inhabit these marshes and shores. The combination of cover provided by the vegetation, the food arising from numerous insects, invertebrate animals and microscopic plants, and the absence of man's disturbance supply the necessary home or habitat for these birds and many other species. Each year, many thousands of waterfowl rest, or feed, on these wetland complexes. . . .

Beneath the waters, shellfish including crabs, oysters and clams feed upon the minute organisms found only in the fertile brackish waters of estuarine zones. And more than 60 species of finfish spawn and feed and grow in the bays and channels of this wetland complex.

Any changes in the ecology of the wetland complex can erase the smaller, living units of the food chain, and those creatures dependent upon them. . . .

Between 1954 and 1964, a total of 4,635 acres of wetlands were lost in just Nassau County alone. All of Long Island's wetlands are threatened.

And that's only Long Island. Just how stupid can we go on being?

The annual "rivers and harbors" bill, even high school civics students know, is the "pork barrel" bill for Congressmen. The Corps of Engineers is the most nearly untouchable empire in the United States, as powerful in its field as the FBI or the CIA and as difficult to oppose. But unless America learns to oppose its Engineers, Ronald Reagan's remark about Vietnam—that it ought to be paved as a parking lot and a white line painted down the middle—will apply to the United States of America first.

Not, of course, that all the Engineers are in the Army. On the Little Tennessee River in Tennessee is some of the last free-flowing, unspoiled river country of the Southeast, famous for trout fishing and for scenic values. The Engineers of TVA are about to destroy it with the Tellico Dam. In Florida, several real estate operators are agitating for the building of causeways to undeveloped keys, ignorant of or unconcerned about the fact that the entire flow of water in Biscayne Bay will be ruined and the beauty of the entire area possibly destroyed. The Duke Power Company will threaten the entire Savannah River and destroy four of its wild tributaries—the Toxaway, the Whitewater, the Horsepasture and the Thompson—with a development in South Carolina. The Interior Department had to intervene before the Federal Power Commission to get the power company to provide safeguards for archeological exploration and some protection for fish and wildlife resources; even so, the area is now removed from consideration for inclusion in the National Wild Rivers System, and temperature changes in the water as a result of operating the power plant may have completely unpredicted effects on the fish and smaller forms of life in the rivers.

In a later chapter, we will look more closely at what may be the most fantastic Engineers' scheme yet: the totally pointless construction of Rampart Dam in Alaska at a cost of at least $1.5 billion and probably much more. To provide hydroelectric power that Alaska can't possibly use and in the hope of attracting industry which has already said it won't go, the Engineers plan to flood an area larger than New Jersey, change the entire ecology of central Alaska, and completely wipe out the nesting grounds of a million and a half ducks, 12,500 geese and 10,000 little brown cranes (not to mention the destruction of habitats for moose, wolves, peregrine falcons, salmon, martens, wolverines, weasels, lynx, muskrat, mink, beaver, otter and 1,200 Athabaskan Indians).

Even when begged, the Engineers refused to look at what they were doing. If fact, they went so far as to suppress studies which said that the dam was a bad idea. Finally, conservation groups collected money to finance their own study, which, according to Dr. Richard Goodwin of the Nature Conservancy, "clearly indicated that this plan is not well conceived to fill our present and immediate future economic requirements, while at the same time it would be extremely destructive to our fisheries and wildlife resources." The U.S. Fish and Wildlife Service was less polite in its language: "Nowhere in the history of water development in

North America have the fish and wildlife losses anticipated to result from a single project been so overwhelming."

But Rampart Dam is still very much alive as a proposal, and so are dams along the trout stream headwaters of North Carolina's French Broad River and on Virginia's historic Rappahannock.

If it isn't a dam, it's a highway. In New Jersey—the fourth smallest state in the union—studies now project 40 additional superhighway lanes across the state in the next few years. A proposed Federal parkway will destroy Vermont's famous Long Trail on the ridgetops of the Green Mountains. Another is aimed through the wilderness of the Spruce Knob-Seneca Rocks National Recreation Area in West Virginia. Still other projects will pave Franconia Notch in New Hampshire and Cumberland Gap, between Virginia and Kentucky, for interstate highways. And yet another will ram Interstate 70 through the Gore Range-Eagle Nest Primitive Area in Colorado, despite the existence of an excellent alternate route over Vail Pass, which would even be cheaper.

The New York Thruway was cut directly through the center of the Montezuma Wildlife Refuge. Only last-minute action by Republican Representative John Saylor kept a Pennsylvania six-laner from cutting right through the middle of the nation's largest fish hatchery. In California, the Highway Commission still insists on running a freeway through the middle of a virgin redwood stand in a state park.

They are everywhere, the Engineers—even in the National Park Service, where, in the middle of a wilderness area near Mammoth Cave in Kentucky, they are teaching young men to operate bulldozers and earth-moving equipment. They plan two dams that will destroy the only tiny stretch of the mighty Missouri River that still flows as it did when Lewis and Clark saw it (if you don't think the engineering mentality has taken over America, get an atlas with good state maps and follow the course of the Missouri, state by state).

Every dam, every superhighway, every lumber access road for that matter, creates a new ecology and destroys at least part of an old one. The Engineers don't care.

Dr. John C. Calhoun, Jr., vice chancellor of Texas A. & M., describes arguments that he says have been raging for years over possible construction of a dam near his home on the Navasota River. They argue, he says, over the advantages to water supply, the added recreational values or the loss in land values, but "at no time during the discussion have I heard arguments pro or con concerning the effect of this installation upon the natural biological system. Is there anything worth protecting in the living world that would be affected by this dam? I don't know and apparently neither does anyone else."

Setting aside for the moment any questions about moose or fish, wilderness or ecosystems or genetic information, there is plenty of evidence that the Engineers don't know what they're doing even *in their own terms*. Happily for us and unfortunately for them, the Corps of Engineers has to make some of its financial data public—and a close look at it turns up some interesting information.

A Duke University economist named Robert Haveman took such a look recently, specifically studying 147 Corps of Engineers projects in ten Southern states between 1946 and 1962. He notes the effect of the cozy relationship between the Engineers and the Southerners in Congress: Out of $7.5 billion spent in the Engineers' general construction program for those years, $1.5 billion was spent in those ten Southern states.

But the real point is that most of it was misspent. What Haveman does in his study is to take the accounting methods used by the Engineers to justify their projects and submit them to a number of criticisms raised by economists over the years. In order to get a project through Congress, the Engineers have to show that the "benefit," computed through a complex formula, is equal to the "cost." Their method of figuring out this "cost-benefit ratio" has often been criticized. Haveman took five of the most respectable criticisms and, using the methods suggested by the critics, recalculated the cost-benefit ratios. It turned out that many of the projects could not pass even one of the five "tests." This was Haveman's conclusion:

According to this approach, then, it appears that 63 of the 147 projects, representing $1,169,000,000 of committed Federal funds, or 44.2 percent of the total, are devoted to projects which should not have been undertaken: projects the construction of which has led to a misallocation of national resources and economic waste.

It should be noted that Haveman's study accepts something this book rejects. He says that the goal of government programs is "the maximization of total social welfare," but for want of a better way to measure, Haveman makes that equal to "the maximization of national income." Esthetic values, for example, or scientific values like the conservation of genetic information—neither of which has anything *directly* or measurably to do with national income—thus get left out. The point is that Haveman takes the Engineers apart without even figuring these less tangible things into the account.

A smaller and less abstract example of the Engineers' grotesque inefficiency—and while we might expect Engineers to be insensitive we at least expect them to be efficient—is the "low-flow augmentation program" planned for the Potomac River. Like Rampart Dam, this is a project still very much alive in spite of the fact that it has been clearly shown to be preposterous. Scientists spent several years and $2 million on a study of the Delaware River estuary—a study that was never completed, but in which scientists managed to learn a great deal about how water operates in the lower part of the river. While that study was going on, the Corps of Engineers was coming up with its plan for the Potomac—a plan to cost more than a half *billion* dollars with a large chunk of it going for low-flow augmentation. The idea is simple enough: You back up the water when it's high, then when it's low you release water to "augment" the flow and thus, presumably, to help carry off some of the Potomac's famous pollution.

In 1966, Dr. Abel Wolman, professor emeritus at Johns Hopkins and a frequent consultant to government agencies on ecological questions, appeared before Congress to apply the results of the Delaware study to the Corps' Potomac project. In the simplest possible terms, it just plain won't work. But the Engineers' project is still before Congress, and may yet be approved.

In the face of all this, Republican Representative Frank Horton of New York has introduced legislation aimed at ending pollution in Lake Erie—by authorizing the Corps of Engineers to make a study of water resources in the Great Lakes. This is approximately analogous to asking Jack the Ripper to make a study of prostitution.

So pervasive in our nation is the Engineers' mentality that a law passed in 1966 to establish a "co-ordinated, long-range national program in marine science" is called the Marine Resources and Engineering Development Act. California Democrat George E. Brown, Jr., during a Congressional hearing touching on the shortage of ecologists, suggested facetiously that we might give in to the engineering mentality altogether:

"Might I suggest that we could solve the problem . . . if we retitled these ecologists as biological systems engineers and let the Department of Defense finance them?"

V · YOU GO THROUGH SEDRO WOOLLEY

SOME ATLASES SHOW it as Highway 17A, but it's marked as Washington State Route 20. Rod Pegues of the Sierra Club in Seattle told me that it was the best road to take if I wanted to see unspoiled land in the Great Cascades without getting out of my Avis car to go tramping across the snowy mountains in February. "If you go through Sedro Woolley," he said, "you're on the right highway."

I never found out where the little town of Sedro Woolley got its name, but I found the road. It escapes the shoreline civilization quickly, and winds lazily up the lovely and unspoiled Skagit River, a deep and enchanting mint-green with the beginnings of spring runoff, now loafing its way through a wide valley, now hurtling whitely through a narrow gorge. On both sides of the river and the road, creeks as varied as their names, and falls ranging from tiny trickles to crashing cataracts, contribute their share of the precious and beautiful water to the river.

The occasional towns seem a sacrilege, but they are few, and in fact, with one exception (a town called Concrete, which is as attractive as it sounds), they seem to have made their peace with the towering mountains and the cold and lovely river. The Engineers and their angry steel-and-concrete rapine seemed far away. I couldn't see the steelhead in the Skagit, but I knew they were there—they and the hundreds of forms of river life that make up the ecosystem of which they are an exciting, dynamic part.

But there is, of course, no escaping the Engineers. Atop the Skagit, within Mount Baker National Forest, are the three dams of the Seattle Power and Light Company—"City Light" to Washingtonians. Every one is ugly, and the river grows stunted and ugly as you approach the first of them. They have spawned an ugly town, Newhalem, with the depressing standardized look of company towns everywhere.

Behind the dams are the lakes (and one resort), unquestionably lovely themselves but disturbing to look at. Trees partly under water around the shores of Diablo Lake testify to the drowned ecology of the shoreline. The road, new from here on, has to climb away from the water, but I could see changes in the vegetation where life is struggling to adjust. Life will win, but it will not be the same.

This area is north of the newly designated Great Cascades National Park and the wilderness area included in it, but the land is the same, and as I got out of the car on a bridge that crosses an arm of Diablo Lake that was once a creek, I could only do what thousands have done before me: stare at the awesome mountains and wonder what kind of idiots we are.

The ugliest thing on the upper Skagit is not a dam or a town; it is the chain of metal towers that support the power lines bringing to the lowlands the power from Gorge Dam and Diablo Dam and Ross Dam. For a few million dollars these lines could be hidden. In Seattle, electricity bills would go up a few cents. Most people would pay it happily if they drove once up the Skagit on Route 20.

But I had to remind myself that my musing was beside the point. I stared at the vastness of the Cascades, and I was forced to admit that the dams were not really hurting anything. The Skagit it as beautiful today a little way below Gorge Dam as it ever was, the fish still swim, the microorganisms still thrive. And would I give up the electricity that drives the typewriter on which I write, that lights the paper I write on, that powers the record player through which the Mamas and the Papas softly sing behind me? Hydroelectric power generation at least pours no sulfur dioxide into the air I breathe. And if we are to live as we want to live, there must be some dams, some "thermal pollution," even some sulfur dioxide—and some fish who can't make it home to their spawning grounds.

A few feet from where I stood on the bridge, the Forest Service is building a picnicking area, carefully cleared in tiny patches beneath the firs. There are lavatories, and I wondered idly whether, over a period of time, their nutrients will change the land and perhaps the lake; but surely this beauty is to be seen and enjoyed, and not only by the hardy. The road at whose temporary end I had stopped will eventually cut its way all across the range; it was the subject of a conservationist fight, now lost, and of course it will change, as any road changes, the meaning of the land it touches. But can I believe that it will seriously damage the Great Cascades?

"They call us preservationists," Stewart Brandborg told me in Washington. "It's supposed to be a kind of a dirty word. They say we're trying to 'lock up' the land. But all we think is that some of it ought to be left completely alone."

Brandborg is executive director of the Wilderness Society, which is just what it sounds like. The high point of the Society's existence to date was passage in 1964 of the Wilderness Act, which froze 54 areas within national forests as "wilderness areas," to remain essentially untouched by man, and provided for the possible designation of a number of other areas now within national parks, wildlife refuges or other Federally owned and administered lands. Proposed areas include 1,000,000 acres within Everglades National Park, 200,000 acres within Mount Baker National Forest, a few thousand acres (since designated) in the Great Swamp of New Jersey.

According to the act, the areas designated are to be administered "in such manner as will leave them unimpaired for future use and enjoyment as wilderness, and so as to provide for the protection of these areas [and] the preservation of their wilderness character." A wilderness, says the act poetically, is "an area where the earth and its community of life are untrammeled by man, where man himself is a visitor who does not remain." More prosaically, a wilderness area is

an area of undeveloped Federal land retaining its primeval character and influence, without permanent improvements or human habitation, which is protected and managed so as to preserve its natural conditions and which (1) generally appears to have been affected primarily by the forces of nature, with the imprint of man's work substantially unnoticeable; (2) has outstanding opportunities for solitude or a primitive and unconfined type of recreation; (3) has at least five thousand acres of land or is of sufficient size as to make practicable its preservation and use in an unimpaired condition; and (4) may also contain ecological, geological, or other features of scientific, educational, scenic, or historical value.

Ecology is there, thrown in as virtually an afterthought but obviously not the point of the whole thing as far as an apparently recreation-minded Congress was concerned (tourists bring more money than ecologists). Nor does ecology seem, from the group's literature, to be a primary concern of the Wilderness Society, which talks a lot about "our physical and spiritual regeneration" and about "intangible values"—all of which is of course important—but very little about ecology. The Forest Service's own description of the 54 wilderness areas set up by the act of 1964 mentions only three as having specific ecological interest.

Anyway, the idea is that a wilderness area is supposed to be just that: wilderness, left alone, with no roads, no buildings, no formal campsites. As a result, a lot of people are extremely unhappy about it. Among them—since the already designated wilderness areas are mostly in national forests—are lumbermen. John Buchanan of Del Norte, Colorado, a lumber industry representative, was outspoken about it in a talk he gave late in 1966, in Albuquerque:

The miners, stockmen, water users, the vast majority of our recreationists, timber harvesters [they love that word "harvesters"], and public land managers ask only that resource facts prevail over resource folly. A forest, like a city, is an ever-changing, living organism. Lock up the western forests in barren, single-use preservation, neglect them, subject them to non-management, look the other way when they are ravaged by uncontrolled fire, disease and insects, and as surely as God made them, they will suffer the blight and devastation of our cities.

As surely as God made them, of course, he made them a long time before Mr. Buchanan or his forefathers showed up—and they have managed to survive. He even made them in such a way that fire plays an important ecological role in keeping them alive. But lumbermen and their satellites are good at myths; the mayor of Sedro Woolley, William O. Pearson, came up with the simple-country-farmer myth in the spring of 1967:

Iowa grows corn, Kansas grows wheat, the South grows tobacco and cotton and harvests these crops. In the Pacific Northwest, we grow and harvest trees. Our economy depends on it. It certainly is not in the national interest to let vast stands of mature timber rot and become infested with disease and bugs when they can be managed and harvested as a crop.

Aside from the fact that, from the two quotations, credit for the origin of the forests seems to be a toss-up between God and Mayor Pearson, the important thing is that all that rotting and all those bugs are a vitally necessary part of the ecological process. Olin Industries—a vast firm whose money comes in part from paper and chemicals—has run a two-page, four-color ad with a picture of a forest and the caption, "If you think it's beautiful now, wait until we chop it down." The copy goes on to explain that "Most virgin forests are already doomed. They're waging a constant, losing battle against disease, insects and wildlife. A battle where death always more than offsets growth."

It becomes difficult to convince people that the forests were larger, not smaller, before the lumbermen came.

There are other, similar myths put forth by other interests. In *Fishing and Hunting News,* for example—a publication devoted to the narrower interests of sportsmen—an editorial says that national parks are an outmoded idea, because while you can preserve rocks, mountains and scenery, you can't stockpile animals (so hunters should be allowed in the parks to restore the balance of nature!). But the point of all the myths is about the same. Mr. Buchanan and Mayor Pearson want to cut—excuse me, harvest —the trees; and in a national forest, if an area is not designated as a wilderness area, they can do so.

And there isn't really anything wrong with what they want to do. We cannot save all of our forests and ask for wood as well. Far better that the John Buchanans should do their "harvesting" under the careful control of the foresters of the Department of Agriculture—who will see (as the industry-controlled state forestry agencies usually do not) that the logging is more or less selective, that some new seeding is done, that roads are not built up the middle of streams and that forest stands are reseeded, too, after their immediate use—than that the slopes should be logged bare and left to erode, the roads left in the streams to destroy the life there.

In his office in the Everglades, Roger Allin (echoing the philosophy of his boss, the current head of the National Park System) vigorously resisted any suggestion of mine, however facetious, that the Everglades would be better off if the people went away. "The park is here for the people," the superintendent insisted. "The problem is not to keep the people out and that way to save the park—the problem is to save the park for the people." Allin was proud of the fact that in the park, as he put it, "a little old lady in a wheelchair can come here and really see the Everglades."

She can, too. And she should be able to, as she should be able to see the Great Swamp or the Great Smokies or the Great Cascades. But the Pinchot-Muir fight is still going on.

The Sierra Club and the Wilderness Society, their opponents charge, are made up of "backpack snobs"—people with the time and the money (and the youth and the energy) to go on mule trips or afoot into the deep wilderness, and who consequently want it saved for themselves, although the great majority of American vacationers expect, and have a right to, more of the amenities—including the right to see the Cascades as I did, with my car in sight and its warmth to retreat to.

Those critics are at least partly right. There was a hearing, for example, on the Park Service's proposal to include part of California's Lassen Volcanic National Park under the Wilderness Act. The Wilderness Society, urging its members to demand a larger wilderness area than the Park Service had proposed, said in part that "the Horseshoe Lake road should be closed in order to provide a quality wilderness camping opportunity that would afford some relief from the standard, congested campgrounds."

The Park Service was already proposing some 50,000 acres of wilderness in Lassen. But the Society made no argument that the additional area had any special wilderness value, much less any ecological value; there was only the snobbish-sounding appeal for a "quality" area away from the "standard" wilderness where the peasants go. (Incidentally, there are Engineers in Lassen, too; on private land inside the park boundaries, there is a proposal for a geyser steam plant.)

Such an emphasis is, in the long run, unfortunate for all of us, because it makes possible blanket criticisms of the whole wilderness concept, like this rather clever version by an attorney for ski-resort interests of what was being proposed in the Cascades:

If a large park and additional wilderness areas are established we can say to the people that want to use them: "Here is one million acres of forest and mountains in their pristine glory. You can't get into it by car, because roads are prohibited. We have a few trails, but we should tell you that the forest is rotting and the trees may fall down and kill you. There is some superb mountain scenery to see, but you have to hike 12 miles over a very difficult trail in order to get above timberline to a vantage point where you can see this scenery. Also, we can only let in a certain number of people each day because if more go, the trail will be damaged through compaction. If too many people walk on the alpine meadows at the end of the trail, they will be destroyed. And one further warning—in going through the forest along this trail, be very careful that you do not wander off more than a hundred yards because you will then be in a virtually impenetrable jungle crisscrossed with wind thrown trees."

This is, of course, the insidious nonsense of careful exaggeration; but the speaker's opponents invite such attacks. The hearing records tend to degenerate into arguments between those who want to cut down the trees and ski down the slopes and those whose entire recreational lives are dedicated to the hiking trip, the sleeping bag and the unspoiled wilderness. In the middle are all the rest of us—who want to see the Everglades and the Cascades, who take spirit from the untouched land, but who spend other parts of our leisure time crowding the city theaters, jamming into Monterey for the Jazz Festival, even clogging the roads to Watkins Glen for the highly technological recreation of an International Grand Prix.

There is no need for such conflict, no point in an argument between me with my Avis car on Diablo Lake and the backpacker who wants to preserve the Glacier Peak Wilderness Area—and we can have lumber besides. There is no need foolishly to fight every work of man, such as City Light's dams or *any* cross-Cascades road. A trip up Route 20 proves that we can have dams and the Skagit too; the ecology doesn't have to be ripped apart every time men build something, if care is shown. And where the ecological pattern is repeated again and again, we can spare one riverhead to the demands of urban convenience—we can have a road for spoiled city dwellers or people in a hurry (like me) and still have plenty of space in the Great Cascades for the backpackers.

If the interests of narrow and selfish men often seem to triumph, it is at least partly because we are so busy bickering with each other like sectarian leftist political groups of the 1920s. The Wilderness Act is a major, even an astonishing, accomplishment. The National Park System is a thing of wonder, to be applauded and enjoyed and encouraged. The work of the Forest Service in maintaining the sustained use of our forests while preserving their beauty is worthy of our highest praise. This is not to say that everything these groups do is right, or that we should refrain from criticism. It is to say that the real enemies are elsewhere—and that a lot is left to do.

There is, for instance, a horrible, gaping hole in the Wilderness Act that may very well mean a horrible, gaping hole in the Great Cascades.

When the proposed act was reported out of the House Committee on Interior and Insular Affairs in 1964—the Senate had already passed a bill identical to the one the committee started with—it had been disfigured by three special-interest amendments, all of them urged by the committee's chairman, Democrat Wayne Aspinall of Colorado.

One of them would have excluded from the bill 3,500 acres of the San Gorgonio Wild Area in southern California, because somebody wanted to build a ski lift there. Representative John Saylor of Pennsylvania moved to amend this amendment out of the bill again, and won the fight by a 73–39 vote.

A second amendment concerned areas in the national forests now classified as "primitive areas," which, under the original bill, have to come up for study as possible wilderness areas within a given period of time, and are supposed to remain as they are until then. The amendment would have allowed the Secretary of Agriculture, at his discretion, to declassify any primitive area—meaning that he, or a successor, could open it up to commercial development before Congress could consider it for wilderness classification.

Saylor came back with another amendment to the amendment, this one saying that sure, the Secretary can declassify the areas—

by recommending declassification to the President, who will then ask Congress, who will then decide one way or the other. In the meantime, nobody touches it. Saylor won that one too, 67–38.

But the third amendment was something else again. It said that mining and mineral leasing, which is okay in national forests generally, would not have to stop in wilderness areas until December 31, 1989. Democratic Representative Henry Reuss of Wisconsin said that mining "is one use which simply cannot be compatible with the concept of wilderness as outlined in the bill." Democrat Frank Clark of Pennsylvania said, "You cannot have mining in wilderness and still preserve wilderness." Democrat John Fogarty of Rhode Island, Republican Silvio Conte of Massachusetts, Republican John Anderson of Illinois all argued against the provision.

Westerners, however, were conspicuously silent, and Aspinall —who is a conservationist like Doris Day is a B-52 pilot, and who owes his prominent Congressional seat as much to mining interests as to anyone—sat back smiling. This time he had the votes and he knew it. Saylor and the other wilderness advocates didn't even offer an amendment, but pinned their hopes on the House-Senate conference committee, which would meet to iron out the differences between the two bills.

They pinned their hopes in the wrong place. All the conference committee did was cut the mining extension from twenty-five to nineteen years, so that it expires on December 31, 1983. Until then, you can explore for minerals, stake mining claims, patent mining claims and dig holes in the ground to your heart's content, wilderness area or no.

A few miners, Congressman Aspinall and three or four other people will tell you that the act contains provisions against undue exploitation, and that miners can't do anything that will really hurt the wilderness. Judge for yourself; this is the "protection":

Mineral leases, permits, and licenses covering lands within national forest wilderness areas designated by this Act shall contain such reasonable stipulations as may be prescribed by the Secretary of Agriculture for the protection of the wilderness character of the land consistent with the use of the land for the purposes for which they are leased, permitted, or licensed.

In other words, the Secretary of Agriculture can stop you from doing things to harm the wilderness, unless what you're doing is necessary to mining. If you have a good Secretary of Agriculture, then fine. One Ezra Taft Benson type, however, and you might as well sell the wilderness areas to the copper companies.

Like, for instance, Kennecott.

Between 1954 and 1958, the Bear Creek Mining Company quietly bought up a bunch of mining claims in the Miner's Creek and Suiattle valleys of Washington, near Glacier Peak. A little later, the claims were transferred to the Ridge Mining Corporation. In 1959, the Forest Service decided that it might like to create the Glacier Peak Wilderness Area (under the pre-1964 definition of "wilderness area"—actually the same thing as the "primitive area" mentioned two pages back) out of parts of Mount Baker and Wenatchee National Forests. Most people wouldn't have minded that—it's still a national forest and you could still mine there—but the Wilderness Act was already being talked about, and you can never tell what these nutty conservationists will do next.

Thus, in October, 1959, when the Forest Service held hearings in Wenatchee on the proposal, three exploration geologists turned up to give their own private opinions that the wilderness area should not be created. Somebody asked one of them whether he was employed by the Kennecott Copper Corporation; he refused to answer. The other two volunteered that they worked for Bear Creek Mining. Nobody volunteered that both Bear Creek and Ridge are wholly owned subsidiaries of Kennecott.

Kennecott now holds 350 acres of patented claims and 2,650 acres of unpatented claims in the area. An unpatented claim gives you an uncontested mining right in the land; you can patent it—i.e., confirm it, make it permanent and beyond the Government's right to withdraw it—by mining it. That's an oversimplification, but it conveys the general idea. In 1966, word leaked out that Kennecott was planning an open-pit copper mine in the heart of the Glacier Peak Wilderness.

If you have never seen an open-pit mine, hunt up a picture of one. Kennecott has a monster of an example at Bingham, Utah—bigger than the proposed pit in Washington, it's true, but the same kind of monstrously ugly scar on the countryside (and, as the

Sierra Club once pointed out, the Washington pit *would* be big enough to be seen from the moon). It's hard to imagine anything uglier.

By now, of course, the Glacier Peak Wilderness Area is included in the Wilderness Act. The mine doesn't look as though it would take up much space—the Glacier Park Wilderness Area includes more than 458,000 acres. But wait.

In the first place, it would be visible for miles around, not only from the moon, and would effectively destroy a whole section—and a relatively accessible section at that—of the wilderness area. In the second place, that sneaky little Aspinall Amendment doesn't say only that you can tear up your claimed 3,000 acres; your claim includes:

such reasonable regulations governing ingress and egress as may be prescribed by the Secretary of Agriculture consistent with the use of the land for mineral location and development and exploration, drilling, and production, and use of land for transmission lines, waterlines, telephone lines, or facilities necessary in exploring, drilling, producing, mining, and processing operations, including where essential the use of mechanized ground or air equipment. . . .

In this case, reasonable ingress and egress seems to mean to Kennecott one hell of a big road up the Suiattle River and then up Miner's Creek, and the other provisions seem to mean one hell of a big processing mill. They also mean—according to C. D. Michaelson, vice president of Kennecott in charge of mining—"hopefully thirty years of blasting." He meant that he hoped it wouldn't be *more* than thirty years.

At the most, the mine will produce as much copper as the United States uses in two days. That ought to be all the argument that's necessary, but it is by no means all that Kennecott's Engineers are willing to do to Glacier Peak for the profits on two days' copper.

When they dig that open pit, two-thirds of what they take out of it won't be ore at all; it will be nothing but waste rock, which they'll dump at the edge of the pit. The one-third that's left will be 1 percent copper. They'll take that 99-to-1 ore down to their mill on Miner's Creek, where they'll use 5,000 tons of water a day to concentrate it to 36 percent copper before carrying it out of the area to their smelter at Tacoma. What's left is called "tailings," which Kennecott will thoughtfully dump on 200 acres of your wilderness area.

If, as Kennecott suggests, the final yield is to be 15,000 tons of copper, that means—if I haven't forgotten my fifth grade arithmetic—that they will dump almost 1.5 million tons of tailings from the concentration process, and about 3 million tons of waste rock near the pit in the first place: 4.5 million tons of junk for two days' copper. If Al Capp had invented it and set the scene in Dogpatch, we'd laugh ourselves into a good mood every morning for a week.

The tailings won't pollute the water as mine tailings have done elsewhere, Mr. Michaelson has said, because they will be kept behind bulkheads. This has been tried before in Washington—at the Holden mine on Railroad Creek. The surrounding vegetation is all dead, the fish in Railroad Creek are all dead, and the tailings are now polluting Lake Chelan, ten miles away.

The pit, Mr. Michaelson has said, will probably fill in, and avalanches and slides will remove the road, and after a while "none of this will be noticeable." Another Kennecott wheel with an Engineer's mind has suggested that the pit be filled with water and a lovely man-made lake be created. The excavated rock will be "indistinguishable from natural talus piles." And the tailings and the dump will be pretty anyway, because Kennecott will plant Australian vetch on it.

Even leaving aside these obvious public-relations fulminations (the Australian vetch would be illegal; you can't introduce an exotic into a wilderness area), the whole thing is patently ridiculous.

In the first place, we don't need the copper. Kennecott has made a big deal out of the national copper shortage, and they have even dragged in support for the boys overseas. The company points out that the Federal Government is engaged in a Copper Production Expansion Program. And indeed it is. The Copper Production Expansion Program, however, has nothing to do with the war in Vietnam—it's designed to produce copper for the nation's emergency stockpile, not because there's any present or immediately foreseen need for it. And more important, the nation doesn't want Kennecott's Glacier Peak copper even for the stockpile.

John G. Harlan, Jr., commissioner of the General Services Administration, made the nation's position quite clear in a letter dated March 31, 1967, written to then Assistant Secretary of Defense Paul R. Ignatius:

The objective of the Expansion Program [Commissioner Harlan wrote in part] was to encourage maximum increased production in the shortest time possible. This project could not contribute sufficiently to qualify for assistance because of the length of time necessary to bring the mine into production and the relatively small amount of additional copper which would result therefrom. It should also be pointed out that even if the project had otherwise qualified for Federal assistance, it is doubtful that the contribution it would make to the critical copper supply situation would have been sufficient to outweigh other important considerations, such as the inevitable damage to the natural beauty of the wilderness area.

And Assistant Secretary Ignatius, whose job was Installations and Logistics and who might have been expected to know something about what the country needs, wrote, when he sent the letter along to Senator Henry Jackson of Washington, that "I am in agreement with the point of view expressed by Mr. Harlan."

Mr. Harlan, by the way, also said something else. He said that Kennecott had never asked that the Glacier Peak operation be qualified under the Copper Production Expansion Program. So much for our boys overseas.

In 1967 Secretary of Agriculture Freeman openly asked Kennecott to save everybody a lot of trouble and abandon Glacier Peak. Regional Forester J. Herbert Stone, who heads the region, called the mine proposal "incompatible." But Kennecott is so completely determined that the whole thing may wind up in court.

Under those reasonable ingress and egress regulations, and the reasonable stipulations that the Secretary of Agriculture is allowed to make, the Forest Service and Secretary Freeman have proposed that Kennecott try an underground mine instead of an open pit, and use a narrow-gauge railroad instead of building a road. So far, Kennecott has said no—and Cal Dunnell, recreation and land use staff director of the Mount Baker National Forest, thinks maybe he knows why.

"The company apparently feels," Dunnell said, "that our requests would increase their costs of operating to an unreasonable degree. They have the right to take us to court to try to prove that the requests are unreasonable. We expect that they will."

If they do, it will be a case that deals with a lot more than the reasonableness of a request for a narrow-gauge railroad. It will be *the* test case concerning the Forest Service's powers in regulating a wilderness area under the present act and its Aspinall Amendment.

Kennecott may yet withdraw, of course, but they seem to be spoiling for an all-out fight (they have been appearing in opposition to the U.S. Geological Survey at a lot of hearings on proposed wilderness areas elsewhere in the country, including some in which they have no holdings). There is also a theory that the company is trying to blackmail the United States into buying its claims at some inflated figure, but there is no real evidence for it.

And there is a third possibility (one that should be remembered, every Election Day, by people in the Second Congressional District of Washington). Representative Lloyd Meeds, who is from that district, has come up with a bill that would authorize the Secretary of Agriculture to condemn property now owned by mining companies in the Glacier Peak Wilderness Area, to withdraw unpatented mining claims, to forbid further prospecting, and to provide just compensation (not overinflated compensation) to the owners.

Of course, the bill will probably wind up in Aspinall's committee, and that will be that. But it's still a possibility.

It would seem that there must be something more than 15,000 tons of copper involved, because Kennecott could earn a fortune in good will by simply quitting—and they certainly don't need the measly couple of million they might make. For instance: Until 1964, Kennecott owned the Braden Copper Company, which operated near Santiago, Chile. In that year, the Chilean Government bought 51% of the company—for $80 million. Production went up to 280,000 tons at about that time, and Kennecott still owns 49%.

There are Kennecott copper mines in Utah, Nevada, Arizona and New Mexico, and one in Alaska that's expected to start producing in 1970. Mining properties are in production, about to begin production or are under serious exploitation in North Carolina (open pit, phosphate), Puerto Rico (copper), British Columbia (open pit, molybdenum, and some copper drilling), Quebec and Australia. The company owns properties in Nigeria and has an option on a 20-percent interest in a mining operation in South Africa (where miners cash in on *apartheid*-style labor).

Besides all that, it owns part of Kaiser Aluminum and a few other firms. In 1965 its consolidated *net* income was $102 million, and it isn't getting any smaller; the net income for the *first half* of 1967 was almost as much: $94,200,000.

No such statistics can be summoned for the steelhead in the Suiattle—the same steelhead that populate the Skagit farther north, after traveling the Skagit-Sauk-Suiattle pathway to their breeding grounds. The breeding grounds will almost certainly disappear under the impact of the road and the mine tailings, as waterways everywhere in the country have gone when pit- or strip-mining operations are nearby.

"The basic question is to try to establish a proper balance of the use of our two billion acres of land mass in this country." So wrote Frank R. Milliken, president of Kennecott Copper. He was quite right. He then went on to ask, "Is it necessary, if minerals are discovered in other wilderness areas, that each case must be tried in the press?"

Of course it is. If each case isn't described (not "tried") in the press, if we don't talk about it out loud and get the arguments in each case into the open, how is the "proper balance" to be struck? The answer is that it will be struck in favor of the Engineers and their anything-for-a-buck bosses, and we will all wake up, very soon now, surrounded by dams where there used to be rivers and open-pit mines where there used to be wilderness.

Certainly we need copper. I wouldn't, and probably couldn't, be without it. But we don't need *that* crummy little chunk of copper at *that* expense, and Mr. Milliken would probably know it if he weren't on the receiving end of the project. We have enough troubles trying to figure out how best to use such a magnificent resource as Mount Baker National Forest, so that wilderness (and ecological integrity) will remain while recreational space for other uses continues to be available.

The need for that space already so presses upon us that saving any wilderness at all is going to be increasingly difficult, and that means that the wilderness advocates—the backpackers—are going to have to start seeking allies by backing up people who want to use other land for other things, from artificial lakes for fishing to road racing courses. The demands on Yosemite and the Great Smokies are already too great. We must have either additional facilities—at the expense of wilderness—or alternative destinations for the vacationer with a car, with small children, with elderly parents. We can of course kill a national park or a national forest by choking it to death with campsites; before that happens, we must somehow ensure that some of the cars, some of the little old ladies, go elsewhere this year.

And it must be somewhere nearer home. "The fact that there will remain thousands of acres of empty land in Wyoming," noted William H. Whyte, Jr., "is not going to help the man living in Teaneck, New Jersey." Geographer Noel Eichhorn had an even more dramatic point to make:

If the national parks are to continue to serve their purpose, the number of visitors to any given park must be held to no more than that park can stand without being markedly changed. If the people of the country continue to hold the philosophy that everyone must be able to see everything, ways will have to be found to display the parks, perhaps by television, without actually letting very many people inside.

The specific idea probably wouldn't work: it's at least as likely that seeing a place on television, particularly color television, may simply make people that much more anxious to see it in person. But the alternatives may not be limited to cutting off the little old lady and making the land available only to the backpacker. In some locations, perhaps, a simple restriction of access might help. The two lanes of State Highway 1 in California, for example, along the coast north of San Francisco, get pretty crowded during the summer; but there is an absolute limit to the number of cars (and consequently of people) that can fit on the highway at all. By not making the highway any larger, the number of people visiting the area could be restricted without discrimination in favor of a particular *kind* of people, and the same principle could be used in some other places.

There are semantic possibilities as well, if governmental rivalries can be sufficiently set aside. Some beautiful but nonessential areas—areas, for example, in the national forests that surround Great Smoky Mountains National Park—can be called "national parks"; access or visitation could be restricted only in those places which have serious ecological importance or will be irreversibly damaged by overuse, and many of the campers and hikers wouldn't care that much.

But in any case, something must be done to distribute the recreational load on the land, and it cannot be done without cooperation among the varied groups involved. "Wilderness enthusiasts," Michael Frome wrote in *Holiday,* "should support the motorcyclists in their desire for specialized recreation areas. . . ." Well, of course—and the boaters, and the fishermen, and the hurried visitors with rented cars. We not only should have, but we *need,* both motorcycle hill-climbing areas and wildlife refuges, both untouched Everglades and trails where children can gaze popeyed at alligators, both unsullied watersheds and artificial lakes behind dams for boating and swimming, both roads through the Great Cascades and sections of the Great Cascades left forever wild.

And we have to help each other get them. If it means the Park Service's 50,000 acres of wilderness in Lassen Park instead of the 101,000 acres the Wilderness Society demands, then that is what it has to mean.

Dr. F. H. Bormann, of the department of biological sciences at Dartmouth, gave an example of what happens when uses come into conflict:

The northern hardwood forest ecosystem covers most of the land area of northern New England and is basic to the economy of the region. During the past 10 years, working with state groups in New Hampshire and Vermont, I have attempted to locate good examples of old age, relatively undisturbed northern hardwood forest. . . . Recently the best stand has been greatly impaired by the construction of a lake conceived and developed by the state fish and game commission.

How much better if all the people concerned with conserving something had learned to see the land in terms of its ecosystems.

Surely the needs of fish and game are not incompatible with the need for preservation and study of an important environmental area. After all, it all existed together before we came along.

The most disturbing fact about the Wilderness Act is not the Aspinall Amendment, destructive though that is. It is that no one—not the act's authors, not the Wilderness Society, not the local groups who fight for this or that area—seems to understand that the best reason for the preservation of wilderness areas is not esthetics but ecology: the *need,* not just the desirability, of preserving ecosystems, and sometimes vast ones, for study.

The Wilderness Act would be a great deal better if it specifically noted that ecologists doing field studies *must* alter at least small parts of the environment in the course of doing controlled experiments (they will even screw it up once in a while, though on nothing like the scale practiced by the Engineers). It would be better, too, if the Government showed some sign of understanding that the living species that make up part of an ecosystem can't read the signs that show the boundaries of the official wilderness area; some provision could be made for protection that would extend beyond those official lines, possibly even into nearby areas with roads and campsites.

On my way back from the top of the Skagit, I stopped at a tiny restaurant, which is the only building in Newhalem not owned by Seattle Power and Light, and I talked with the couple who operate it. It's open only two hours a day during the winter months, serving only City Light personnel, but during the summer it hums with tourists. In 1966, I learned, the power company took 24,-000 people through a tour it operates for visitors; easily twice that many, perhaps more, must have visited the area, and visited it deliberately, because the road did not yet go anywhere else.

"Is that too many people?" I asked, because the woman behind the counter obviously loves the stark and snow-clad mountains and the green and gentle river.

"No," she replied, after a moment. "But one of these years it will be."

INTERLUDE: GOODBY, RUBY TUESDAY

> Goodby, Ruby Tuesday,
> Who can hang a name on you
> When you change with every new day?—
> Still I'm gonna miss you.
> —THE ROLLING STONES

SAVE THE CABLE CARS.

Save the Grand Canyon.

Save the Metropolitan Opera House.

Save the upper Selway, the roseate spoonbill, the striped bass, the Missouri, Lake Erie, the coyote, the epiphytic algae.

What shall we save, and why?

On the Florida coast is a monument to the memory of Guy M. Bradley. When the craze for egret plumes threatened the existence of that snowy bird, the Audubon Society paid the wardens who protected the egret from illegal poaching. In Monroe County, Warden Bradley arrested a plume poacher and was shot dead. Before the fight of the feathers was over, another warden, Columbus McLeod, had also been killed.

Would anyone die for the roseate spoonbill?

Probably. And probably as ignorantly, for it is doubtful whether Bradley or McLeod had even as much knowledge as is available today—little as that is—about the ecological role of the snowy egret. It is doubtful whether they had any concept of the conservation of genetic information. They knew only that the birds were beautiful and ought not to die.

The people who want to preserve things to keep them "natural" are caught in a contradiction, as their opponents love to point out.

For in nature, too, species become extinct, and fire or flood occasionally destroys a forest stand. The Wilderness Act provides for fire control (as it should—there will be people hiking and camping in the wilderness areas); there is no question, even in the mind of the most ardent preservationist, of simply letting nature take its course.

We need a reason to save things, and not alone because they are pretty. There are pretty highways—as any advertisement for American automobiles or Greyhound buses makes clear. There are pretty bridges and pretty dams and pretty artificial lakes. Some of the best fishing is in artificially stocked streams, and some of the best camping is in artificially managed forests.

In San Francisco a few years ago, cries of esthetic horror went up when a Texas group constructed a new hotel, the Jack Tar, which embodies the epitome of architectural awfulness. Fifty years hence, when somebody wants to build something else on the site, we can foresee a later generation mounting a campaign to save the Jack Tar, as an architecturally unique example not without its grotesque charm. What shall we save?

I have before me, as I write, a stack of literature begging me, or anyone else who will listen, to save 250,000 acres of wilderness on the upper Selway River in Idaho. A vast area of land has been put into wilderness, but a corridor has been left, which is now, according to one leaflet, "threatened by logging and roads!" Nowhere in this literature is there any argument as to *why* I should try to help save it, except simply to keep it from being logged.

But *something* has to be logged, and without roads I, for one, will probably never see *any* of the upper Selway. I am willing to urge—I would be willing to urge right now—that the upper Selway ought to be saved, if someone points out that logging this particular corridor will somehow endanger the watershed ecology, or make a meaningful difference to the rest of the already selected wilderness area. It very well may be true, and perhaps it should be saved. But none of the literature makes that point, and I have to reply that we can't save everything.

If an ecological sense can do nothing else for us, it can provide us with some understanding of what needs to be saved and why. Circular 223 of the Bureau of Sport Fisheries and Wildlife, issued in 1965, lists more than 200 forms of vertebrate animals in the United States and Puerto Rico as at least threatened; the numbers of endangered invertebrates and plants must be much larger. It's easy enough to want to save the Grand Canyon or the crocodile; Nevada's nearly barren Great Basin or the roseate spoonbill demand a little more dedication; to want to save a swamp or a salt marsh (or, perhaps, the coyote), you need a pretty good reason.

Not long ago, *The New York Times* carried a story about a cooperative effort, involving the Smithsonian Institution, that will attempt to study (with the idea of saving) the elephants of Ceylon. On the same day it also carried a story about the formation of the Committee for the Preservation of the United States Capitol. Everybody wants to save something, for one reason or another.

But without a sense of the ecosystem, we will not only fail to rally support for particular projects; we will fail to save some of the things that ought to be saved. The beauty and the uniqueness of redwood stands, or of the Grand Canyon, are obvious; but there is no overwhelming conservationist support for the proposed Great Basin National Park, which would preserve an ecosystem not duplicated anywhere in the world.

In *The Destruction of California,* Raymond Dasmann came up with another candidate nobody thinks about:

The larger species of wild animals, or the more glamorous ones, have hosts of defenders. Forests have their friends, and even individual species of trees have organizations to protect them. But it is difficult to find friends for grass. . . . We have no grassland reserves or primitive areas, and most of us don't even know what a good range should look like. Even in state and national parks the grasslands are often allowed to deteriorate or grow up in alien species without anyone being aware of the change. Yet natural grasslands are surely as valuable from a scientific viewpoint as natural forests.

Durward Allen of Purdue, another friend of grass, writes that as recently as 1963 the Senate tabled indefinitely a proposal for a Prairie National Park in the tall-grass region of northeastern Kansas. And yet, says Dr. Allen, "one of the greatest needs we have, I think, one of the greatest challenges in wilderness restoration and preservation, is that of creating at least one major national park in our grasslands."

Not, of course, that that would be easy. As another ecologist, A. Starker Leopold, has pointed out, such a park would take thousands of acres—and while people may be willing to give us impassable chunks of the Rocky Mountains for national parks, a few thousand acres of fertile prairie is something else again.

Nobody much wants to save chaparral along the Rio Grande, either. The typical Western thicket of shrubs and thorny bushes has been cleared out to plant cotton and vegetables and citrus trees, except for about a thousand acres scattered around. In those thousand acres are concentrated nestings of white-winged doves, and, says Dr. Allen, they are "a unique habitat in the United States for jaguarundi and ocelot, several species of hawks, and various Mexican birds." Personally, I'd rather have one ocelot than a lot of the products of Texas, but you may disagree with me.

Happily, the World Wildlife Fund has decided to buy up this particular hunk of chaparral, and is also trying to buy up some grassland on the Gulf Coast of Texas in the hope of saving the Attwater prairie chicken, which lives only there and whose 1963 population was down to 1,335 because its habitat is disappearing.

But private money won't do it, especially when what is to be saved has a high monetary value or is little understood. And, unfortunately, we have a tendency to put available government money into the popular instead of the necessary. In a newspaper article, Dasmann noted that "the Government did not have to build Disneyland in order for such a venture to be carried through," and added that it would be irresponsible for the Government to build more Disneylands. But:

. . . government support is needed for those forms of public outdoor recreation that are not popular, because the level of public awareness and education does not yet create a demand for them, yet are essential if the level of public appreciation of its natural heritage is to be expanded.

There are better motives than that, but the point is clear. Public money has to support the conservation of what we have to save, because private money won't, despite the occasional and welcome examples provided by the World Wildlife Fund and a few other organizations. And public money won't do a lot of it at all—grasslands, for instance—and won't do the rest of it right, unless we have some overall idea of what we *have* to save and why.

In fact, even the long-raging fight over the redwoods is almost sure to be lost on this point. There will be a Redwoods National Park, but unless something drastic changes, it won't be where it should be. The situation changes too often and too rapidly to keep up with in a book, but the important thing is that everybody has just about decided to reject the original Sierra Club proposal for a park, and the Sierra Club has shown itself ready to compromise.

The Sierra Club's original proposal was for a 93,000-acre park on Redwood Creek, which would cost about $140 million. Secretary of the Interior Stewart Udall was on one occasion quite outspoken about it; the Redwood Creek proposal, he said would "break the back of the conservation fund."

"We can't have a national recreation and park program by putting all the money into redwoods," he added. And noting that the lumber industry is opposed (surprise!), he said further that "we would be picking a fight instead of picking a park."

It's a nice phrase. How does the Sierra Club answer it? In their Fact Sheet No. 2 on the argument, they made these pitches for Redwood Creek:

In the valley of lower Redwood Creek, the team found the largest large stand of surviving virgin redwoods yet unprotected. Here they found the world's tallest known tree. Since, reports of even taller trees have been made in that area. . . .

[Mill Creek] lacks stands of record dimensions. It does not have herds of Roosevelt elk nor long, wide beaches, such as the Gold Bluffs Beach.

No doubt arguments like this are necessary to whip up support, but they aren't going to convince a money-conscious Secretary or a money-conscious Congress. Herds of Roosevelt elk are nice and should be saved, as should all species, but there is no indication that Roosevelt elk will die out.

The real importance of the Redwood Creek proposal—the full Sierra Club proposal, embracing all 93,000 acres and regardless of how much it costs—was that it marked the last chance to save a complete, or nearly complete, redwood ecosystem. The topography ranges from sea level to 2,500 feet; the proposed park area embraced nearly all of the watershed of Redwood Creek, while the Park approved by Congress takes in only small parts of the watersheds involved—and those parts at the bottom. The park visitor, except for saying "ooh!" when he reads a plaque at the tree's base, doesn't really know whether he's seeing the world's tallest tree or its tenth or twentieth tallest. But he knows whether he is seeing a tree.

On Bull Creek—a tributary of the South Fork of the Eel River, farther south in California—stood, until a decade or so ago, Rockefeller Forest, a state-owned stand of virgin redwoods, maintained in preservation. Between 1947 and 1954, the unprotected area above Rockefeller Forest was logged by private lumber companies; a fire followed their activities, and in the winter of 1954–55, northern California was hit by severe storms.

Any storm, of course, results in a certain amount of stream-bottom erosion when the water is unusually high. But the naked slopes of upper Bull Creek couldn't hold the water they had once retained, and in the classic pattern of erosion the river rose even higher, and in its turn undercut its banks to create more erosion, the circle ever widening until finally, in the Rockefeller Forest, the ground was cut from under the mighty—and "protected"—redwoods, and hundreds of them fell to the gnawing water. Logging has ceased now on upper Bull Creek—but every winter more redwoods fall.

Bull Creek is the reason why the Redwoods National Park should not only be on Redwood Creek but should embrace the entire 93,000-acre proposal of the Sierra Club—not because the trees are taller or because there is a pretty beach. The preservation of the entire watershed area is not only the one sure way to protect the redwoods; it is also the only plan that makes the redwood ecosystem available to the future. A few trees at the bottom of a river are not an ecosystem in the redwood country, and if you kill the ecosystem you're only kidding yourself about saving the trees.

I don't mean to imply that the Sierra Club people don't know all this; they do, and sometimes they even say it. What I deplore is that the final decision should be made on the basis of either which location is prettier or which costs more. Both criteria are beside the point.

So, incidentally, is any criterion based on the use or preservation of "resources," as Professor Sanford Farness of Michigan State has said rather well:

> . . . we commonly speak in our planning studies and reports today of "natural resources" and "human resources." Now when we apply the concept "resource" to something we have already classified it as a "means"—an instrumental value toward our ends. At this point we have already assumed the economic attitude and are geared primarily for economic decision making.

To decide what to save on the basis of an economic decision is the sheerest folly.

To save the United States Capitol, or the cable cars, or the Metropolitan Opera House, or the Jack Tar Hotel, is one kind of thing. If it became important enough, we could even tear them all down and then, later, duplicate them. But in Europe, some experimenters in animal husbandry are trying, through selective breeding, to re-create a live aurochs—the evolutionary ancestor of the cow. It is a worthwhile experiment, for a great deal is being learned; but it is also an ironic one, because they will never know whether they have succeeded. "Habitat preservation," Dr. Cain has written, "is the key to species preservation, whether it be a microscopic flatworm on the underside of a water-lily leaf or a thousand-pound moose browsing water lilies at the edge of a wilderness lake." The aurochs—like the redwood, and like you and me—does not exist alone. You can't re-create an ecosystem.

In New York, the Adirondack Forest Preserve—2.6 million acres —is protected by the state constitution, which says that it must remain in its wild state. New York, however, has been trying to devise a new state constitution, and conservationists are mobilized to make sure that the "forever wild" clause stays in. "They could do some terrible things," one of them said to me. "They could put it into the constitution, for instance, that Negroes can't own property, or that everybody has to pay a 50 percent income tax—and of course I'd fight those things. But if they went into the constitution, then in a year, or two years, or five years, we could get those provisions out again. Once the loggers get their saws to work, we can't put the Adirondack Forest back by rewriting the constitution."

We can't put the redwoods back in Rockefeller Forest either. That, it would seem, is the key to answering the question "What should we save?" We should save—not everything we can't replace, for we can't replace a single stone or blade of grass— but everything that is ecologically meaningful, every living species, every remaining essentially undisturbed ecosystem, from Redwood Creek to the Great Basin to the Great Swamp.

We should seek the knowledge we need to make use of these principles, too. Ian McHarg, a landscape architect, told a group of ecologists what *he'd* like to know, for example, about all the varying environments of the United States:

I would like to know . . . the degree to which these environments are prohibitive to intervention, or permissive. . . .

One would like to know, of all lands, which lands can best support man or his interventions of one sort or another. And which cannot. For any region, where can man intervene in a massive way? Where can he not intervene at all?

We don't know, and we won't know until we develop what Aldo Leopold called an "ecological conscience," the concept that we don't own the world or any part of it, but that man is, as another ecologist put it, "the holder of a life rent, bearing the responsibility so to order his activities that he turns over to his successors the biological capital with which the world is endowed in at least as good condition as when he got it."

VI · EVERYBODY SHOULD BREAK AN ANKLE

IN A LAWSUIT in San Francisco a few years ago, an attorney was trying to recover damages for a workman who had broken his ankle on the job, and on the stand a doctor testifying for the insurance company was vigorously insisting that no permanent damage had been done. The ankle, the doctor insisted, was as good as new.

"In fact," the doctor argued, "the cartilage that has grown up at the point of fracture is actually stronger than the original bone."

The attorney turned to the jury, raised an eloquent eyebrow, and turned back to fix the doctor with a withering stare. "Tell me, doctor," he asked, "do you recommend this type of fracture to all your patients?"

All across the United States, the Engineers (and particularly the Engineers who work for private industry) are recommending fractures as improvements on the national ankles. In fact, if Engineers across the country are engaged in rapine, it is in private industry particularly that they find their public relations colleagues eager to assure the public that rape is really a therapeutic treatment designed to soothe anxiety, improve circulation and whiten the teeth. They are experts at finding ingenious ways to convince you that fractures are good for you.

Willard F. Cheley, assistant to the board chairman of the Georgia-Pacific Corporation, told *The New York Times* that "the corporation is so interested in conservation that it plants five trees for every one it chops down in its lumber business—sometimes it plants ten and fifteen trees. We are very conservation minded." That the trees cut down are sometimes in irreplaceable virgin Douglas fir stands, Mr. Cheley omits to say.

The Arcata Redwood Company—which did its best to cut down the redwoods along Redwood Creek before anybody could protect them in a park—posts signs along the highway when the ruinous consequences of its work cannot be hidden. They read: OVERMATURE TIMBER HARVESTED HERE. Overmature timber, of course, is any tree big enough to cut down and make a profit on.

Among the best of the fracture-sellers are the giant utility companies. The largest of them—California's Pacific Gas and Electric Company—not only spends huge amounts every year to keep its "image" clean (through such activities as a sizable annual contribution to the San Francisco Museum of Art, for instance), but "encourages" its executives in every northern California town to become unselfish civic leaders.

With every monthly utility bill, the PG&E customer gets a copy of a slick, eight-page publication called *PG&E Progress,* and in every *PG&E Progress* there is a profile of a fortyish, eager, energetic young man who's a member of the local housing commission, heads a troop of Boy Scouts, plays in the local chamber music group, heads the local Lions Club, and somehow puts in a few hours a day as a local PG&E executive. The profiles are virtually identical (for one thing, outside the two or three largest cities these active executives are all white males), and so are the messages: Look at us, we're such good guys.

And then there's Con Ed.

Everybody knows about the Consolidated Edison Company, because some years ago they made one of the greatest public relations goofs in major corporate history. Because they serve New York City (as well as a number of surrounding areas) and because in New York City the electric lines are underground and because Manhattan keeps building new buildings of massive size (and ugliness), Con Ed is constantly having to dig up the streets. So, of course, do the street department and the subway people and a few other diggers, and—Manhattan being only twelve blocks wide in its busy midtown area—people are constantly running into a crew digging a hole in whatever street they happen to be hurrying along. Deciding to make a virtue of necessity, Con Ed came up with a cartoon of a happy-looking little man in a construction helmet and the cheery slogan, "Dig we must!" Humorists leaped on it, the cartoonists who toil for *The New Yorker* made it nationally famous, and as a result Con Ed is blamed for every excavation that momentarily slows a cab in heavily overcrowded Manhattan. Now they're trying to get rid of the slogan.

With a little luck, they'll be more successful with that public relations campaign (in which, I confess, they have my sympathy) than with a couple of others that haven't done so well—and shouldn't: Indian Point and Storm King.

Indian Point, on the Hudson River, is the site of a nuclear power station opened by Con Ed, with great fanfare, in 1963. A lot of people don't like *any* nuclear power plants, and with some reason —the general idea is that utility company Engineers are in a great rush to build the damned things, while nobody really knows enough yet about what their effects might be—but there wasn't any really great outcry about Indian Point. Like all reactors so far, it is a thermal polluter—it raises the temperature of the river at its site by using river water as a coolant and then dumping the warmed water back into the riverbed—but the Hudson is so fouled up anyway that a lot of people have given up on it.

The only problem was that after the plant opened, somebody noticed a bunch of crows around a dump near the new power station—more crows by far than usual. When this kept up for a while, somebody got in touch with the Long Island League of Saltwater Sportsmen, a group which—in marked contrast to a lot of sportsmen's groups—happened to retain a consulting biologist. His name is Dominick Pirone, and he went to take a look at the dump.

Although Con Ed didn't want him to look, he managed to see bulldozers at work, shoving dead bass into twelve-foot-high piles, where lime was being dumped on them to hasten their decomposition. And he saw a line of trucks, bringing new loads of dead bass. Pirone decided to follow the trucks, and found himself at Indian Point.

"I saw and smelled," he said, "some 10,000 dead and dying fish under the dock."

The seven-degree rise in the temperature of the water, after the plant has sucked in Hudson River water and spat it back out again, is enough to attract spawning bass. They were trapped under the dock and ultimately suffocated. Intake pipes sucked them up into wire baskets, the baskets were dumped into the trucks—and before Con Ed, under pressure, put up a fine-mesh screen around the dock, 2,000,000 bass had been killed.

Con Ed did its best to kill the story. New York's Representative Richard Ottinger (who would probably have leprosy by now if somebody on the Con Ed staff had the Evil Eye) described it this way:

The story of the Indian Point fish kill is strangely obscure. There are reports of truckloads of fish carted away secretly; fish graveyards limed to hasten the destruction of evidence and guarded by Burns detectives to prevent witnesses' access to see the size of the kill. There are stories of pictures suppressed by State officials and State employees pressured into silence.

That was before Pirone's visit blew it wide open. I've seen some of those once-suppressed pictures and talked to a couple of those state employees. And I've also learned that fine-mesh screens may prevent spectacular fish kills—but they don't necessarily protect fish, as will become clear when we get to Storm King.

Before that, though, let us turn to Wesley Marx, from whose book the Indian Point account is largely taken. He uses it, as it must be used, as an example of the need for an ecological sense, an ecological conscience—not as a moral imperative but as a practical need in an increasingly hungry world where every salmon, bass and shad may be of literally vital importance:

To be fully effective any program designed to preserve anadromous fish [salt-water fish who go up fresh-water streams to spawn] from extinction in the twentieth century must encompass the entire environment of the fish, from the international waters of the open ocean to the headwaters of mountain streams. Every human activity along this vast range, from fishing to waste disposal to water storage, must meet the breathing, feeding, and spawning requirements of the fish. Wherever these requirements clash with human activity, it would have to cease or a duplicate environment for the fish created [sic]. A program of anadromous conservation thus runs up against every conceivable political and economic obstacle in modern life.

But it's been done on the Columbia, and it could be done on the Hudson. The biggest "political and economic obstacle" is Con Ed.

On a foggy January afternoon, I drove slowly up Route 9D in New York, a winding, occasionally dangerous road that follows the east bank of the Hudson. To my immediate left, railroad yards, dumps and frequent junk piles occupied the foreground; in the middle distance the brown and dirty but still-impressive river went past in the other direction, as much as three and a half miles wide at Haverstraw Bay; beyond, in the distance, the false fronts of the Palisades, looming and impressive even though I knew that their backs have been quarried away, looked somberly down.

I did not think about Henry Hudson and the tiny *Half Moon*, probing 350 years ago for a passageway to the western sea, nor about Benson Lossing a century ago, paddling and sketching and taking notes for his still-beautiful book on the river. Instead, I found myself thinking about the desperate people of Manhattan, where for a time I lived, and whose citizens seemed to share an almost frantic need to get out, to get away, at every opportunity, while at the same time they cannot or will not give up the fantastic complexity and excitement of that filthy, exciting, lonely, exhilarating city. I thought of the power blackout, through which I had lived, and how amiably New Yorkers had borne it—and of how dramatically it demonstrated the city's total dependence on electricity and on the Consolidated Edison Company.

Where a tunnel pokes through Breakneck Ridge, I stopped, left the car in the parking lot of the deserted Breakneck Lodge, and climbed down the bank to walk across the New York Central tracks and stand on the shore. Across the Hudson—narrow and hurrying at this point—was Storm King Mountain.

The ridge behind me was, and is, 295 feet higher than Storm King's 1,340 feet; I remember thinking irrelevantly that the highest point in my native hilly San Francisco is less than 1,000 feet above sea level. But Breakneck Ridge is simply there. Storm King rises directly and abruptly from the rushing river, and in its presence, even from the other side of the river, I felt that sense of helpless puniness that men are apt to feel in the presence of nature at its most impressive.

The Engineers of the Consolidated Edison Company feel no such puniness. Like all of the Engineers, they know of mountains and rivers only that they are there to be used, changed, managed. Storm King, they have decided, is the ideal place for a pump storage plant.

A pump storage plant is a simple thing, though not in itself an economical one. Its function is to suck up water, and to pump it to a high reservoir. Then, at peak periods when the company needs to deliver a lot of power, the reservoir releases the water to fall back into the river, and the plant uses the falling water to generate electricity.

The drawings for the plant, which was to be on the north slope of Storm King, showed no particular esthetic damage to the site, but then of course they wouldn't. When conservationists protested the plans to build the plant, Con Ed promptly responded, not only that "we need the power" and that taxes and payroll would benefit the town of Cornwall (which rose magnificently to the bait), but that the care which Con Ed would give the site would actually improve its scenic values.

The company also said it would build the town of Cornwall, in which Storm King is located, a riverfront park (since they have to dump all that dirt somewhere, they plan simply to dump it into the river—which says enough about their concern for bass spawning grounds and shoreline ecology—and then to build the park on it)—which the town welcomed, partly because a park built without state or Federal funds could be restricted to local citizens. The town fathers call this being free from "urban pressures." What it really means is that they can keep out not only Negroes and Puerto Ricans from New York City, but even the nearest black citizens, from Newburgh.

By now, however, we have heard all this nonsense about improving the scenery before. A seacoast away, the proposal of PG&E to deface California's beautiful Bodega Head with a nuclear reactor was billed by the company as "PG&E's Atomic Park." In neither of these two cases, as it happens, did the Engineers get away with the peculiar esthetics of their first attempt; public pressure forced PG&E to surrender its reactor plans (temporarily; it has leased the site to the county as a park for $1 a year, but for only five years), and on the Hudson, Con Ed finally, and grumpily, agreed that it could bury its 800-foot-long plant, pump its water up and let it fall through a tunnel, and put the necessary power lines underground instead of allowing them to march through the town of Yorktown on steel towers.

Now—as major industries usually do—they are taking all the credit for what they were forced to do; the "underground plant" and the "hidden tunnel" are trumpeted as evidence of their concern for the site, and they profess to be bewildered about why everybody doesn't immediately start to love them for improving Storm King. They have even taken, as New Yorkers will have noticed, to calling it the "Cornwall project" instead of the "Storm King project," a device known to anthropologists and metalinguists as word magic.

But while they are talking fast, loud and long about the great underground hidden operation that no one can see, and simultaneously claiming that it will improve the site, they are hoping that nobody will notice a few other things, and they profoundly wish—with understandable sensitivity after what happened at Indian Point—that everybody would stop talking about fish.

Storm King is uniquely beautiful, and it is of unique historical importance; those facts are actually outside the scope of this book, which is primarily concerned with ecosystems and genetic information. If I go on talking about Storm King's uniqueness a little, it is only because Storm King is such a perfect illustration of an industry's explanation that fractures are better than unbroken ankles. Fish, however, are not outside the scope of this book, and anyone who thinks that a few screens (or, in this case, a whole massive network of screens, a lot of them visible) are going to make it all right just doesn't dig fish.

Testimony from the State Conservation Department should, in a rational world, be enough; and according to New York's Joint Legislative Committee on Natural Resources, "The State Conservation Department admitted that it could not project the effect of the Storm King project on fish life."

Con Ed's paid experts can, of course, and have done so; they say it will be all right. At the first Federal Power Commission hearing on the proposal, someone unkindly pointed out that striped bass—beloved of fishermen from Long Island to South Carolina—go up the Hudson to spawn, and that something like 85 percent of them spawn in the Storm King area. That gigantic "straw" through which Con Ed plans to suck up as much as 1,000,000 cubic feet of water *per minute* from the Hudson can suck up fish and larvae and fish eggs just as easily—and while everybody now knows about the 2,000,000 bass killed at Indian Point, nobody much mentions eggs or larvae.

The FPC ruled once that such warnings were "untimely," and that "the project will not adversely affect the fish resources of the Hudson provided adequate protective facilities are installed." You can't argue with that. The project won't hurt anything provided you build it so that it won't hurt anything. The problem is that you can't do that. An Interior Department spokesman, James McBroom, told a Congressional committee flatly that "practical means of protection of eggs and larvae stages have yet to be devised." Screens just won't do it.

Screens, however, are what Con Ed proposes—and for those who care what all this looks like, the screens include a permanent, but movable, crane to lift them out of the water for cleaning at periodic intervals. What will be lifted out of the water, it appears, are 96 pieces of screen, each 9 feet wide and more than 40 feet deep. They'll hang out there somewhere to mark the site of Washday-on-the-Hudson.

The FPC once granted Con Ed the permit to build this monstrosity, but—happily for the bass and the Hudson—a group called the Scenic Hudson Preservation Conference had come into being, and had hired as executive director a hard-talking, hard-fighting publicist named Rod Vandivert. With the aid of a number of other people, notably attorney David Sive, Vandivert took the FPC to court, and won from the United States Court of Appeals a historic decision:

In this case, as in many others, the Commission has claimed to be the representative of the public interest. This role does not permit it to act as an umpire blandly calling balls and strikes for adversaries appearing before it; the right of the public must receive active and affirmative protection at the hands of the Commission.

The court ruled that the FPC must take scenic, historic and recreational values into account; that it has to care about the fish; that it has to listen to testimony—such as that offered by former New York City engineer Alexander Lurkis—about alternative methods of providing the power if New York City needs it:

Especially in a case of this type, where public interest and concern is so great, the Commission's refusal to receive the Lurkis testimony, as well as proffered information on fish protection devices and underground transmission facilities, exhibits a disregard of the statute and of judicial mandates instructing the Commission to probe all feasible alternatives.

Finally, the opinion, written by Judge Paul R. Hays, broke a little new ground in giving explicit directions to the Commission:

The Commission's renewed proceedings must include as a basic concern the preservation of natural beauty and of national historic shrines, keeping in mind that, in our affluent society, the cost of a project is but one of several factors to be considered.

Nothing could be better calculated to drive the Engineers out of their minds. When the FPC began new hearings in response to the court's order, for instance, *Electrical World,* an industry magazine, said that the "Cornwall project" (they don't call it "Storm King" either, apparently by coincidence) was "tediously being drawn through new but repetitious hearings," and sneered at Con Ed witnesses' being "asked, more or less, to define 'beauty'—in 25 words or less."

To make matters even worse for the Engineers, the Supreme Court came down in early 1967 with what is known as the "High Mountain Sheep decision," concerning a private power company's proposed dam on the Snake River. Secretary of the Interior Stewart Udall had asked the FPC to turn down the application to build the dam, arguing that it might damage fish and wildlife. The FPC said no, and Udall went to court—all the way to the United States Supreme Court. A 7–2 decision said that the test of a hydroelectric project is "whether the project will be in the public interest," and that you determine the public interest by considering

future power demand and supply, alternate sources of power, the public interest in preserving reaches of wild rivers and wilderness areas, the preservation of anadromous fish for commercial and recreational purposes and the protection of wildlife.

The court also noted, importantly for our purposes:

The importance of salmon and steelhead in our outdoor life as well as in commerce is so important that there certainly comes a time when their destruction might necessitate a halt in the so-called "improvement" or "development" of waterways.

Striped bass, too, are anadromous fish, and the same argument applies.

Although the FPC doesn't really like all this—it has long since passed from *regulating* public utilities to accommodating them, and thus can be counted as still, more or less, likely to be on Con Ed's side—it is nevertheless true that Con Ed liked it all even less. To the public, the company insistently advertised that "Cornwall represents conservation at its best" (without saying that anything was being conserved—more word magic), and insisted, in italics, that *"It would not damage the wonderful scenery of the Hudson River; being underground, it would not damage the landscape."*

Of course not. Except that—well, for one thing, there's the tailrace.

The spot at Breakneck Ridge from which I first saw Storm King is not the best place. The gap between Storm King and Breakneck is one of the few places—and by far the most impressive and accessible—at which a mountain river breaks through the Appalachian wall to the sea, and the place from which to see it, by land or on the water, is from the north (or from the top of Storm King itself, but we'll get to that later). Here, though you can't see the vital bass, you can see best the majesty and the beauty of the scene.

On the north face, or slope, of Storm King (Con Ed witnesses sometimes argued that the project isn't "on the mountain" at all, but merely on the slope leading up to it, which is still more word magic) is where construction of the project's tailrace—the channel for the water the plant will use—will gouge away several million cubic feet of the mountain.

The river frontage of Storm King is about 6,000 feet. The tailrace gouge will tear away 560 feet of this, and there will be, in addition, "130 feet of supporting concrete abutment at the east end of the bridge and 125 to 150 feet at the west end." In other words, something like 800 feet of the shoreline of Storm King is to be torn away; in place of 560 feet of that shoreline, there will be a hole.

This gouge would go back into the mountain for from 200 to 280 feet—which means, in turn, that the cutting and bulldozing will make a hole back to where the elevation is 70 feet above the river. This is the "underground" project that "would not damage the landscape."

Con Ed has promised replanting, and one of the landscape architects who testified for them—another living demonstration of the "engineering mentality" in another profession—said that "the concrete bridges at the mouth of the tailrace will be treated so that they will blend in with the background." Camouflage paint, no doubt.

But that isn't all. There is a big "recreational plan" in the works, too, to be built on the mountain itself (no argument about that, this time). Lest I be accused of unfairness, let's let some of this be described by one of the men who designed it and who testified for Con Ed:

The visitors' information building will contain a reception room, display area, a seminar room and a small auditorium, together with necessary sanitary facilities. It will also contain an elevator which will provide a means of access to an observation room located far below in the power plant itself. . . .

An access road from Route 218 to the general site will be constructed. Thirty individual picnic units each consisting of a table, benches and fireplace will be built, together with a group picnic shelter with sanitary facilities, fireplace and terraces. A parking lot with space for 40 cars will be provided at the site of the shelter. Along the hard surface entrance road of approximately one mile, a number of two car turnoffs will be constructed. Additionally, lawn areas will be available where group games may be played and outdoor concerts held.

None of which will mar the landscape, of course.

The visitors' information center (according to a Con Ed exhibit) will be 150 feet long and 37 feet high, and "several appropriately landscaped observation terraces will be placed adjacent to the building to afford panoramic views of the Hudson River and the surrounding countryside." In addition, there'll be another section of parking lot; together, the two sections will have a capacity of 120 automobiles and three buses.

But it's okay. They're going to plant something around all of it. One of the landscape Engineers said that "the planting around the Visitors' Information Center will make the Center virtually invisible from the river and from the opposite shore"—but it will have panoramic views. Presumably through peepholes.

Actually, Con Ed's own exhibits contradict the invisibility claim, and the same landscaper admitted that between October 15 and May 15, the planting will *not,* in fact, make the center invisible, virtually or otherwise. One would suppose, in addition, that it is during the remaining months, between May and October, that we might expect to find the most people using those 31 invisible fireplaces. But the mountain will be prettier, anyway—even though it is already impressive enough to have moved James Fenimore Cooper to thoughts of Creation and to have inspired Washington Irving.

And then there's Cornwall's lily-white park. It will be 57 acres in size; there will be about a mile of roadway with "appropriate parking space," 10 acres of open lawn, 30 picnic units (each with a fireplace), some paved areas, two group picnic shelters and sanitary facilities. None of which anybody even claims will be invisible (another 30 invisible fireplaces would apparently be too much even for Con Ed's word magicians). It will just be prettier.

It will, too. The base of Storm King today, as the Engineers are fond of pointing out, is not all that pretty up close. It is piled up with junk, in fact. But you can pick up junk without dumping millions of tons of mountain into the river and making a phony shoreline. "The disposal of fill to base up the park," testified

Charles W. Eliot II—a fairly well-known landscape architect in his own right—"will replace two long sections of *natural* shoreline with practically straight line rip-rap or rock wall [his emphasis]," and he continued:

. . . the artificiality of the new rip-rap shore, together with what is typical of the usual city park, will further emphasize the interference of the whole project with the natural conditions along the river and Storm King.

As a glance at the exhibits shows, the park will also wreck the curve of the bank out of which the Storm King promontory now so dramatically thrusts. And then there's the reservoir. Con Ed's ads don't even *mention* the reservoir, and I don't blame them.

The reservoir is in the valley between Mount Misery and White Horse Mountain, in part of the Black Rock Forest. It is necessary because, of course, when they suck up 1,000,000 cubic feet of the Hudson every minute or so, they have to put it somewhere. They've decided to cover a treasured forest that is used as a study area by Harvard's botany department and includes trails maintained by the New York-New Jersey Trail Conference (although Con Ed's experts say it's full of rattlesnakes).

Again, let's let a Con Ed witness describe this additional piece of rape-as-therapy:

The project reservoir will be formed by the construction of five dikes of varying sizes in saddles between ridges which presently form a natural basin in the Hudson Highlands in the area of Mount Misery and White Horse Mountain, about 10,000 feet southwest of the underground [*sic*] power plant. The reservoir will occupy a surface area of approximately 240 acres and, at maximum water elevation of 1,160 feet above mean sea level, will have a storage capacity of 25,000 acre-feet, or approximately eight billion gallons.

That word is not "million." It's "billion."

Dr. Eliot, who was *not* testifying for Storm King (or, rather, he *was* testifying for Storm King; he was not testifying for Con Ed), looked at it, however, from a different angle:

Standing in the area to be flooded, one can get some idea of the size of the future reservoir by imagining water almost to the top of White

Horse Mountain and Mount Misery. The water surface will be wider than the Hudson River between Storm King and Breakneck. This huge, manmade water body, almost literally on top of a mountain, will dwarf the scale of Storm King and Crow's Nest. . . .

The main dam across Black Rock Hollow is shown on the plans as 2250 feet long and over 275 feet high at the deepest point. The western slope is shown as extending 500 feet from the face. The other dams required include about 3000 feet on the northeast parallel with Highway 9W; 750 feet east of Mount Misery on the southeast; and 500 plus feet on the north.

None of this testimony was contradicted at the hearing—in fact, Dr. Eliot took the information from the company's own exhibits. But you haven't read about any of this in Con Ed's full-page ads, either.

Their house landscape Engineer said that they might try to disguise the outsides and tops of those "dikes" (a good public relations firm watches every word), but even he had to admit that you can't disguise the inside mud walls as the water rises and falls. The reservoir, incidentally, will be "not safe for recreation uses and therefore it will be necessary to exclude the public from its use." It'll have a fence around it—presumably a fence disguised as a set of ninepins, or a row of forest rangers, or something.

But the 240-acre mud pile and its ugly mud walls will be visible from about fifteen high points in the part of the area that Con Ed will allow people to go on using—a prospect that doesn't bother the Engineer Con Ed presents as its landscape architect. "Any large lake," he said during the hearings, "is handsomer than a small lake."

And in case fifteen high points aren't enough:

The Company plans to construct a scenic overlook where none presently exists at a point close to Route 9W. This overlook will provide a panoramic view of the Hudson River in one direction and of the project reservoir in the other. The total acreage involved in development is approximately 36 acres. . . . A shelter building with toilets and 24 picnic units with appropriate facilities [fireplaces?] will be constructed for both the overlook and picnic areas.

All invisible, of course. Con Ed's critics insist that, from the company's own plans, the geography of those who planned that overlook is as bad as their esthetics. But there isn't any point in going on with this. There remains only the question: Do we need the power, and if so, what could Con Ed do instead?

At one point, somewhere back in the proceedings, Con Ed gave the cost of Storm King project as $162 million. By the figures of their own expert, the least it can cost them to put the transmission lines underground is $44.5 million. But a company that can put a 70-by-560-foot hole in the side of a mountain and call it "invisible" has little trouble confusing a lay journalist with figures. Because the court ordered the FPC to consider alternatives, the FPC considered alternatives—quite a few of them. And since the court made it quite clear that "it's cheaper" is not, by itself, sufficient excuse for chewing up bass eggs and mountains, a lot of attention was paid to figures.

The minimum differential between Storm King and the next cheapest alternative to provide the same power (I'm assuming that the power is needed, since I haven't really investigated *those* figures) is, according to Con Ed witness Walter Fisk, just under $79 million over twenty years. Con Ed vice president M. L. Waring seems to have gotten this up to $119 million later on. But some of this wasn't too clear, because the Rev. William Hogan, a Fordham economist who was called to bolster Con Ed's position, used the $79-million figure—in fact and to be fair, he spoke of "a cost differential . . . ranging from $78,692,000 to as high as $362,886,000"—but on the same page of testimony he said:

The alternative closest to the Cornwall project [they call it that at Fordham, too, apparently] in aggregate costs as indicated by Exhibit 257 was the alternative numbered 4A. . . . This alternate . . . would cost . . . $56 million more than the proposed plant at Cornwall.

Well, maybe that's not important. What I really wanted to be sure you don't miss is Father Hogan's reasons why the plant should be built on and in Storm King rather than somewhere else —because you may not realize the far-reaching implications of all this. You see, there are "social implications as well as economic ones involved here." For one thing, 22 percent of the population of New York City is either black or Puerto Rican, and a lot of those blacks and Puerto Ricans are underprivileged. A more expensive alternative to Storm King would—or at least might—mean higher utility rates for these underprivileged people, whereas Storm King might keep their electricity bills down. "Reasonable utility rates," Father Hogan went on, "would encourage the purchase of . . . appliances." These "appliances" would very likely include air conditioning. Air conditioning would give these underprivileged black and Puerto Rican New Yorkers "the prospect of a fuller life," and that would mean that "the threat of hot summers with all their attending implications could be avoided."

In other words, if the FPC will kindly let avuncular old Con Ed build its public service invisible facility at Storm King, it will stop riots in Harlem.

Still granting Con Ed's relative-cost figures to be correct, it turns out, on examination, that even if Con Ed were to lower everybody's electricity bill to match the difference in cost between Storm King and the next cheapest alternative, that underprivileged black family in Harlem will save somewhere between a dime and four bits a year. For fifty cents a year they're all going to buy air conditioners in Harlem, and all the trouble will go away.

There is one further little economic problem here. The alternative in question involves construction, not on Storm King but in New York City itself. That, in turn, means that Con Ed would pay taxes, not to Orange County (where the lily-white Cornwall park would be), but to New York City. And another economist testified that "$83,000,000 more in local property taxes would be paid to New York City with the alternative" than with Storm King.

You can't buy an air conditioner for four bits a week, but New York City could, if it would, do something about the troubles of the people in Harlem with another 83 million bucks.

Con Ed's concern for being sure that everyone has a broken ankle finally shows up in the rather dry-sounding testimony of Professor Reynold Sachs, a Columbia economist:

Since, however, estimated costs and taxes extending twenty years into the future necessarily involve forecasts subject to error, the present values described above . . . are not statistically distinguishable. It is accepted scientific practice not to distinguish summary data whose differences are less than the probable errors of measurement inherent in the underlying statistics. In this statistical sense, therefore, and taking account of total costs and benefits attendant upon either proposal, and *using the Applicant's own cost figures,* I can find no statistical basis for distinguishing between the Project and the Alternative [emphasis added].

In other words, keep your eye on the pea.

The new hearings ended on May 23, 1967, a bookshelf full of briefs have been filed, and the FPC staff is still in there pitching for Con Ed. For instance, at page 13 in the staff brief, it says, "Despite the fact that the powerhouse and appurtenant works would no longer be seen at all, opposition still persisted. . . ." Even the Con Ed witnesses never made that claim. The FPC staff, instead of reading the Con Ed testimony and accepting it, apparently devoted itself to reading the Con Ed ads in *The New York Times.*

Following closely the arguments in the staff brief, the Hearing Examiner for the FPC recommended, in mid-1968, that the plant be built. In October briefs were filed by both sides. No matter how the Commission finally rules, the whole thing will probably go to court, and the argument may go on for years—because Con Ed is clearly going to go on insisting that concepts like beauty, history and ecology have no place in the construction of a technological society.

After a while you have to get off the subject. You can take just so much solemn testimony and public relations balderdash about holes improving mountains and cartilage being stronger than bone. Anger starts to set in, and you want to talk about something else. You can't, though. Everywhere you look, everywhere where there is something that really ought to be saved, there is someone to assure us that we would be better off if the ankle were broken —and other industries are almost as good at it as utilities.

A few years ago, Governor (now Senator) Gaylord Nelson of Wisconsin discovered that 32 percent of the shallow wells in Wisconsin were polluted by detergents. The resulting investigation showed that the pollution was present in wells all over the country.

The detergents—made from a petroleum-based chemical, alkyl benzene sulfonate—resisted attack by the bacteria in sewage and waste water, and simply wouldn't break down (in scientific language, it was non-biodegradable). They poured out of sewage disposal plants in their original form, and poured down rivers and into lakes as mountains of foam. In March, 1965, the Milwaukee River near West Bend, Wisconsin, was covered with a mountain of detergent foam 40 feet high. A community-owned well in Yuba City, California, had to be abandoned because of ABS pollution. The United States Fish and Wildlife Service reported that ABS detergents "were toxic to eggs and larvae of clams and oysters at concentrations of 0.6 parts per million or less." And of course, as water is used and reused, detergent concentrations become higher.

The detergent industry, however, insisted loudly and publicly that there was nothing to worry about. In fact, they insisted on recommending fractures to all their patients. The board of directors of the Soap and Detergent Association met in April, 1963, and E. Scott Pattison issued a press release following their meeting, arguing that detergent foam in wastes "serves in many cases to warn that other less feasible [sic] and more dangerous pollutants are present."

Six months later, the Monsanto Company published an article stating that detergent pollution had never, ever hurt anybody, and suggesting that ABS "may be valuable as a tracer which indicates that more dangerous sewage ingredients, including disease organisms, may be reaching the water supply." They did not go quite so far as to suggest that drinking All would prevent or cure cholera, but they did argue that legislative remedy was a ridiculous idea. Specifically, they argued against a bill introduced by Senators Nelson and Maurine Neuberger of Oregon, which set a deadline of June 30, 1965, by which the manufacturers had to make the detergents biodegradable or quit making them at all. That was asking for the impossible, the manufacturers insisted; the cost would be millions, and the legislation would impede scientific progress.

They did it, though—just as the auto makers met safety standards when they were forced to, although that was impossible too. By June of 1965, the Soap and Detergent Association's members had "voluntarily" changed over their detergent manufacture so that today's detergents are based on linear alkylate sulfonate —a "soft," or biodegradable, compound.

Even LAS is not as good as it might be, and further refinement of detergents is under way. But the point is that left to themselves, the soap people, like the auto people and the public utilities people, are among the leading advocates of that great Engineers' concept immortalized by Joseph Heller as "catch-22": They have a right to do anything we can't stop them from doing.

The broken-ankles-are-better philosophy often comes out—as it did in the speech by lumberman Buchanan—as the philosophy of "maximum use" (or, sometimes, "multiple use"). Industrial polluters of water, in the words of the Conservation Foundation's Russell Train, put it this way:

"A stream has a natural capacity to assimilate waste. This assimilative capacity (which depends upon the availability of free oxygen in the stream) is a natural resource. Conservation means wise multiple use of natural resources. Therefore, it is 'true conservation' to use the assimilative capacity."

Sound like "Cornwall represents conservation at its best"?

Having quoted it, Train proceeds to tear it apart, but it hardly seems necessary; the sophism is self-evident. It is similar to the argument that underground transmission lines shouldn't be used because they raise the cost of power, or that pollution abatement devices can't be installed because they raise the price of manufactured goods. "Following this approach," Train said in a different speech, "child labor would never have been abolished."

But there is no stopping them. *The Washington Star* noted early in 1967 that billboard companies were still objecting to a proposed control law because signs would have to be kept 2,000 feet away from on- and off-ramps, and that in commercial and industrial areas signs would have to be spaced at least 500 feet apart. At that distance, you would pass ten signs a minute if you were driving at 60 miles an hour—and that was a billboard "control" bill, unacceptable to the industry.

Over a hundred years ago, Henry David Thoreau gazed with sick horror on the work of Engineers on the Concord River, and wrote: "Poor shad, where is thy redress . . . who hears the fishes when they cry?" Today, approximately a hundred miles away, the Nature Conservancy's Dr. Richard Goodwin reports that "the Yankee atomic [power] plant on the lower Connecticut River is very likely to destroy the highly productive shad run in the river. What provisions have been made to avoid this? A study—to be made only through the industry, whose profits are involved, to determine whether damage is done. Only then will cooling towers be installed. By this time, it is not at all unlikely that remedial action will be too late."

The Engineers of private profit on the Connecticut use the same argument as the Engineers of the Army on canal C-111 in the Everglades: we'll do it first and see what happens. Neither ecology nor beauty enters into their calculations. In 1966, a House sub-committee held lengthy hearings on the general subject of pollution. Through the hundreds of pages of testimony one theme recurs again and again: Industries reject or resist pollution abatement devices, because they are an investment without an immediate return.

In the meantime, the profitmakers and their Engineers march on: electric plants on the upper Savannah and the beautiful St. Croix, pulp mills pouring their garbage into the Great Lakes, lumbermen nibbling at the forests and waiting for the regulators to look the other way. Even the Adirondack Forest Preserve, described briefly in the previous chapter, has been quietly, but legally, invaded. During World War II, because of the emergency, New York allowed the Tahawus Railroad to be built, to haul out precious titanium ore from a mine operated by the National Lead Company. Militantly, the state insisted that the agreement be written to cover only the time of national war emergency, though they allowed a fifteen-year margin at the end to allow for making other arrangements, ripping out tracks, etc. About three years ago, without a word being said in public, the state of New York (in violation of its own constitution) quietly extended the agreement for 100 years. The Federal Government was just involved enough so that strict legalities were observed and the state's constitution, with its "forever wild" clause, could be overridden. Where there is a buck, someone will do his best to find a way; and if he's caught, he'll find a way to tell you that it's all, really, good for you.

The Kennecott Copper Corporation—aside from a spokesman's occasional and nonsensical reference to the war in Vietnam—has not yet told us how its open-pit mine will improve the scenic value of the Cascades or make the steelhead in the rivers healthier. But pollutants can be tracers for disease organisms; a Con Ed pump storage plant can improve the impressive majesty of the Hudson's gorge at Storm King; PG&E can propose an "atomic park", and I have just heard a radio commercial for "San Mateo's *beautiful* Hillsdale shopping center, where there are acres of free parking just a few steps away." Certainly we can expect some word magic from the copper kings any day now about how we'd all be better off with broken ankles.

VII · THE EFFLUENT SOCIETY

ONCE UPON A TIME there was a lake.

It was a thing of magnificent beauty, left a breathtaking blue by departing glaciers. It was 30 miles wide in some places, nearly 60 in others, and more than 240 miles long. Ten thousand square miles of lake, more than 200 feet deep, it lived on a still larger sister to the north, and fed a somewhat smaller sister to the east. Indians lived with it, calmly and in peace most of the time, in conflict occasionally; one tribe, later given by whites the same name as the lake, was almost wiped out in a 1656 war with the Iroquois Federation.

Thirteen years later, a white man—Louis Joliet or Jolliet—saw the lake, and soon forts and settlements sprang up.

Today, Lake Erie is virtually dead. Detroit, Cleveland, Buffalo, Akron, Toledo and a dozen other cities pour millions of *tons* of sewage into the lake *every day*. Some of it is fairly carefully treated; much of it is not.

The Detroit River, which feeds Lake Erie, carries *every day,* in addition to Detroit's largely untreated sewage, 19,000 gallons of oil, 100,000 pounds of iron, 200,000 pounds of various acids, and 2,000,000 pounds of chemical salts. The fertilizer used on the farms of Ohio and Pennsylvania and New York drains into streams that pour into the Erie. Paper mills in the Monroe area of Michigan pour volumes of pollutant waste into the lake. Steelmakers pour in mill scale and oil and grease and pickling solution and rinse water. The Engineers of the Army dredge the harbors and channels of the area and dump the sludge into the middle of Lake Erie.

The results are manifold, and all bad. "When strong winds blow in from the east toward the beaches in my district," said former Congressman Weston Vivian, who represented the southeast corner of Michigan, "the beaches become littered with various and sundry forms of marine growth and sludge from the lower levels of the lake. Even on quiet days, the water is turbid. Along the beaches signs are posted year after year saying 'Not safe for swimming.'"

Estimates for "cleaning up" Lake Erie range from the billion dollars mentioned at a hearing by Representative John Blatnik of Minnesota to another estimate, compiled for Vivian by various Federal agencies, of $5 billion over twenty years ($20 billion for all the Great Lakes, of which Erie is merely the worst; at least $100 billion for all the inland waters of America). But the fact is that nobody knows how to clean it up, because nobody knows exactly what's wrong with it.

One thing everybody knows: Lake Erie is eutrophic as hell. "Eutrophic" and "BOD" are a couple of not very complicated terms you soon learn in order to talk about water pollution. A eutrophic lake is simply one that's biologically too good, one that has too many nutrients in it. It happens to every lake sooner or later, but it usually takes a few thousand years more than it's taken in Lake Erie.

Normally, a lake receives from various sources a certain amount of nutrient material, which is consumed by plankton or algae or bottom vegetation or bacteria. The fish eat the plankton and the algae, the bacteria mess around with the nitrogen, a couple of hundred other processes simultaneously take place, and it all works out pretty well.

So you dump a bunch of sewage or fertilizer or other biologically rich material into the water, and the algae, for instance, grow faster than the fish can eat them. Algae are life forms just like you and me, but (like you and me) in large numbers they stink. They also use up whatever free oxygen might be in the water, which makes it tough for the other life forms. Beaches become covered with algae in the form of slime, and so does the surface of the lake. The lake, in ecological terms, "dies."

In Lake Erie, the dominant genus of algae is *Cladophora*. Normally microscopic, it grows in Lake Erie in 50-foot swatches, and, writes Gladwin Hill, it "looks as if it had dropped off the Ancient Mariner and smells terrible." One of the things that make

Cladophora grow like that is an abundance of phosphates; there are a lot of phosphates in municipal sewage, and detergents are something like 70 percent phosphate. Tons and tons of detergent waste pour into Lake Erie every year, and Hill points out that every pound of detergent waste will propagate 700 pounds of algae.

In the meantime, fish like pike, which need a lot of oxygen, disappear (taking an important commercial fishing operation with them), and "trash" fish like carp, which need little oxygen, take their place—for as long as any fish can live at all. The point is that as long as there's enough free oxygen in the water to go around, things can usually be worked out. But some pollutants, like sewage, bring about an increase in a few life forms, like algae, that use up the oxygen. Other kinds of pollutants tie up the oxygen in chemical combination so that it's not available to the life forms in the lake. When the "biological oxygen demand" (that's the BOD) gets too high, you've had it.

Lake Erie has had it.

The southern end of Lake Michigan, near Chicago, has also had it (though mostly it's not Chicago's fault; it pollutes the Mississippi instead), and so has the part around Green Bay and Saginaw. Lake Ontario is in trouble, and the other Great Lakes aren't far behind. Erie happens to be both the most densely populated and the shallowest of the Great Lakes, and so it's out in front in the eutrophia derby. It's not irreparable (or at least a lot of people believe it's not), but it will certainly cost billions if anyone wants to repair it, and if anybody ever figures out how. It may cost millions just to figure out how.

Not only the sewage and the fertilizer are involved, but the chemical wastes of the manufacturing plants. Nobody quite knows what their combined ecological effect might be, or the effect of one of them minus the others (for all we know, one could be holding another in check and mitigating its effects; it could be that removing one pollutant and leaving the others would make the lake even worse). Therefore, nobody knows how to go backwards to undo the mess.

On the other hand, that's not the world's most difficult problem. This is one place where no matter what we do, it isn't going to get *enough* worse to matter; it can't. The more important problem is that, despite a number of official voices raised in alarm every now and then, nobody really seems to give a damn.

At a Federal-state hearing in 1965, for instance, Michigan's Democratic Representative John Dingell thundered that "neither the city of Detroit nor any other municipalities or industries concerned have any God-given right to befoul the waters of the Detroit River or Lake Erie!" But at the same hearing, Detroit city officials adamantly refused to provide secondary treatment for the 6.5 million pounds of sewage they dump into the river every day (primary treatment is rudimentary and removes few pollutants); it would cost $100 million, they said. The much smaller city of Houston spent a third of that to build the Astrodome for ball games.

"It is a strange anomaly," another Congressman said sadly, "to have water officials from the city of Detroit attempt to minimize the problem of Detroit River pollution and suggest that secondary sewage treatment would be a waste of money. . . . This kind of horse-and-buggy economy is largely responsible for the situation we find ourselves in, and if it continues, would diminish the development of the Detroit metropolitan area by astronomical amounts."

It didn't matter that those sentiments came from House Minority Leader Gerald R. Ford, Jr., the conservatives' friend (who is also from Michigan). Detroit ignored him anyway.

As if the absence of secondary sewage treatment weren't bad enough—and even secondary treatment is only about 80 to 85 percent effective in removing pollutants—Detroit, like almost every other large American city, dumps *completely* untreated sewage whenever there is an unexpected high runoff from a large storm. Storm drains and sewers are usually the same pipes, and most cities have a "bypass" to take care of unexpectedly high runoffs.

The industrial types don't care much either. Representative Charles Vanik, Cleveland Democrat, says that "the Great Lakes steelmaking industries do not utilize any visible devices for the removal of mill scale, oil and grease, and . . . the Great Lakes steelmaking industries provide practically no treatment of spent pickling solutions and rinse water developed in the steelmaking process. The steel industries almost universally use these processes for water pollution control except where the steel industry is located on the Great Lakes."

Representative Vivian matched Vanik's steelmakers with his own district's paper mills:

Second after second, they pour volumes of what can best be labeled as "goop" into the local waters which flow into the lake. The paper mills do have facilities for cleaning the effluent from the mills. Now when the officials of the mills know I'm about to visit, these facilities are always operating. But when I visit unannounced, they're shut off. . . . And Lake Erie continues to be filled up with more of this goop.

If it isn't industrial Engineers or city Engineers, it's some other Engineers. Republican Representative Charles Mosher of Cleveland says, "It is frequently alleged by people in my district that the Army Corps of Engineers is one of the worst polluters of Lake Erie. I am referring to the dredging of sludges from harbors and rivers and dumping it into Lake Erie."

At first glance, the solution seems easy: Stop. It may not save the lake, but at least it can be kept from getting any worse. Simply make it illegal for anybody at all to put anything into the lake that can remotely be construed as a pollutant.

Except that there's another problem. If you don't put it into the lake, what are you going to do with it? As Congressman Vivian pointed out, some of the pollution is unnecessary; and Detroit could provide better treatment for its sewage. Furthermore, there are a number of sophisticated techniques for dealing with a lot of water pollution. There's sand-bed filtering. There's a method called electrodialysis (one sizable California town, some of whose citizens don't know what they're drinking, gets all of its water from the electrodialysis of "waste water," mostly irrigation runoff and sewage). There's another called reverse osmosis.

The hangup here is that every method leaves you with *something*. John D. Parkhurst, who works for Los Angeles County as a sanitation engineer, is an enthusiast for reverse osmosis (which I won't try to explain here), although it still costs a lot. "You're taking perfectly pure water out of the waste, not taking wastes out of the water," he says. "This process gets the water away from everything—nitrates, bacteria, phenols, detergents, the lot."

But Mr. Parkhurst is, alas, an Engineer, and Engineers solve one problem at a time and deal with the consequences later. After you've taken the water out, what do you do with the nitrates, bacteria, phenols, detergents and the lot? Bury them? An urban unit of 1,000,000 people produces, believe it or not, 500,-000 tons of sewage a day; even after you take the water out, you'll need a pretty big cemetery.

Burn them? We have enough air pollution problems as it is.

Sewage aside, that same urban unit of 1,000,000 people produces, every day, another 2,000 tons of solid waste that has to be disposed of. On top of that, it throws into the air, every day, 1,000 tons of particles, sulfur dioxide, nitrogen oxides, hydrocarbons and carbon dioxide. In 1963, American mines, every day, discarded 90,400,000 tons of waste rock and tailings. In 1965, every day, more than 16,000 automobiles were scrapped (joining from 25 to 40 million already on junk piles).

There are engineers, with a small "e," who are capable of seeing more than one problem at a time, and one of them, Ray K. Linsley, heads the department of civil engineering at Stanford. He once explained to a Congressional committee the scientific principle of the conservation of matter—which says that matter cannot be destroyed, only changed—and added:

We would not be far wrong if we drew from this a principle of conservation of pollution which said that waste materials, once produced, are with us always. With the exception of that relatively small fraction of waste materials which man reclaims for his own use, and the portion of waste materials which are converted by natural processes into useful material, the principle of conservation of pollution is essentially valid. When man burns solid waste, he does not eliminate it, he merely converts it to gases and particulate matter which may pollute the atmosphere. If we dump pollutants in the ocean, we are not eliminating them, we are simply putting them where we cannot see them.

Despite a lot of vocalized concern, the attitude of most of us toward the pollution of our world remains that of the Lake Tahoe resident who told *Saturday Evening Post* reporter John Bird that the lake is "so clear you can see a beer can thirty, forty feet down." Beer drinker or Engineer, we have the same problem:

We go ahead and do things when we don't know what we're doing. Those few who shout warnings seem as far away as Seneca, reviling the "heavy air of Rome and the stench of its smoky chimneys"; those who offend seem to us no more to be criminals against the environment then the fourteenth-century Londoner who was hanged for violating a law against burning sea coal.

Californians and Arizonans, among others, have fought bitterly for years over the water of the Colorado. Few of them know that in 1956 and 1957, fish in the San Miguel River were 98 times as radioactive as natural background levels, or that bottom fauna from the Animas River contained radium contaminations thirty times greater than normal. The San Miguel (via the Dolores) and the Animas (via the San Juan) flow into the Colorado.

Murray Stein, chief enforcement officer for the Federal Water Pollution Control Administration, said at the time that he thought there was a serious danger to drinking water and to irrigation potential. The Public Health Service agreed. A Senate committee thought so too. The radioactivity was coming from uranium mine tailings alongside the rivers, but the Engineers of the Atomic Energy Commission pooh-poohed the whole thing.

"The safety standards," Senator E. L. (Bob) Bartlett of Alaska said angrily, "have been administered largely by the men who make the radiation." They still are. The mines and the tailings are still there, too.

Not only is a cure unlikely for the pollution of the air, the water and the land; it will all probably get worse before it gets better, no matter what we begin to do. In the Public Health Service there's an Office of Solid Wastes. Its chief, W. E. Gilbertson, says that every one of us in the United States generates about 4½ pounds of solid waste a day, in one form or another (in the cities, it's about 6 or 7 pounds per capita). It adds up to somewhere between 800 million and a billion pounds, every day—and by 1980, Gilbertson says, it will go up by about a pound or a pound and a half, per person, per day. When you figure out the arithmetic, don't forget to add in the population increase.

Gilbertson stresses, by the way, that those are *collection* figures. They don't include sewage, or any solid waste that isn't picked up by some kind of garbage man. Of course it used to be that you could throw away a Kleenex or a paper bag in the woods, and rain and bacteria would eventually break it down and add it to the soil. Even glass is primarily a natural mineral substance. But bacteria have a problem with Saran Wrap, plastic disposable bottles, and cans made out of aluminum (which nobody tries to reclaim) instead of steel (which can be used again as scrap, or rusts into iron oxide).

Waste is already a major urban problem. New York City expects to run out of landfill sites for rubbish disposal before the year 2000, and it's no surprise: One day's refuse from New York City would fill a freight train seven miles long.

Paris—where a garbage disposal unit cannot be put in the sink in even the finest house because the sewers cannot carry off the resulting waste—comes up every day with three tons of garbage per square kilometer, the world's highest density. London is building the world's largest incinerator at Deephams, and hopes that by 1970 it will not only get rid of 700 truckloads of garbage every day but produce about 30 million watts of electricity.

Tokyo dumps most of its garbage (9,000 tons a day) into Tokyo Bay, but a few officials have begun to understand what they are doing to the bay, and they have started a move to build incinerators. The populace is unhappy because they don't want to live near burning garbage. West Berlin has a political problem along with its garbage problem: It has been dumping its garbage inside the city limits for years, because it would otherwise have to dump it in East Germany; they're now considering incinerators also.

Mexico City—with a mere 400 (collected) tons a day—comes closest to a modern solution. Their garbage is buried in the dry bed of Lake Texcoco, but first it's gone over by the ragpickers of Ixtapalapa, who remove anything that might have any value—including paper, cardboard, rags, iron scraps, tin, enamel and china. Only what is left is buried.

San Francisco—currently worrying about a "garbage crisis"—is perhaps typical of American cities. Its three quarters of a million people produce about 1,500 tons of garbage every day, which it has traditionally dumped in a fill-and-cover operation near Brisbane, just south of the city limits on San Francisco Bay. Brisbane, a small residential community whose only excuse for existence is its view of the bay, has just decided that it's had enough garbage, and San Francisco is looking for something else to do with its waste.

Various visionaries have suggested everything from loading it on freight trains (which would also serve other Bay Area cities) and hauling it to a burial spot in the Nevada desert—which is okay if you consider the Nevada desert unimportant; some people don't—to loading it on barges and polluting the ocean with it. The Federal Government has come up with $117,000 to help build an incinerator (an experimental, low-air-pollution type) which will take care of 100 tons a day or so, but the rest of the problem isn't solved.

Two members of the San Francisco Board of Supervisors have proposed an audaciously terrible scheme to use the garbage to fill in the ocean, after construction of a couple of breakwaters. They talk about renewing "the entire ocean frontage by constituting it a prime recreational area," but apparently they never go to the beach; it's really quite lovely the way it is, and a lot of people use it. It may be more important that, if the fill-and-cover behind the breakwaters were completed to surface (which is not in the supervisors' plan but would surely be in someone else's very soon), you could build single-family residences on it, just like those now near the beach, and add about $350 million to the city's real estate values.

This particular piece of nonsense is mentioned here more as an indication of the desperation to which the waste problem is reducing cities than as a serious proposal for San Francisco. The supervisors in question obviously know nothing about littoral drift or the reaction of the ocean (Wesley Marx's chapter on beaches is herewith recommended), and they may have overlooked the fact that San Francisco is kept cool by winds from the ocean—and that moisture makes garbage smell. Even more important, garbage effluent would almost certainly seep through the breakwaters and pollute not only the ocean but beaches far down the coast, as, indeed, the breakwaters themselves would undoubtedly cause the erosion of beaches in San Mateo County and probably farther south.

Along with garbage in the cities, we still have the problem of pesticides in the country. We could stop tomorrow the use of any kind of pesticide, and pesticide pollution would still be a major problem. Dr. Robert Ayres of the Hudson Institute is one scientist who worries about it:

Since a good many of these pesticides are chlorinated hydrocarbons and the whole toxigens group have long lifetimes in the soil, it is probably fair to say that the soil burden is . . . growing roughly 7 percent a year. This will continue to increase until such time as it reaches an equilibrium with the environment, at which point as much of this toxic stuff will be washed away into streams each year as we have.

We have not reached that equilibrium point. In terms of the damage these pesticides have done today, I rather shudder to think of what the situation may be when we do reach that equilibrium.

"The damage these pesticides have done today" has been pretty well covered by Rachel Carson, but it is worth remembering the fish of the lower Mississippi. In the early 1960s the drum, buffalofish, catfish and shad of the area were all afflicted with a mysterious disease that nobody could figure out. Although routine analysis showed the river to be no more polluted than usual, the strange illness spread until in late 1963, it killed about 5,000,-000 fish.

Eventually, far more sophisticated methods of analysis found pesticides not only in the raw river water but in the water supplies of Vicksburg and New Orleans. The fish were killed, the Public Health Service decided, by a pesticide called endrin (a chlorinated hydrocarbon such as Dr. Ayres was talking about) —and it has now been determined that buffalo, shad and catfish can be killed by two-tenths of one part of endrin to one billion parts of water: a concentration of one in *five billion*.

Most of the endrin in the Mississippi seems to have come from the plant of the Velsicol Chemical Corporation at Memphis, a city that doesn't treat its sewage. The company has since installed control facilities, but endrin has been used on cotton and sugar cane all over the South, and presumably a lot of it has not run off into the streams yet, if Dr. Ayres is right.

In 1965, sprayers in Argyle, Minnesota, discovered that they had used the wrong insecticide by mistake—and the town was evacuated for a day. There is no way of knowing, of course, how many mistakes go uncaught. In 1967, the Environmental Defense Fund, a conservationist group, went to court to try to stop the state of Michigan from using a deadly pesticide, dieldrin, in fields at the edge of Lake Michigan, because pollution of the lake might kill birds and fish. The Fund lost the case; it is still too soon to know about the birds and fish.

In the Imperial Valley of California, a mass spraying intended to kill bollworms also wiped out 10,000 hives of bees and hundreds of doves, quail and hawks. Not far away, in October, 1967, a truck trailer overturned and spilled 60 gallons of 80% pure parathion—enough of one of the world's deadliest poisons to kill every Californian. The truck that was pulling the trailer went on to deliver its cargo of frozen foods to Arizona (there's no law against food and parathion in the same shipment; they could legally have been together in the overturned trailer) after the driver and some highway patrolmen washed the parathion off the road into an adjoining field. Only when an employee of the State Bureau of Occupational Health arrived, several hours later, was a call put in for the manufacturer and a team sent out to neutralize the parathion with soda ash.

The truck driver, incidentally, had had no idea of what he was carrying, and thus took no special care to protect himself or anyone else during or after the accident. Shortly before his accident, and not far across the border in Mexico, 17 children died in Tijuana from eating bread prepared with flour that had been contaminated by parathion.

There is no question of the dangers from the pollution of our water, and no question that President Johnson was correct when he said that every one of our major lakes and river systems is seriously polluted. In fact, he was correct—at least in principle— some years ago, when he came forth with my all-time favorite Lyndon Johnson sentence: "America cannot sweep water under the carpet and hope that the problem will be blotted out."

The pollution of the air is the form of pollution that most people know most about, but ecologists have some concern here, too. Nobody knows, for instance, what happens if you take one pollutant out of the witches' brew that city dwellers breathe; the chemical interactions are so complex that to take away the hydrocarbons and nitrous oxides that come out of automobile exhausts may lead to difficulties with the remaining pollutants that no one can now predict.

In Los Angeles, the automobile exhaust appears to be the chief contributor, by volume, to air pollution; in New York, it's sulfur dioxide, a lot of it from Con Ed. They and other industrial users across the country pour 23 or 24 million tons of sulfur oxides into the air every year—despite the fact that sulfur is an element in short supply, with only 8,800,000 tons produced every year. The sulfur that literally goes up in smoke every year is worth, at today's prices, about $300 million.

Cleveland's Congressman Vanik describes a more or less typical urban situation:

The muriatic acid which etches the windows of Cleveland homes can only have its origin in the steelmaking process. The graphite dust which settles over vast residential areas during the quiet of the night can only come from industries which push it into the atmosphere under great pressure. The yellow iron oxide dust which blankets large areas of the city with certain changes of the wind can only have its origin from industrial operations.

There is a tendency, among writers on pollution, to blame the automobile a little too much and industry not enough. Except in Los Angeles, the auto is probably not the major contributor to urban air pollution, although it certainly contributes everywhere. In preparing the lead article for a special issue of *Saturday Review* on pollution, C. W. Griffin, Jr., for example, devotes more space to automobile exhausts than to industrial pollution of the air. This is an important error, because it leads to further errors in planning. Discussing the mass transit system now under construction in the San Francisco Bay Area, for instance, Griffin writes:

Rush-hour drivers who now spend forty-three anguished minutes crawling along in bumper-to-bumper traffic through San Francisco and Oakland can then speed through a trans-bay subway tunnel in eight minutes. And the rapid transit system will keep hundreds of tons of pollutants out of San Francisco's air every day.

The trouble is that the tunnel further wrecks the ecology of San Francisco Bay. There is, incidentally, no 43-minute journey by car that will be reduced to 8 minutes by the Bay Area Rapid Transit System.

But that's not the point either. The point is that there's no assurance that the car drivers will use BART and the truck users certainly won't, and BART will necessitate the use of many more buses. As a transit system it has enough problems; as an answer to air pollution in the San Francisco Bay Area it's a drop in the bucket.

While we search, perhaps not as frantically as we should but at least with increasing concern, for someplace to put our solid, liquid and gaseous wastes, the Engineers gaily produce new ones. In the rush to find new sources of clean water, the technique that has most captured the popular imagination is the desalinization of sea water: actually the process of removing from the water a number of different kinds of mineral salts.

This is an Engineers' project if there ever was one—a ridiculous and one-faceted approach to a problem we don't even know whether we have. The best that can be said for it was probably said in a recorded dialogue between economist Kenneth Boulding and geographer Gilbert White:

BOULDING: Desalinization is a will-o'-the-wisp. Let's face it. It is non-sense. The energy requirements are enormous; the transport costs are enormous. The whole trouble with the oceans is that they are terribly low. It is all right for Kuwait, it is all right for high industrial purposes. But this idea of desalinization giving us unlimited quantities of water everywhere in the world is bunk.

WHITE: . . . Why is it so easy for our scientists and technicians and government to sell these extravagant research programs for desalting to legislators and intelligent administrators? Why does it catch the imagination of the popular press . . . ? I wonder if it doesn't reflect perhaps the last glorious demonstration of reliance on technology, massive technology as a means of solving any problem that we have [been] presented by nature.

BOULDING: It is the wrong technology. You can teach vegetables to like salt much more easily than you can take salt out of the water. The Japanese have the idea. Seaweed is delicious.

WHITE: I think this is just the point, Kenneth: that we tend to rely on a massive engineering measure, a single-purpose kind of measure.

Indeed we do.

Beyond questions of cost and efficiency, when you have finished desalinizing—even in Kuwait—what you have left is a bunch of hot brine. You can't dump it back in the ocean on the spot; you'll raise the temperature considerably and thus endanger all the off-shore life, and besides you'll simply raise the salt concentration to a fantastic point and just have to take it all out again in your next batch. Eventually you run into the law of diminishing returns. Doubtless the Engineers will come up with a plan for taking it farther out and dumping it into the ocean—that's the last garbage dump left. But it would be nice if they knew what they were doing first.

Irrigation, unknown to most of us city folk, creates a similar problem. When the water of the San Joaquin River in California, for instance, is run through a few irrigation ditches, it leaches mineral salts from the soil and carries them back to the river. They build up—to the point where California is now considering a plan to *pipe* the San Joaquin River water up the river channel to its San Francisco Bay outlet, and eventually to pipe it through the bay to the ocean! Otherwise it will be too polluted with the mineral salts from earlier irrigation runoff to be of any use far-ther downstream.

In some irrigated areas, especially those where there isn't too much available water to start with, the process works the other way. The plants (and evaporation) use up all the water—and soluble salts, present in the water in minute amounts, stay in the soil. After a while they build up, and—depending on what kind of salts they are—you get salt flats or alkali flats.

This salinization of irrigated lands is an obvious matter to an ecologist, but ours is not the only culture that has let Engineers decide its approach to problems, and one culture after another has had to learn about salinization the hard way. During the earliest days of history, salinization of irrigated land drove populations from the plains of the Indus River. It is interesting that today, not far away, West Pakistan is being forced to abandon hundreds of thousands of acres that they began to irrigate seventy-five years ago. Salinization has taken over again.

The Engineers assure us that we can get rid of sulfur dioxide in the air and stop the ecological damage done by big dams on watersheds if we will only turn to nuclear power. But nuclear plants create two new problems: radioactive wastes and what Assistant Secretary Stanley Cain calls "thermal pollution."

You don't hear much about radioactive wastes any more, but that isn't because the problem has gone away. Most of the wastes are simply held at reactor sites, or encased in lead and then in concrete and sunk somewhere in the ocean. That this doesn't work too well is indicated in a reminiscence by California Democrat George P. Miller, who heads the House Committee on Science and Astronautics:

As I understand it, the people in the three west coast states wanted to deposit the atomic waste in the ocean. It just didn't work out even though this was to be a very slight concentration. They were supposed to dump the waste in a thousand fathoms of water. The material was deposited in steel drums covered with concrete and was supposed to sink to the bottom of the ocean. The division of fish and game in California duplicated these drums, sunk them, and found that they were floating at 400 fathoms rather than a thousand.

Off the shore of New Jersey two of these drums had been supposedly dumped in a thousand fathoms of water, but became snagged in the nets of some fishermen.

A Pacific Gas and Electric power plant near Monterey, which uses ocean water as a coolant (dumping it back into the ocean at a higher temperature), has caused serious changes in the marine biology of the region, even though a study beforehand suggested that no such thing would happen. Thermal pollution from the Yankee atomic power plant is what's killing the shad on the Connecticut.

The tendency of some conservationists to blame all this on the Atomic Energy Commission may be unfair. Wesley Marx quotes an exchange from a Congressional hearing between Congressman John Dingell and Harold Price, director of regulation for the AEC:

MR. DINGELL: Assuming as a matter of fact that you were to find that a project you were licensing was going to raise the temperature of a major river by ten degrees, and this was going to have an enormously destructive effect on, let's say, a major salmon and trout stream, would the Atomic Energy Commission go ahead then and license that plant, in spite of that fact?

MR. PRICE: Under the present law, I don't believe we could deny the license for that reason.

If the project were a power plant, of course, the Federal Power Commission could—and under the High Mountain Sheep decision possibly should—veto the project. Under the previously mentioned bill proposed by Representative Ottinger, the Secretary of the Interior would be able to do it (or, as with High Mountain Sheep, he can take the FPC to court). But the AEC may have other than legal motives. Its bureaucratic existence depends on the continued growth of nuclear power—and Mr. Price went on in that hearing to say that thermal regulation "would impose a burden on the nuclear industry that is not imposed on the conventional power plants." Again, the FPC could even out that inequity.

Even sewage, spewed out in large enough amounts, raises water temperature. "Sharks have appeared in waters off southern California," Congressman Miller points out, "where they never previously appeared, and the studies made indicated that the slight rise in temperature through the disposal of sewage changed the ecology and caused the water to become suitable for the sharks. These are the things," Mr. Miller added in the understatement of his career, "that we don't know very much about."

As a Californian, Miller tends to be most concerned about ecological problems when they affect his own state, but over a period of time he has raised some interesting questions about things that will get worse before they get better. In a committee hearing, for instance, the following exchange took place between Miller and Dr. Walter R. Hibbard, Jr., director of the Bureau of Mines:

MR. MILLER: I'm conscious of the fact that in California, when Shasta

Dam was built, they had to seal off a number of old copper mines. I have often wondered how long the seals of those mines are going to last under heavy heads of water. What will happen if these seals break?

DR. HIBBARD: I don't know, but it will be very unfortunate.

The Shasta Dam, of course, restrains the upper reaches of the lengthy and important Sacramento River.

Even as we fight radioactive mine tailings and worry about a future pollution by sealed copper mines, new problems arise. Dr. Gerald Berg of the Taft Sanitary Engineering Center in Cincinnati came up with this cheerful note:

We know there are viruses in sewage—we have isolated many kinds from effluents of sewage plants, even after chlorination. We have also found them in rivers miles below the outfalls. There is no doubt that conventional water-treatment processes don't remove all the viruses— they aren't designed to.

Infectious hepatitis, it's known, can be waterborne. In Georgia, several cases were traced to oyster smugglers (the Savannah River is in such horrible shape that in most places you can't eat what oysters are left—at least not legally). Disease-causing salmonella bacteria can get into water tables through septic tank seepage (it happened in Riverside, California). If any of us were to try to live rational, healthy lives—if, that is, we were to quit smoking, refuse to drive a car, and avoid foods that might be contaminated with pesticide residues—one of the things we'd have to do is to treat our tap water exactly as though we were drinking from an unfriendly-looking pond in a strange and alien jungle.

The work of the Engineers takes almost no time to make itself felt—as Europe has learned to its dismay. A United Nations commission recently reported that in the Netherlands—where 100,000 salmon were delivered to the retail trade in 1875 from fisheries on the Rhine—the catch by 1915 was down to 20,000 a year, and by 1930 there was for all practical purposes no salmon fishing at all. M. Maurice Lalloy reported to the French Senate in 1964 that the Grand-Morin, a tributary of the Marne, which as recently as 1954 was a widely known trout stream, is now empty of the fish. "Today," said Senator Lalloy, "the river is dead and covered with filthy rainbow-colored greases and hydrocarbons. Less than ten years were needed for this."

In the United States, Dr. Victor Shelford of the University of Chicago studied the Dead River, near Waukegan, Illinois, in 1909, and made an extensive report on the fish life. In 1960, Dr. Rezneat M. Darnell of Marquette went back to the same place and repeated Dr. Shelford's study. He reported:

A number of the changes . . . are directly attributable to human activities, and most of these changes may be thought of as deleterious in the sense of substitutions of a pollution-tolerant garbage feeding community in place of the clean-water balanced community. The elimination and restriction of native species is obvious. In a few years, as the area becomes urbanized, the stream will be replaced by a culvert and then a pipe, and the natural community will have disappeared entirely.

I have a feeling at times that the Dr. Shelfords must have taken more pleasure from their work than the Dr. Darnells do—or can.

Off Raritan Bay in New Jersey is a connecting body of water called Arthur Kill—a spot to which Engineers might be condemned for their sins. You can search Arthur Kill to your heart's content, but you won't find any form of life at all, in the water or on the bottom. All you'll find is a mass of grease and sludge.

Arthur Kill is the measure of the direction in which the Engineers are taking all of America.

As noted before, some of the Engineers work for us, in theory at least. The largest purchaser of coal in the country, for example, is the Tennessee Valley Authority. Some years ago, the U.S. Forest Service suggested that the TVA, when it contracts for coal, could include in the contract a provision for land restoration by the miners and thus contribute to the reduction of pollution generally. TVA refused, did its best to get its coal as cheaply as possible—and out of another pocket you and I are paying $36 million for strip-mine reclamation under the Appalachian Redevelopment Act.

In the meantime, even art suffers from pollution. *Science and Technology* for June, 1965, reported pollution damage to "Mission of Gabriel," a fresco by Giotto in Padua, Italy. Sulfur dioxide, oxidized and hydrated in the air to sulfuric acid, is attacking the lime in the underlying plaster.

These are the prices we pay for convenience and ease. Today's no-deposit, no-return bottle is tomorrow's solid waste. An auto manufacturer reports that air pollution can be reduced slightly by a device that returns to the gas tank the small amount of gas that remains, when a car is stopped, in the carburetor bowl (from which some of it evaporates into the air); but they won't put it on cars because it would mean that the car would take a minute longer to start, and the customers won't stand for it.

Every year, America manufactures 48 billion cans, 26 billion bottles and jars, 65 billion metal and plastic caps, virtually all of which become, almost immediately, waste (and unnecessarily; both cans and bottles could be reused if we so desired). Of the 8 billion pounds of plastics we produce, only 10 percent is reclaimed. Of the 1.75 million *tons* of rubber products, only 15% is reclaimed.

The citizen of Manhattan pays approximately $5 per story in additional rent just to get above the noise, to see occasionally the sun and the moon, and to escape some of the polluted air. To no avail: On the city's East Side, 80 tons of dust and soot fall, every month, on every square mile. The city's Air Pollution Control Board got about $1 million in 1965, which reporter Charles Bennett says is "like fighting a five-alarm fire in the Empire State Building with a single hand extinguisher." And, he writes further, Air Pollution Control Commissioner Arthur J. Benline "concedes that he worries over the possibility of the kind of thermal inversion that could endanger the lungs—and the lives—of city residents with the full force of the poisons of air contamination."

New York had an inversion, in 1953, that was blamed for the deaths of about 200 older people and tiny babies. And the situation is a lot worse today than it was in 1953.

In Houston, where the official position is that there isn't any pollution problem at all, they nevertheless have an Air and Water Pollution Control Section in the county health department. Its director, W. A. Quebedeaux, Jr., says that children who play in some of the parks near Brays Bayou can expect waterborne diseases during the summer. And A. W. Busch, a professor of environmental engineering (!) at Rice University who worked with the Houston Chamber of Commerce on a study, says that the

50-mile ship channel that links Houston to the Gulf of Mexico needs close study. "Given a strong north wind and lots of rain and runoff," he says, "there can be fish kills in the lower reaches of the channel and in Galveston Bay."

The examples can, of course, be multiplied until we get tired of stringing them out. But the point is that virtually every example is an instance of what happens when the Engineers—the engineering mentality—are turned loose on what somebody dimly perceives as a problem. A straight-line question (what shall we do with the pickling acid?) gets a straight-line answer (dump it in the river), and then the guy with an economic interest in that answer wins a no-contest fight with balkanized governments and unorganized citizens—and, most of all, with the long-suffering but not inexhaustible environment.

A "research management advisory panel" to a House subcommittee—a panel consisting of both businessmen and scientists—reported in 1966 on the problems of doing something about all the myriad forms of pollution that the Engineers have brought upon us. First of all, they said, "without more knowledge of an ecological baseline, and without the ability to predict the results of man-made changes in the environment," there isn't any way to figure out just what ought to be done. This, of course—the establishment of just such baseline data—is why ecologists are so anxious to preserve examples of various ecosystems. Of course people want to save the Everglades and the Grand Canyon because they are uniquely beautiful. But they *must* be saved because they are unique ecosystems. The entire redwood ecosystem remaining on Redwood Creek must be saved, because without a variety of ecosystems with which to work, no one can establish the ecological "baselines" that are needed—and we can quit worrying about how to cure pollution problems because they simply aren't going to be cured.

It may seem a long jump from spending a few million more dollars on Redwood Creek to saving many times that much by curbing pollution, but it's actually not a jump at all; it's a clearly marked path once the vision of an ecological conscience is there to light the way. It is precisely the hope of establishing such ecological baseline data as the Congressional advisers said they need that every new project of the Engineers causes to flicker just that much more dimly.

The panel did bravely try to make some recommendations, however. For the gross treatment of mine drainages, they said, there is simply no present technology that will help (and of course, no one has any economic interest in developing such a technology, which in the world's leading capitalist society probably means that nobody will). The same is true for the elimination of nitrous oxides from automobile exhausts (present-day "smog devices" deal only with unburned hydrocarbons, which are only a small part of automobile exhaust pollution, and they don't even do that very well).

There is only a partial technology for the treatment of sewage, for other elements of automobile exhaust, and for some industrial pollutants. The solid-waste problem is simply a question of either space or reclamation, and there is little technology (or, as of right now, motivation) for reclamation. In still other cases, including the recovery of sulfur dioxide from stack gases, the technology exists but is extremely expensive.

Manufacturers, by and large, vigorously resist any attempt to force them to install the technological devices that exist; more often than not, they use the one-problem-at-a-time arguments of the Engineers. When Congressman Vanik suggested that the Federal Government might set industry-by-industry standards for pollution control, every industrial representative before the committee holding the hearings made a noise like a baby guinea pig with his foot caught in his cage.

Typical was John O. Logan, an executive vice president of Olin Mathieson, who appeared for the Manufacturing Chemists Association. "The problem of discharging one ton of waste on the North Fork of the Holston [Tennessee] River," he argued, "is very substantially different than it is on the Mississippi or the Ohio." The argument was that there is more water in the Mississippi or the Ohio. But of course there are more factories, and more sewage-spewing towns, as well—and besides, it is the nature as well as the amount of waste that is important in ecology. Mr. Logan, one suspects, is not overly interested in ecology.

In fact, Assistant Secretary Cain recently told Congress flatly that with a few exceptions, "industry, including mining and manufacturing industries, is almost completely without an ecological philosophy or concern." The exceptions he cited were industries like petroleum and timber, which have learned enough ecology to husband their own resources, whatever their attitudes may be toward the rest of us. Most of industry, however, simply threatens to leave the area and take its payroll with it whenever someone suggests regulation. Even the strip miners of Appalachia have tried that on a number of towns and counties.

In 1967, in *The Nation*, Paul Good took a look at the strip miners of Appalachia and at the havoc they have brought (and also looked at the social consequences of their rapine, a subject which I have regretfully but firmly left out of a lot of my own examples). He describes a group called the Appalachian Group to Save the Land and People, who did a little investigation into this economic threatening and came up with a question-and-answer fact sheet. Some excerpts, as Good gives them:

Q. Doesn't strip mining employ lots of Eastern Kentuckians?
A. No. A very large strip-mining operation bringing millions of dollars of profit to the operator can be run with a handful of men. They are paid whatever the operator feels he can get away with.
Q. Doesn't strip mining help our economy in other ways?
A. No. In fact it costs the taxpayers of this state about a dollar every time a ton of coal is strip mined. That figures out to millions of dollars a year—in expensive reclamation and reforestation, in road repairs [laden coal trucks chew up highways while their overloads are winked at by county judges "sympathethic" to the operators], flood-control projects, water-pollution control. We pay the strip miners to destroy us.
Q. What will happen to Eastern Kentucky if strip mining isn't stopped?
A. In a few years, every coal-mining county will be a crisscross of shattered mountains and ruined valleys. Thousands of people will have to leave.

The bracketed comment is Good's.

But if the threat to move is meaningless elsewhere as it is in Appalachia—and it is; it costs a lot of money to move—the threat from *not* fighting pollution is quite real. In Pittsburgh, one of the few cities to have made genuine strides in fighting pollution, a beginning was made in 1945 because forty industrial firms had decided to leave; the smoke and rotten air, plus threats from floods and contaminated water, were driving them out. In that same year, Pittsburgh led the cities of the United States in deaths from pneumonia.

In 1952, a saving of $26 million was estimated for the citizens of Pittsburgh—in cleaning bills alone! Household laundry bills dropped another $5.5 million. And visibility, which has no monetary value, was up 77 percent over 1945. That can be done with present technology, we know: Pittsburgh did it.

Doing something about pollution, of course, is expensive; but it's not impossible, if the polluter can be identified and if he exists in the same political jurisdiction as the people suffering from the pollution. California got tough with paper mills (although they, too, threatened to leave), and the Kimberly-Clark Corporation accepted the restrictions when they built a pulp mill near Mount Shasta. The company built a waste-purifying plant, the final stage of which is a tank into which its waste effluent flows and in which fingerling salmon and steelhead swim happily. The law required Kimberly-Clark not to pollute salmon- and trout-hatching waters, and for $2 million Kimberly-Clark was able to obey.

It is not always that easy. Another paper company spent almost exactly the same amount on pollution abatement in North Carolina (though not in a new plant), but the white scum remains on the Pigeon River. An increase in production canceled out the effect of the program—although of course the pollution would be much worse today without it.

Other states are getting into the anti-pollution swing in one way or another. Michigan and Rhode Island have decided on the carrot instead of the stick, and exempt from state taxes (since 1966) any facilities installed to control industrial waste; their wording is mostly directed toward water pollution. South Carolina has a similar law referring to "water and air pollution," and Wisconsin has a complex tax-incentives law relating to water. New York, so far eschewing the tax incentive, has simply passed a law forbidding anybody to put chemicals into the water without a permit from the Water Resources Commission of the state.

Also in 1966, Illinois, Indiana, Michigan and Wisconsin agreed that material dredged from polluted streams will not be dumped into Lake Michigan. The ubiquitous Army Engineers, however, are not party to the agreement; their jurisdiction over navigable inland waterways means that they can go right on doing what the four states have agreed not to do.

California's water resources director has described processes now available for reducing the amount of phosphorus in waste discharges; they are expensive—about $100 per acre-foot of water—but they work, and they're being used at Lake Tahoe, where one of the world's clearest bodies of water is in serious trouble from eutrophia.

The Colorado School of Mines Foundation thinks it has found a way to eliminate the smelting step in sulphite ore production, the biggest source of copper. Smelting is a major source of air pollution. The same new process will enable copper miners to work with lower-grade ores, to the point where it can be used to extract copper from the tailings of already worked copper mines. If it is as good as they say it is, maybe somebody could get two days' copper out of a pile of waste somewhere, and Kennecott can leave Glacier Peak alone without losing the war in Vietnam.

Los Angeles' Whittier Narrows plant purifies 11 million gallons of water a day by tapping a trunk sewer (one that doesn't happen to have much industrial waste in it), putting the sewage through primary and secondary treatment and then spreading it on sand beds. The water sinks into the ground and recharges the water table in the area—and the sand filters out what's left of the pollution, including, for some reason as yet unknown to scientists, the viruses. The whole thing costs a little over half what the county pays for Colorado River water.

Ultimately, it is Whittier Narrows and the ragpickers of Ixtapalapa that hold the only hope for escape from slow death by pollution. The reclamation and reuse of water is already possible, and can be done by some methods without the creation of too much solid waste. John Lear has described a fantastic reclamation program followed in the Ruhr Valley of West Germany:

The Ruhrverband is a cooperative, with 250 riverside towns and cities and 2,200 industries as members. It oversees the repeated use of Ruhr

River water, keeping the water continually potable in passage from town to town. The cost of the process is divided among the membership according to the burden of waste each member adds to the stream. Since 1948, the Ruhrverband has built with its dues and fees 102 water purification plants along the river.

To reduce the Ruhrverband's assessments against them, steel mills along the Ruhr have devised internal recirculation systems which allow a mill to use the same water over and over. As a result, the manufacture of a ton of steel, which once required the use of 130 cubic yards of water, now uses only 2.6 cubic yards of water.

If they can do it, why can't we?

A method is being developed to make it far more economical to reclaim steel from junk cars (and already somebody wants to fill in another 6.5 acres of San Francisco Bay to build a plant to do it in!). Sulfur can be reclaimed, albeit expensively, from the sulfur dioxide of stack gases. San Francisco and other Bay Area cities have for years ignored the offer of a Berkeley fertilizer manufacturer to take their solid refuse and to build a composting plant in the area that would make use of it for fertilizer.

Electric automobiles, still a difficult conception for most of us, can be a reality any time. The Bureau of Mines operated a three-quarter-ton electric truck in Pennsylvania for 7,724 miles over a three-year period, and matched it against a gasoline-powered truck of the same size, doing the same work. The electric truck cost between 1.5 and 2.65 cents a mile for its energy; the gas truck cost 5.8 cents a mile (at 29 cents a gallon, at that).

The Rowan Controller Corporation in Baltimore has claimed that they are not only going to produce electric cars, but—unlike the tiny runabouts being shown as prototypes so far—they are going to produce one that's slightly larger than a Volkswagen Karmann-Ghia. It will, they say, have a range of 200 miles on normal lead-acid batteries (the usual figure for electric cars is about 50 miles), and it will cost about $1,500. From what is known of the present state of electric-car technology, that all sounds a little fantastic. But Rowan must be serious; they went to Italy and bought the entire Ghia body plant for $625,000.

If the electric car doesn't work out, however (there is now some evidence that the power requirements for recharging batteries would be so high that the production of that power would pollute the air more than today's cars do), there is still steam—a simple, practical and remarkably clean way to power an automobile, and one that offers more potential and fewer problems than any other. General Motors is paying for the conversion by a Pennsylvania firm of six Oldsmobiles to steam power, to be tested by the California Highway Patrol, and for installation of a steam engine in a Chevrolet Chevelle by a firm in Oakland, California, that made steam cars 40 years ago.

At any rate, there *is* enough technology to make genuine strides in the fight against pollution. Now all we need is to know what we're doing—both when we fight pollution and when we pollute. Because we do have to "pollute" something, or give up steel and electricity, transportation and communication, even the quality of food to which we are accustomed however poor we may be. We will have nuclear power—when they solve a couple more problems I'll be all for it—and we will have to heat the water in some rivers or along some shorelines; it's a matter of picking the spot where it will do the least ecological damage. We will always have some waste, and we will have to do something with it.

It is a question of planning—overall planning, in this case, so that a copper company is not fighting the Forest Service over here while the Interior Department tangles with a lumber company over there—so that every proposal doesn't have to start a whole new set of arguments over again.

If I were not such a confirmed cynic about the power of the Engineers, I would go along with Wallace Stegner in his enthusiasm for scrapping the Interior Department and substituting a Department of Natural Resources, which would be charged

with all the land and water management functions of the federal government. This would mean transfer to the new department of the National Forest Service, now in Agriculture, and the presumed removal of the bones of contention between Forest Service and National Park Service. It would mean transfer of the functions of the Corps of Engineers, now in the Department of the Army, to Natural Resources —in effect merging the Corps with the Bureau of Reclamation. It would mean other transfers: the Federal Power Commission, now in Commerce; the Tennessee Valley Authority, now a public corporation; and the water-pollution control activities that are now in Health, Education and Welfare. The Bureau of Indian Affairs and the Office of Territories, now in Interior, would be moved over into HEW.

In a Senate hearing early in 1966, Gaylord Nelson of Wisconsin talked with Assistant Secretary of the Interior Stanley Cain:

SEN. NELSON: I notice that they have now filled in 200 square miles of San Francisco Bay. It was about 520 square miles and it is now down to 300-and-some square miles of water. . . .

SEC. CAIN: To my knowledge there is no general ecological study being made of the bay and the damage of this filling. I can say, however, that the Bureau of Commercial Fisheries has been engaged for a few years now on a study of Tampa Bay, where perhaps between 15 and 20 percent of the bay has been filled behind bulkheads and, in producing the material for the fill, there has been about an equal percentage of the bay that has been dredged. These studies reveal that after 10 years of dredging, the bottom is, in effect, a biological desert. Here is at least a third, perhaps more, of Tampa Bay that has been completely destroyed from the point of view of natural estuary conditions. Here is a bay in which there must be two dozen species of commercial fish and shellfish that spend part of their life. . . .

SEN. NELSON: So after it is all filled, the ecologists will be able to tell us what happened to it?

VIII · I GOTTA HAVE MY ROAD

*I am not in favor of building any
more roads in the National Parks
than we have to build.*
    —HAROLD L. ICKES

THIS IS THE STORY of a road that's under water, another road that
hasn't been built for a quarter century and probably never should
be, a third road that could enrich a town and ruin a park—and of
the advantages of having the right Congressman in the right place
at the right time.

You would need an old map for this one. On it, you would
find the upper part of a fork of the Little Tennessee River, rising
not in Tennessee but in North Carolina. From the Tennessee border
to the ambitiously named town of Bryson City (1960 pop.: 1,084),
a state road once ran along the north bank of the river. North of
that road were 44,400 acres of privately owned land. And north
of that land was the border of Great Smoky Mountains National
Park. The road along the north bank of the Little Tennessee
was owned and maintained by the state, but it had been built
with bonds issued by Swain County, North Carolina. In 1943,
Swain County still owed money on the bonds.

By 1943, too, the sovereign state of North Carolina had
agreed that the 44,400 acres of privately owned land, just north
of the road, could be added to the national park. Unfortunately,
in 1943 there wasn't a lot of money kicking around for the Park
Service to buy land with. At about that time, along came the
Tennessee Valley Authority.

TVA wanted to build Fontana Dam on the Little Tennessee
River in North Carolina, and to create Fontana Lake behind it.

The problem was that Fontana Lake, of course, would cover the road. Swain County and the state of North Carolina didn't like that.

TVA then said to Swain County: "We'll pay off your bonds."

And TVA said to North Carolina: "We have figured out that you can build another road, just north of the shore of Fontana Lake, for $1,400,000. So we will give you $1,400,000."

But North Carolina took a look, and then replied to TVA: "No, thank you. The road already needs improvement. We would have to build a more expensive road, and that will cost more money."

And Swain County also took a look, and then replied to TVA: "No, thank you. We are obliged to provide services, and therefore access, to our citizens who live along that road. Besides, you will isolate Bryson City." The latter was not strictly true, because U.S. 19 runs right through Bryson City, but it was true that it would be cut off from certain other places.

At this point, the National Park Service stuck its head under the tent and said: "Hey, don't forget us, fellas."

So everybody sat down over an Orange Julius, and a deal was made in the form of a four-way contract, which at this point has to be followed with some attention.

TVA said to the private landowners: "We will purchase or condemn your land." The private landowners didn't get to sign the contract; being citizens, and not agencies, they only got to listen.

TVA said to Swain County: "We will pay off your bonds for $400,000."

TVA said to the National Park Service: "We will donate to you, after we purchase or condemn it, all the land between Fontana Lake and the national park, if you will protect the watershed."

And TVA said to North Carolina: "Now watch the shells carefully and see whether you can find the pea."

North Carolina must have found the pea, because it said to TVA: "It's a deal, because the Park Service can build a new North Shore Road on *its* land, and they can maintain it, and we'll save lots of money. In fact, *we'll* give *you* $100,000 to help buy the land."

Swain County said to TVA: "It's a deal, *if* we get a North Shore Road."

The National Park Service said to TVA: "Thank you for the land, and we promise to protect the watershed."

And the National Park Service said to Swain County: "We'll build a road on the north shore of Fontana Lake, from Bryson City to the Fontana Dam access road, which leads to Fontana Village and from there to the beautiful outside world."

Everybody was happy. TVA had its dam, the Park Service had 44,400 new acres (minus the flooded part), Swain County had its promise, and Bryson City, as noted, wasn't really all that isolated anyway.

Everybody was happy, that is, except the 216 families who lived on the 44,400 acres. Some of them ungraciously went to court, arguing that TVA can't go around condemning land just so they can give it away to the National Park Service. That would seem to make some sense, but the United States Supreme Court, in 1946, reversed a lower court and blandly said that TVA has the power to condemn land whenever necessary for carrying out the purposes of the TVA Act, so there.

In the meantime, or shortly thereafter, everybody moved out of the 44,400 acres. There now being no citizens in the area requiring services from (and therefore access to) the rest of Swain County, there was no need for a North Shore Road.

So nobody built it.

The National Park Service, you understand, can't just go around signing contracts to build roads. It has only a small annual road-building budget to stretch all across the country. What the National Park Service actually did in 1943 was agree to build a Bryson City-Fontana road on the north shore, *provided Congress appropriated the money.*

So far, Congress has not done so. If they had, of course, some Engineer would have built the road whether anybody needed it or not.

So one thing, at least, is clear. The only portion of the 1943 agreement that has not been carried out is the building by the Park Service of a road that nobody needs anyway.

For a while, however, Bryson City and Swain County *wanted* the road, whether they needed it or not, for a very simple reason. The Great Smoky Mountains National Park is one of the largest and loveliest in the eastern United States. The Park Service likes to point out that it is within a day's drive for nearly half the population of the United States (it's a hard day's drive for some of them, but you get the idea). More to the immediate point, the Park is visited by 5,500,000 visitors every year. They buy Cokes and eat hamburgers and stay in motels and spend money in towns near the park—if the towns are handy to the park by car (and in some cases, if the visitors are white).

The easy automotive way into the park right now is on U.S. 441, the only cross-mountain road that goes through the park itself. And the entrance point is on the other side of the mountains from Bryson City, at the once sleepy mountain village of Gatlinburg, Tennessee.

Within living memory, Gatlinburg was "mountaineer Jack Huff's hotel and a general store." Today (1960 pop.: 1,764) it is far from the prettiest town in the mountains, but it is hardly suffering from Appalachian disease. It is, in fact, a neon jungle, a tangle of tossed-together tourist traps and greasy hamburger joints, with a chair-lift ride over the town and, for the devout, a Bible garden, complete with dioramas of the life of Christ. There are even a couple of nice places, including some craft shops, but much more common are trinket stands where the high-priced merchandise is handcrafted in Japan. It's all a highly effective trap filter for tourist dollars. Bryson City and Swain County want some. North Carolina could use a little, too.

Of course, a couple of other things have happened since 1943. In case anybody really wanted to go from Bryson City to Fontana or vice versa—and there probably are such people—North Carolina has constructed (with Federal funds, of course) State Highway 28, around the *south* shore of Fontana Lake. But State 28 is outside the park and open to commercial development, and it wanders pretty far from the lake at times. So no New Yorkers or Illini drive along it and admire the country—with Bryson City as their base. A North Shore Road along the lake would be something else again.

So North Carolina thoughtfully built another state road, a couple of miles long, from Bryson City to the park boundary, and meaningfully cleared its throat, reminding the Park Service that they had a deal. The Park Service, being made up of good guys (and some Engineers), picked up the road and used a little of its own road money to start on around the north shore.

They had gone only 4.6 miles when they quit, partly because of money but mostly because it turned out to be a damned difficult road to build. It also horrified conservationists, since it consists mostly of deep cuts and high fills, and is an ugly scar across the lovely country. Happily, however—although no one would suggest that it was deliberate—the Park Service stopped just short of a lovely potential spot for a campground and marina near the mouth of Noland Creek, at the head of the lake.

If completed, by the way, the road would consist of 25 more miles of expensive cut and fill. Back in 1960, the estimated cost of the road was $16 million—which is slightly more than the Service paid for all of Great Smoky Mountains National Park itself.

So you can now drive from Bryson City to 4.6 miles inside the park, which doesn't do anybody much good at all. In the meantime, however, the local people have taken a few more looks at Gatlinburg, and they've come up with a new idea entirely. This time TVA, being out of it, was not called back in, and the National Park Service does not seem to have received its invitation. Swain County and the state of North Carolina, all by themselves, sat down and "amended" the 1943 agreement. In place of the North Shore Road, they decided, they'll accept a transmountain road from Bryson City to Townsend, Tennessee—right over the hill through the middle of the park.

It will perhaps have occurred to you by now that the whole point of the 1943 agreement—replacement of the road drowned by Fontana Lake—has long since been lost. In fact, some lawyers, and Assistant Secretary of the Interior Stanley Cain, have told me that the Park Service is probably no longer bound by the agreement at all (Dr. Cain is Assistant Secretary for Parks, and this whole thing is his worry). For one thing, there is in the law of contracts a legal doctrine called "frustration of purpose," out of which a pretty good argument can be made. Also, the 4.6 miles of North Shore Road already built, with its huge cuts and fills, apparently contributes some erosion—conservationists say it's a lot of erosion. And in the 1943 agreement, the Park Service promised TVA that it would administer and operate the lands in such a way as to guarantee maximum watershed protection. If it can be shown that the road so far *does* contribute to erosion, then Interior can argue that it would violate the agreement if it built the road (that's not an insoluble paradox, by the way; Interior could make the argument, not to Swain County but to Congress, and thus help to block any appropriation for the road; or they could, as noted above, get out of it in other legal ways).

The Secretary of the Interior has not, repeat not, signed the "amended" agreement, and says he won't. North Carolina and Swain County have said they will take a transmountain road as fulfillment of the 1943 deal, but the Secretary hasn't said he will go along. Without a map you'll have to take my word for it, but the proposed transmountain road would probably contribute to erosion and damage to the watershed just as the North Shore Road would.

The next event in our little drama is the 1966 election. A gentleman from Alaska, otherwise unimportant in our story, did not return to his seat in Congress. He was a member of the House Committee on Interior and Insular Affairs and was, in fact, chairman of the subcommittee on national parks. Into this chairmanship, in January, 1967, moved the next ranking Democrat: Representative Roy Taylor—of Swain County, North Carolina.

"He's a fine gentleman," Assistant Secretary Cain told me, quite seriously and without irony. "He will do all he can for the Park Service. He has only one problem. If you mention the Great Smokies, all he can say is, 'I gotta have my road.'"

Actually, as a visit to the area (or even careful study of a good map) clearly shows, Representative Taylor does *not* gotta have his road, if various governmental agencies can get together. There are other ways to relieve congestion on U.S. 441, provide for a lot more casual tourism in the Great Smokies, preserve a lot of the park itself as the superb and ecologically important wilderness area it is, and still make Bryson City rich. It would require the cooperation of the state and county, and the Interior, Agriculture and Transportation Departments, but it can be done. In fact, some of it is being done anyway.

One of the Park Service's concerns is that the increasing visitor traffic is jamming U.S. 441, which is also the only way across the mountains for local traffic. But Interstate 40 will now cross the mountains a few miles to the northeast, not through the park but through Cherokee National Forest, an almost equally lovely drive and a far superior route for the driver who merely wants to get from one side to the other.

On the Tennessee side of the park, but outside its boundaries, is being built the Foothills Parkway, which will be a high road with a lovely view, running from Interstate 40 at one end to U.S. 129 —thus paralleling the Tennessee border of the park itself. Millions of tourists will drive the parkway for its magnificent view (and will, incidentally, bypass Gatlinburg by miles).

U.S. 129, however, is low-grade, though it does run back into North Carolina and eventually connects with State 28 to Bryson City. If U.S. 129 and State 28 were upgraded, the Foothills Parkway traffic, coming off Interstate 40, could drive a few more miles around the western end of the park, back along the Little Tennessee south of Fontana Lake, and into Bryson City as a natural stopping place.

Less than ten miles from Bryson City, near the settlement of Oconaluftee, the equally beautiful Blue Ridge Parkway arrives from the northeast, to come to a dead end where it meets U.S. 441. It could easily be extended to the Park's Deep Creek camping area, just outside Bryson City, from which the road to Bryson City already exists. It would be a much more logical end to the parkway for campers (especially if the Park Service expanded the campsite area a little), and the car-bound traveler wouldn't have to drive 441 over the mountains to hit a motel or a restaurant. Again, Bryson City would be the natural stopping place.

For those who just want to get from one side of the mountains to the other, and who aren't park visitors, Interstate 40 isn't the only thing that will take some of the load off U.S. 441. To such drivers Gatlinburg is a bottleneck, so a bypass is under construction that will speed things up a little. Also, still another transmountain highway is being built to the southwest, between Robbinsville, N.C., and Tellico Plains, Tennessee.

If Interior were to expand its Deep Creek campsite facilities and complete the "motor nature trail" it is building in that area for the less hardy visitor and if they were to extend the North Shore Road only to the headwaters of the lake and set up a combination campsite and marina (one of the finest ways to see much of the park is by boat from the rivers and creeks of the watershed area), then Bryson City would become a natural gateway to many of the pleasures of the park. Swain County could happily blossom in ugly neon like its transmountain rival, and Representative Taylor wouldn't gotta have his road.

The Great Smokies and Yosemite are probably the national parks that most feel the pressure of population (in 1966, the National Park Service announced that, instead of letting people camp wherever they wanted to camp, it would clearly mark campsites in Yosemite, and in such a way that the number of campers would be reduced by half), but many of the others aren't far behind. The number of people who visited national parks in 1966 is hard to come by—ecologist F. Raymond Fosberg says 95,000,000 and reporter Walter Damtoft says 122,600,000—but in any case it was something like half the population of the United States.

Grand Teton National Park, in Wyoming, had 2,700,000 visitors in 1966, and Yellowstone had 2,000,000. Some people aren't too happy about the way the Park Service handles all this—Peter Farb, for instance:

The National Park Service's stewardship of this park has, in recent years, become an act of official vandalism.

Recently it encouraged the building of a new development which includes a supermarket, trinket shop, laundry, over 1,000 gimcrack cabins—and this eyesore is close to some of the most magnificent scenery on the continent. A parking lot it recently built helped destroy Daisy Geyser, one of the most attractive in the park.

The National Park Service states blandly that only five percent of Yellowstone is taken up by developments such as trailer camps, parking lots, roads, gas stations, motels. But it is clear to any visitor that this five percent has had a traumatic effect on the other 95 percent.

At the risk of belaboring the point: You can't cut down all the trees to make room for the people who want to see the trees. And we do not have to do that yet in the Great Smokies. This is where we ring in the Agriculture Department: Everybody doesn't have to jam into the national park.

From Georgia to Virginia, the entire Tennessee side of the Great Smokies, except for the tiny portion in the park, is included in the Cherokee National Forest. On the North Carolina side, the Nantahala National Forest fills the entire corner formed by the Cherokee Forest, the national park, and the Georgia and South Carolina borders. On the Georgia side, bordering Cherokee and Nantahala to their south, is the Chattahoochee National Forest. The corner of South Carolina that touches Georgia and North Carolina is the Sumter National Forest. Back in North Carolina, most of what's left of the Great Smokies and the Blue Ridge Mountains is part of the Pisgah National Forest.

It all sounds confusing, but on a map it's easy: virtually the entire area, with the national park as a relatively tiny island in the middle of it, is taken up with what is in effect one big national forest. It has different names in different states, and it is broken up for administrative and other accidental reasons, but it is really one huge protected area.

The park, most people agree, is ecologically the most valuable sector, and the one which should, more than any other, be protected from disturbance. The Forest Service of the Agriculture Department can relieve much of the load on the national park by the judicious construction of its own campsites and recreational facilities. Granting that to an ecologist the successional stages of various forest areas in the park are fascinating, what most of the 6,000,000 or so annual park visitors want is an expanse of green and lovely country, and there is plenty of that in the national forests.

The crowding problem of the Great Smokies is given by friends of the park as a reason both for and against Representative Taylor's road. Bryson City druggist Kelly E. Bennett, a lifetime fighter for the park, wants the road "to get these visitors dispersed through and around the park." Anthony Wayne Smith of the National Parks Association says that there shouldn't even be campsites in the park, and that all roads should be dead ends, to keep out through traffic and people "uninterested in what the park really has to offer."

If Mr. Smith had his way, in fact, he would keep cars out entirely and use electric coaches to transport visitors to trail heads and other remote spots. George B. Hartzog, Jr., who directs the National Park Service, agrees about the cars ("The real enemies of the national parks are not people but automobiles"), but his alternatives aren't so popular, either. His occasional mention of monorails or helicopters has brought down so much criticism that he has been heard to grumble, "Any suggestion of change is regarded with skepticism and distrust, particularly one dealing with new techniques for transporting visitors."

Actually, Mr. Hartzog's full-fledged "parks are for people" philosophy is as foolish as—and in the long run even more dangerous than—the worst of backpack snobbery. It is certainly a serious dilution of the idea that has always underlain national parks in the first place—and Peter Farb, who is one of the Park Service's most vocal critics, points out one way in which it can have serious effects for the future. Noting in 1966 that there would probably be 12 new national parks created soon, Farb wrote:

Only one of these areas is a traditional national park. The rest are not wild, not significant, not unique in any way, and, I fear, rarely beautiful. They are recreational areas that will afford entertainment, places equivalent to Jones Beach or any of the hundreds of seashore and lakefront developments around the country. There are even plans for golf courses, boat docks, ski tows, and hunting at some of these new areas.

It is one thing to say that a little old lady ought to be able to see the Everglades. It is quite another thing to say that a national park ought simply to be a place that a little old lady can see.

Hartzog is partly motivated by a concern with money, but what is most important is that he is completely reversing the Interior Department's position of only a few years ago. In 1963 the Leopold Committee, appointed to study the national parks, recommended in part that "the goal of managing the national parks and monuments should be to preserve, or where necessary to recreate, the ecological scene as viewed by the first European visitors." The committee, which included distinguished ecologists, was sharply aware of the difference between an ecologically unique area—like the Everglades, the forest-succession regions of the Great Smokies, or Redwood Creek—and a simply pretty area like the Point Reyes National Seashore north of San Francisco.

Perhaps it is not completely an accident that with the accession to power of a supremely political President, the national park program has increasingly become a matter of pretty pork, with less and less ecological significance. But Mr. Hartzog's own National Park Service still publishes a list of "management principles and administrative policies," which says of "physical developments" that they "shall be limited to those that are necessary and appropriate, and provided only under carefully controlled safeguards against unregulated and indiscriminate use, so that *the least damage to park values will be caused*" [emphasis added].

That doesn't mean helicopters, George.

Monorails, funiculars, boat docks we should perhaps have—in those places where we decide that lots of people can continue to go without causing too much damage (but not, please, in the national parks). We can even build the monorails and the boat docks where they will coax people away from the precious and irreplaceable. A marina on Fontana Lake, for instance (the lake is phony, anyway), can make it possible for visitors to see the unspoiled Great Smokies by boat without serious ecological intrusion, and putting the campsites, and perhaps even the monorails, into the surrounding national forests can take some of the load off the park and distribute it throughout the Great Smokies area —with Bryson City getting its share.

Certainly something must be done to spread the pressure of urban visitors, and not only in the Great Smokies. The number of visitors to Yosemite went up 40 percent between 1961 and 1966, and California state parks in 1965 turned away 1.5 million persons for lack of space.

None of this is to suggest that the National Park Service is a terrible outfit. As the Wilderness Society said, in a statement prepared for hearings that concerned putting some of the Great Smokies Park into wilderness status, "If it were not for the National Park Service and its wilderness preservation work since the creation of the Smokies Park, we could not concern ourselves here today with the question of how much wilderness should be placed in the National Wilderness Preservation System."

Nevertheless, Mr. Hartzog appears to be leaning in the direction of thinking like an Engineer, even if the Assistant Secretary to whom he is responsible is an ecologist. And there are already plenty of Engineers, and Engineer-minded bureaucrats, in the Park Service (*The New York Times* for June 14, 1966, editorializing against the proposed transmountain road from Bryson City, referred to "the Park Service's road-building mania"). Furthermore, above both Engineer and ecologist, the man at the top is—perhaps wisely, perhaps not—a politician. "All of us," Interior Secretary Stewart Udall has said, "overcompromise and therefore fall short of our ideals." Well, sure; and it is probably too much to expect that key positions in the Interior Department will not continue to be filled by political hacks on the insistence of the Democratic National Committee (or the Republican, as the case may be).

But this particular political man would like someday to be a United States Senator from his home state, and his home state is Arizona, and so as Secretary of the Interior he does not oppose the powerful men in that state who want to build dams in the Grand Canyon. His Department can issue a glowing report, pledging that "the chirp of the prairie dog and honk of a Canada goose are not to become oddities heard only on archive tape recorders"—while it supports 600 Government hunters who every year in the West, according to conservation writer Michael Frome, kill 200,000 bobcats, coyotes, foxes, cougars, wolves, pocket gophers and prairie dogs.

It is a political man, not a guardian of our national heritage, who can open the national parks and national wildlife refuges to mineral and oil explorations—stretching beyond all recognition the meaning of the Aspinall Amendment in the Wilderness Act. The act provides that the Geological Survey and the Bureau of Mines (both part of the Interior Department) should investigate mineral supplies in *national forest* areas proposed for wilderness inclusion; but it says national forests, not national parks or national wildlife refuges. Udall simply gave in to oil and mining interests.

Secretary Udall has, of course, done a number of superb things. He was himself one of the leading advocates of the Wilderness Act, he promoted passage of the Land and Water Conservation Fund Act, he has done a lot to make the nation conscious of the very heritage we are talking about. It was he who asked the Leopold Committee for its help, and it was he who pulled Dr. Cain off a university campus and made him an Assistant Secretary. In an earlier day, his function as a political man might have been tolerable—might even have been necessary. But that day is past. There is not enough space, and not enough time, for political compromise to function in this old-fashioned way.

Yet to former Representative and would-be Senator Udall, the strategic location of Congressman Roy Taylor is likely to mean far more than it means to anyone looking at the problem from outside. Possibly for many years to come, almost certainly for as long as Mr. Udall is Secretary of the Interior, Taylor will sit in judgment on any number of Park Service proposals. The easy way out is to give him his road.

Which is what the Engineers in the Park Service have, in effect, proposed to do. Their wilderness proposal is for four areas in the park, totaling 247,000 acres—with a space left for the transmountain road. The *right* way out, though, if there is a right way out, is not to give Representative Taylor his road but to enlarge on the Park Service proposal, possibly following the Wilderness Society's proposal for what are essentially two areas totaling 350,000 acres.

In this case, with vast areas of national forest in the same region that can accommodate some recreational development, Congress is not dealing with the appeasement of "backpack snobs." The Smokies, or at least that part of them within the national park, are ecologically unique. Three separate, distinct types of forest ecology—the Carolinian, the Alleghenian Transition and the Canadian—exist within the park borders. The park harbors, according to the Wilderness Society, 130 native tree species, at least that many woody shrubs and vines, 1,400 different flowering plants, 1,700 types of fungi, 330 species of mosses and liverworts, 230 species of lichens—and 52 species of furbearing animals, 200 of birds, 36 of reptiles, 37 of amphibians and 80 of fish.

The National Park Service itself has a document that says what a wilderness area ought to be, and a part of it deals directly with ecology:

The Service, recognizing the scientific value of wilderness areas as natural outdoor laboratories, would encourage those kinds of research which require such areas for their accomplishment, provided that this research does not itself significantly alter the natural wilderness features and is consistent with established rules and regulations. These areas would serve as unmodified scientific "controls" for comparison with areas elsewhere which have been modified, experimentally or otherwise, by man's activities.

This is about where anybody who understands what's happening in the world had better get into the act. The Ecological Society of America—which is not too often found even at wilderness hearings—was about as blunt as a learned society ever gets in the statement it had to offer about the Great Smokies:

The park has a potential for ecological research which so greatly transcends the usual park needs for interpretive and management research that it puts the Great Smokies in the category of a national ecological resource.

You can't put it more plainly than that.

The Society noted that Congress had recently been told about, and might even be worrying about, the "greenhouse effect" caused by all the carbon dioxide we're throwing into the air—the effect discussed in Chapter II. This, the ecologists said, is a perfect example of "major ecological questions which can best be answered by studies and research programs involving very large areas of undisturbed vegetation." And when that research panel told a Congressional committee that they couldn't really talk about stopping pollution until there had been an opportunity to establish "ecological baseline data," they were quite aware that such data can be gathered only by leaving large, untouched areas like the Great Smokies just the way they are.

The Ecological Society said flatly of the Park Service's proposal (using their own italics) that "the wilderness plan outlined in the proposed management plan for the Great Smoky Mountains National Park *does not* recognize nor take into consideration this major value of the Park's resources." As for that road which Congressman Taylor's gotta have, the Society uncompromisingly calls it "incompatible with the value of and need for the Park as an ecological resource":

Ecologically, such roads have serious long-term effects. The fills and shoulders drain into watersheds and headwaters of streams [and remember, the Park Service has a deal with TVA, too]. In the present case these would be the headwaters of the tributaries of Hazel, Proctor and Forney Creeks which are magnificent primitive and undisturbed streams. The drainage from these road fills includes large quantities of mineral matter released by the combination of crushing and subsequent leaching by rain. Later, as the roads are used regularly, organic compounds of petroleum origin derived from vehicle exhaust systems are also incorporated in the fills and are subsequently leached into the streams. Other organic debris from garbage, picnic tables, etc., soon also enter the stream of alien substances and compounds entering the headwaters. The result of this new and foreign input is a change in the chemical balance of the stream waters which ultimately is reflected in a change of the ecological balance.

And it doesn't take any hundred years, either. Remember that river in France?

Okay, you can't save everything. And some people will find a way to throw a half-eaten hot dog into a stream no matter how remote it is. But a little, the ecosystem can handle. An important road through the middle of an untouched area is more than a little.

In portions of New Jersey's Great Swamp which haven't been touched for a century, you can trace fence lines from the 1700s by still-existing variations in the vegetation. In the Great Smokies themselves, near the foot of Sugarland Mountain, you can still —if you look closely—find the old "Indian Gap Road," a foot trail for the Cherokees two centuries ago. Even without cutting and filling, and without the nitrous oxides and hydrocarbons of a million automobile exhausts, the effect of a road is far from slight.

In 1968, Secretary Udall announced—over the protest of the head of the National Park Service but in response to hundreds of letters, many of them part of a campaign organized by the Wilderness Society—that there will be no transmountain road. But he cannot bind his successors, and Congress has not yet acted on the proposal that would kill the road once and for all.

Bryson City has as much right to greed as Gatlinburg. It is, after all, a hungry Appalachian town. But if Congress—which is supposed to look at the whole record developed in 1966—should decide to put both the transmountain road route and much of the north shore of Fontana Lake into wilderness, thus blocking both road possibilities, that would settle the tired, artificial, political question of the 1943 agreement. Representative Taylor could almost certainly persuade the Park Service to build the additional accommodations mentioned previously, and the Congressmen who represent the citizens of the Northeast, who want to visit and see the Great Smokies, could almost certainly persuade the Forest Service and the highway builders to make the further improvements we described.

It would even provide some employment for the Engineers.

But there is a question whether it is within the understanding of politicians, particularly local politicians (among whom I include Congressmen). Certainly the local politicians, and the citizens, of Swain County have shown no sign of being willing to consider imaginative alternatives—much less of understanding or caring anything about the ecological demands involved.

And it's like that with local politicians, and local citizens, everywhere.

IX · DIZZYLAND, U.S.A., INCLUDING ALASKA

THERE IS, on the drawing boards of the Corps of Engineers, a fantastic project known to *cognoscenti* as "Mike's Ditch." It is an incredible boondoggle that will cost at least $1 billion, drown 90,000 acres of productive dairyland, force 6,000 people out of their homes, lower the level of Lake Erie (as if poor Lake Erie didn't have enough problems) and cause all kinds of troubles to power users in two countries. It is known officially as the Lake Erie-Ohio River Canal, and its accompanying rapine will be committed in order to accomplish nothing whatever, except to satisfy one Congressman, gratify the dreams of a few Engineers, and supply a few Youngstown, Ohio, industries with cheap barge transportation at your expense.

The Congressman is Michael Kirwan of Ohio, now over eighty and a power in the House of Representatives almost from his first day in Congress in 1937. His canal is an Engineers' delight—and indeed, the Corps of Engineers' part in the whole fantastic story is in itself the best possible argument for easing the Corps out of existence.

Kirwan is high on the seniority list of the Appropriations Committee and serves on two subcommittees dealing with public works projects. He is also in charge of the Democratic Congressional Campaign Committee, which decides how much money the party will give to each Congressman up for reelection. Between the two sources of power, Kirwan exerts enough influence to have earned from the press the nickname "Prince of Pork": he decides whether, as a young Congressman, you can bring home a public works project to your district—and he decides whether you'll have any money to run for reelection.

So, when he wants a canal, he gets it. When a bright young freshman Congressman, like Joseph Vigorito of Pennsylvania, stands up and screams that the canal is a total phony, involving "cynically juggled figures to justify an indefensible boondoggle," retribution is swift and certain. Twenty-one other freshman Democrats up for reelection that year got contributions through Kirwan of from $1,500 to $2,000; Vigorito got a token $500.

And the canal—which is opposed by officials of Pennsylvania, Pittsburgh, Cleveland, railroads, labor unions, dairy organizations, and practically everybody else except Congressmen who don't dare offend Kirwan—goes on. Said Mississippi Representative John Bell Williams (whose state gets far more than its share of Engineers' projects) in the 1966 debate on the project: "Let's build this ditch for Mike!" The budget for fiscal 1968 included another $2 million in planning funds for Mike's Ditch.

If Congressmen are bad, city and county governments are even worse. *Cry California* is a quarterly publication of an organization called California Tomorrow, a group of relatively affluent types (mostly northern Californians) who would like to save something of the beauty of their state. But the state's local governments, says a recent *Cry California* study by Samuel Wood and Daryl Lembke, "find it impossible to resist the lure of development":

The parochial urge to "grow bigger," to attain larger populations and building permit totals in competition with other cities and towns, cannot be contained. Legislators at the city and county levels do not know or recognize that they have the right to stop development. For the most part they are businessmen, and they see attempts to control the land development "business" as hostility toward business in general. In far too many cases, local lawmakers profit directly or indirectly from continued, uncontrolled urban sprawl.

The bigger the opponent of ecological good sense, the bigger the government unit that will kowtow to it. Except for occasional flareups of morality like that of former Governor Edward T. Breathitt—who failed of reelection—Kentucky has generally sacrificed the eastern half of itself to the greed of the strip miners, who took out 40 million tons of coal in 1966, increasing sedimentation rates in streams by as much as 30,000 times—that's not a misprint—thereby killing all the fish and wiping out the water supply for small farms. One strip-mining firm in Perry County holds orders from one customer alone—TVA—totaling $100 million.

Montana has long been recognized as "owned" by a copper company much as California was once "owned" by the Southern Pacific Railroad (still a major power and one of the largest and wealthiest landowners). And it takes little political knowledge to figure out what happens in Texas when conservation needs come into conflict with oil interests—or anywhere else in the United States, for that matter.

Another piece of San Francisco Bay is in jeopardy near Benicia, where the local government wants to fill in 137 acres of tidelands to create a "tax base" by making favorable deals with such firms as the Humble Oil Company. Farther south, the Merced County Board of Supervisors is fighting creation of a refuge for one of the few remaining herds of tule elk, because it would take land off the tax rolls.

Nor is it always the local government. Sometimes it's just a local profit-making interest, and sometimes an entire local population sees its own future as tied up with such an interest to the extent that the people won't look past the propaganda that usually takes over the editorial page of the local paper. The same tule elk, for instance, have another potential refuge in the Owens River valley, in southern California, on what is already a public-land withdrawal (the city of Los Angeles owns the water rights); but local stockmen oppose using the land as a refuge, because at the moment they have grazing leases.

A hearing in Riverton, Wyoming, on a proposed Stratified Wilderness Area in what is now a primitive area of the Shoshone National Forest, brought out strong opposition from such persons as lumberman Robert Monson (of Montrose, Colorado, some distance from the area in question) and Charles Arment, district forester [sic] for the Western Wood Products Association. They were backed up, however, by a number of local citizens like Mrs. Margaret Ingram of Riverton, whose opposition was on exactly the same anti-backpack-snob line used elsewhere by lumbermen.

In New Jersey, scientists discovered a set of dinosaur tracks—the best such find so far in New Jersey, and one that is of enormous importance in studying the continent's prehuman history. The people who own the land are cheerfully building a golf course over the dinosaur tracks.

And in northwestern California, where the redwoods grow, David Wilson can report that "the local population, seventy percent of whose economy depends on the lumber industry, is almost childlike in its belief in the sanctity of the timber owners and operators." As will be demonstrated in a moment, it's difficult for a family whose entire livelihood is based on cutting down trees to understand that it might be far better off economically if the trees were saved. At every wilderness hearing, in every struggle for a national or state park, there are a few people who understand that—and ten times as many who don't.

The people in the Park Service and the Forest Service don't always help much. When the Park Service scheduled a hearing early in 1967 on the possible designation of part of the Isle Royale National Park as a wilderness area, they held the hearing in Houghton, Michigan—in the far northern reaches of the state—on January 31, in the middle of winter. The Wilderness Society found it necessary to send out a special bulletin because of its concern "that the mid-winter scheduling of this hearing for a northern community far from major population centers may keep an adequate supportive record from being built at the hearing." If all you get are local people (and the private profit-makers who are not concerned about location, time or expense), then all you'll get is opposition. The Federal courts have even accepted this as a truism when dealing with such things as dams and power projects.

This one fact—the concern of local interests and local populations for their own short-range profits—is probably the greatest single obstacle to the development of a national ecological conscience. And it's true, incidentally, whether we are talking about *opposing* a project, like the Redwoods National Park, or profiting from it, as with Bryson City's attitude toward the irreparable damage that would be done by the transmountain road in the Great Smokies. Local populations living near national parks and other similar areas, says Canadian ecologist Ian McTaggart Cowan,

inevitably view the area as almost solely for their private gain. Because their geographic entity gives them organization and dedication to their purpose, such small groups of individuals have exerted undue influence upon national conservation policy. Searching studies of the social position and political impact of such small towns as Banff and Jasper in the great Canadian Rocky Mountain park system would provide important guidelines for our future reaction to private vested interest within national parks or similar areas.

Dr. Cowan was talking about Canada, but it is obvious that where he says Banff, we can say Bryson City (and when you've got the Congressman in charge of national parks, you don't even need "searching studies"). He might, in fact, be talking about any small town in America that's somewhere near a tourist attraction of any kind—as anyone knows who has ever driven from Miami to the Everglades.

At that Riverton, Wyoming, hearing, rancher Les Shoemaker of nearby Dubois testified that "people in the upper Wind River area are convinced that their destiny lies not in timbering but in the tourist industry." Not so many of them are all that convinced, of course, but even with regard to those who are, their conviction may not be anything to cheer too loudly about.

It may be that what they have in mind is something like Gettysburg, where you can find, and pay to see, an "authentic" Indian village with totem poles and tepees—where there have been no Indians since 1750 and where none ever used either totem poles or tepees. You can also find a Howard Johnson motel "practically in the center of the battlefield," and a place called Fantasyland (with monkeys) facing General Meade's headquarters.

Or it may be that they're thinking of Mount Rushmore, where the visitor runs the gamut of Reptile Gardens, Gravity Hill, Gravity Spot, Dizzyland, U.S.A., the Cosmos, the Horseless Carriage Museum and Fairyland's Bewitched Village. Or they may be thinking of the private concessionaires who seem to be in a race to destroy Yellowstone.

Senator Gaylord Nelson, concerned that increasing tourist traffic to northern Wisconsin would lead local residents to turn the area into "a jungle of neon signs, eat joints, entertainment gimmicks [and] tacky souvenir stores," wrote a letter to hundreds of area residents, which led to a conference on the subject, jointly supported by the University of Wisconsin Extension Division and by Northland College of Ashland. The concern, the response to the letter showed, is there—when there is a concerned leader like Senator Nelson to seek it out—but except for hopeful educational gestures, the tools to stop the proliferation of the neon jungles and the Dizzylands are not.

In their opposition to new parks, wilderness areas and other similar developments, local citizens are often even more short-sighted than the profiteers who so often are manipulating them. While Mayor Pearson of Sedro Woolley worries about losing money that comes now from the lumber industry, park advocates have bypassed rhetoric in favor of gathering some facts about what a North Cascades National Park will mean to the area by 1980:

—Twice as many tourists as would otherwise visit the area (this may or may not be desirable from other points of view, of course).

—$50 million in new income to Washington, $33 million to the park area.

—3,000 new jobs in Washington, 2,000 of them in the park area.

—$2 million in new tax revenue to the state.

—6 new dollars and 7 new jobs in the state, 4 new dollars and 5 new jobs in the park area, for every dollar and job lost.

Within fifteen years after New York City set aside Central Park, the value of real estate in the city went up 100%—but the value of land adjoining the park went up 800%. Warinanco Park in New Jersey's Union County paid for itself in five years by bringing in $1.2 million in additional taxes from the surrounding neighborhood.

Local interests—often builders—like to argue economics, because they know that their opponents don't often have the facts. In October, 1963, a group of builders in Westchester County, New York, claimed that zoning and other policies which restrict their activities were costing the county $15 million in construction and 270,000 man-hours of carpentry labor. But this argument belongs with Kennecott's earnest plea that if you don't let us ruin the mountains, you won't get a free man-made lake.

How, for instance, do you measure the decision of a major company to locate a branch or a plant in one county rather than another because the preferred area is *not* a welter of jerry-built houses or a neon mess? A spokesman for the Prudential Insurance Company, for example, put it like this: "With each new office we have had to face the problem of transferring key employees. One of the motivating forces that attract people to one place over another is the availability of attractive recreation outlets."

And there are other benefits as well. After the establishment of Cape Hatteras National Seashore in North Carolina, not only did the assessed valuation of real estate in the area double in eight years, but in six years there was a 100 percent increase in business volume and bank deposits. When Hearst Castle in California was made a state park, the local tax rate went *down* within five years because of increased revenue from higher-valued land near the park and facilities that were constructed to meet the tourist demand.

It isn't only that local people don't know what to be *for;* they often don't know what to be *against.* Planner Dennis Durden has made an extensive study of the "second home resort colony"—an operation in which a fast-buck operator buys some otherwise useless rural land at low prices, builds a "community" which has no functional purpose (but which is either near a lake or near a place where a man-made lake can be created), sells small lots and jerry-built houses to urban dwellers (often with massive television and/or newspaper promotion) and gets out before the sewage problems start or the paint begins to peel. Aside from the fact that such operations are usually ecological horrors (and architectural horrors, and sociological horrors), they constitute, as Durden notes, " 'jumping-off places' or 'launching pads' for assaults on conservation areas—especially those that, up to the present, have been relatively remote."

But there is no opposition to this from the existing residents of those areas—who presumably would rather sell beer to the vacationers than remember that they themselves live in those areas precisely because the areas *are* away from the urban-suburban bustle that the developments will imitate. Nor is there opposition from Congress, which seems about ready to include such "second homes" in the category of purchases for which FHA financing will be available.

Even local economic interests often seem not to know what they ought to be against. Commercial fishermen in New York State, for example, brought in 1,467,000 pounds of fresh-water and anadromous fish in 1958; five years later, the catch was 884,000 pounds—due directly to water pollution. Yet the commercial fishermen have not clamored for legislation that would limit the pollution, any more than in Canada—where St. Lawrence Valley lumbering has all but ruined the salmon industry—they have clamored for simple changes in the pattern of lumbering that would have enabled both industries to exist side by side.

The biggest example—literally the biggest—of a project designed solely for the benefit of local interests, to the absolute detriment of the people of the United States generally and to the total despair not only of ecologists but of anyone with a grain of intelligence who takes even the briefest look at the facts, is the proposed Rampart Dam in Alaska.

This Engineers' plaything on the Yukon River is so big (the dam itself would be 530 feet high and 4,700 feet long) that it will create, behind it, a lake larger than the state of New Jersey, larger even than Lake Erie. This lake will drown the breeding grounds of more waterfowl than are produced in all the forty-eight contiguous states (Senator Ernest Gruening says the waterfowl "can nest all over the other 98% of Alaska"; he may be great on Vietnam, but he's pretty bad on the geography of his own state—the statement is ridiculous). In addition, says editor-conservationist Paul Brooks (using figures from the Bureau of Sport Fisheries and Wildlife):

The moose range, with an estimated eventual carrying capacity of 12,000 animals, would of course disappear. So would martens, wolverines, weasels, lynx, muskrat, mink, beaver, otter, which taken together represent an annual harvest of some 40,000 pelts, or about seven percent of the entire Alaska fur production—a sizable item to write off in any state's economy, which is, nevertheless, far below the future potential.

Besides, it would wipe out the salmon run (270,000 salmon a year), drown seven villages, force the evacuation of 1,200 natives, and—because of the salmon—destroy the livelihoods of five or six thousand other Alaskans besides. It would probably destroy, for those who care about such things, the last breeding place of the peregrine falcon. It will probably kill off the wolves who would be essential to the ecology of eastern Alaska—if the project were going to leave anything of the ecology of eastern Alaska.

"Nowhere in the history of water development in North America," says the Bureau in its report on the project, "have the fish and wildlife losses anticipated to result from a single project been so overwhelming." And that's saying quite a bit.

As if that weren't enough, there have even been some suggestions that the creation of an Erie-sized lake on the Arctic Circle may have a drastic effect on the entire climate of the world. But that, of course, is not the kind of question that an Engineer would even bother to investigate.

The point of all this, according to the dam's proponents—who include not only the dam-happy Engineers but virtually all the politicians in or from Alaska, and a lot of just plain Alaskans who have been conned by the propaganda—is to produce 5 million kilowatts of electric power at something like three mills per kilowatt-hour. This, in turn, is supposed to provide for "Alaska's future"—and it is on this point that Alaskans have been sold and resold.

But don't you believe it. In the first place, there's not a user in sight for any of this power (before Grand Coulee Dam was built, in contrast, there were firm contracts for the sale of all the power it would generate). Arthur D. Little, Inc., a renowned consulting firm, reported to the state of Alaska in 1962 that "low-cost hydroelectric power" is a meaningless semantic jumble by itself, because "low-cost for any particular project must be accompanied by high-volume use," and such projects as Rampart Dam will, if built, "produce a quantity of power many times the ability of present Alaskan industry, commerce and population to absorb." Even a project producing one-fifth the amount of power that would come from Rampart, the Little firm reported, would produce too much, "unless several electric-intensive industries appeared on the scene within a short period of time. This is, of course, a possibility, but not a very realistic expectation."

But it *is* realistic, the Alaskan politicians insist (they went out and bought themselves another study with more favorable comments, which is the one they like to distribute). Why, shucks, we're going to have a big aluminum industry.

When the president of the Aluminum Company of America said that the company is eliminating its dependence on hydro-electric power and now favors steam power, and that Alcoa is therefore building in the Ohio Valley, the Alaskans ignored him. When the Department of the Interior said that there aren't as many mineral deposits in Alaska as people believe and that the timber industry in Alaska will actually suffer if the dam is built, the Alaskans ignored the Department, too.

The possibility of nuclear power aside, there are plenty of other places in Alaska where smaller, more practical hydroelectric dams can be built without killing off all the animals and ruining one of the ecologically most important areas still available in the United States for study. The justifications for Rampart, as fast as they are made, disappear under examination. (The recreational facilities described by the dam's promoters are almost funny: On the Arctic Circle the ice will break in late June or early July, oceangoing vessels are required on a lake that size, and if they weren't, there is still a "drawdown" problem that may leave a mile of mud between boat and marina.)

So—the compulsions of Engineers aside—why do it? Paul Brooks thinks he knows, and his argument makes sense. With taxes going up and the military construction boom (the DEW line, for example) dwindling, there's a genuine economic problem in Alaska.

Employment [Brooks writes] needs a shot in the arm. If the dam is built, the amount of Federal money spent on construction in the five years preceding initial power production would, according to the D&R report [the more favorable report mentioned earlier], exceed the total amount spent for military construction in Alaska from 1950 to 1955. The whole job will pour a minimum of one and a third billion dollars into Alaska, and probably a great deal more. As one legislator is said to have remarked privately, Rampart Dam will have served its purpose if it is blown up the day it is finished.

The money, of course, won't go the the displaced Alaskans, who don't have the skills to work on the dam and, you can be quite sure, won't be trained in them. A lot of the money won't go to any Alaskans at all, but to construction workers, mostly from the contiguous 48 states, who will of course spend a lot of it in Alaska but who will also take a lot of it out. Why not leave the dam unbuilt and simply give $1.4 billion to Alaskans, divided on a per capita basis? It makes just as much sense, and it saves, for the moment at least, the peregrine falcon.

It is triply ironic to think of spending billions ($1.4 billion is, actually, a low estimate) on an unnecessary dam in Alaska, violating every tenet of sensible land use and intelligent economics, while the things that need to be done are dying for lack of funds. In the middle of the land designated as part of California's Point Reyes National Seashore, for instance, a private landowner, Richard Chase, plans a 12-acre subdivision. Secretary Udall is reportedly very upset and thinks the subdivision might put the whole project in "serious jeopardy" (local officials, of course, think it's peachy; it will go on the tax rolls, those sacred tax rolls). Yet the National Park Service had to tell Chase (who would have sold) that his property was "extremely low on the acquisition list" and that there "was no possibility of purchasing his property in the foreseeable future." Twelve lousy acres.

A similar project on a private inholding in Washington's Olympic National Park was narrowly prevented in 1967 when the Nature Conservancy bought thirteen acres in the Quinault Valley from the Grays Harbor Asphalt Company. The Interior Department couldn't even come up with funds for an option (the Conservancy will hold the land until Interior can buy it). Temporary purchases of this kind by private groups have saved other areas and are obviously commendable (get together with some friends and save a piece of land in *your* state), but it is obviously not a mechanism we can rely on—and you can't stop Rampart Dam by buying the Yukon Flats.

Cape May Point in New Jersey is losing its beaches (thanks partly to faulty projects by Engineers farther up the coast), but it can't come up with the money to save them, and the Corps of Engineers won't spend the necessary $1 million. The Corps' Frank Sivaro explained that "it comes down to the fact that Atlantic City serves more people than the beaches of Cape May Point would; therefore, it can get more Federal aid. This is one of the facts of life. It is a brutal fact."

The reason it's a fact, of course, is that Congressmen from New Jersey, like Congressmen from Alaska or North Carolina or anywhere else, rarely know what they're doing. They'll build a canal or a dam—or vote for someone else's canal or dam—without even taking fifteen minutes to learn what the ecological consequences might be. Most of them have yet to learn what the phrase "ecological consequences" means.

In the office of Representative John Saylor of Pennsylvania, a Republican who is recognized as one of the Congress' leading conservationists, I asked how many members of the House, in his opinion, had any real understanding of conservationist issues (there are 435 members of the House).

"Not many," he said after a minute of thought. "Perhaps a hundred."

"And how many do you think have any real concept of ecology or of an ecological approach to problems?"

Saylor bears a slight resemblance to the British actor Nigel Bruce, who once played Dr. Watson to Basil Rathbone's Sherlock Holmes. At my question, he heightened the resemblance by duplicating Bruce's owlish, head-down-eyebrows-up stare. "I think," he said, "you've gone beyond the understanding of most members of Congress."

Later, curious about the upper house, I tried the same question about ecological understanding on Wisconsin's Senator Nelson, who has introduced legislation to set up an Ecological Surveys and Research Division within the Department of the Interior.

Nelson shook his head sadly. "All we can do is try" was his only answer.

Finally, I asked the same question about local legislators—directing it to a Congressman who happens to be a longtime acquaintance, who has served on the local level, and whose name I omit because the question was asked unofficially over a bottle of his better brandy.

He, too, shook his head. "Look," he said, "*I* don't know very much about it—and you know damned well I'm a hell of a lot smarter than most of those bastards."

X · THE MASSIVE FUND-RAISERS

IF THERE IS A GOD of the Engineers, then his idea of Chartres is probably a dam in the Grand Canyon.

The whole idea of damming this excruciatingly beautiful, world-famous gorge and drowning under a needless "reservoir" 600 feet of the earth's history going back to before the beginning of even the simplest forms of life so boggles the mind of anyone who is not fanatically an Engineer that it is impossible to write about it with even a momentary pretense of dispassion. To read the debates in newspapers and magazines, in pamphlets and in *The Congressional Record,* and to find grown and otherwise responsible men discussing such a project as though they were talking about a footbridge across the upper reaches of Wildcat Creek, is to realize the cosmic reach of Herbert J. Muller's remark that no animal is so stupid as a human fool.

When, after only a few minutes' concentrated study, a reporter realizes that the Engineers want to build these hydroelectric dams neither because anyone needs the water nor because anyone needs the power, the idea of writing about it seems as impossible as a satire on Dienbienphu. Still, there they are, the Engineers of the Bureau of Reclamation in this case, with their bosses in the Interior Department apparently all out behind them, the chairman of the House Committee on Interior and Insular Affairs (our old friend Wayne Aspinall) whooping it up for the "project," the Congressmen from all the surrounding states falling all over themselves to endorse the dams and still insisting that they should be built despite a defeat in the 1968 Congress.

One has to start somewhere. Perhaps we can begin with the Cambrian era, which may have been 500 million years ago or so, because it is easier to describe. It was an unstable time, with a lot of churning of land masses and sea bottom, but the climate was generally mild, and most of the earth was covered with seas. Life had taken hold. Trilobites—tiny invertebrate marine animals with their bodies divided into three lobes—were probably the most numerous life forms, but the idea of a skeleton was beginning to make its appearance; the first shells existed on primitive snails. Algae that concentrated calcium existed, and in some regions lichens had appeared.

That's all there was. The first primitive vertebrates were not to appear for another 80 million years or so (and of course, we do not know enough to be sure of the figures; they are gross approximations). But if you go in a boat down the Colorado River, through the Grand Canyon, and look directly to one side or the other, you will see a piece of the earth that was there *one billion years* before the Cambrian era began.

Even to a geologist, trained to think in millions of years, that is extremely difficult to comprehend. To an Engineer, it is obviously impossible. And since it is impossible, it is all right to put that bit of earth under water—and eventually under 600 feet of silt.

Most Americans believe that all of the Grand Canyon is a national park and is somehow "protected." It is not. The vagaries of men who name things make it difficult to say, even, where the Grand Canyon begins and ends; but what is done is done, and that makes it easier.

Where the Colorado River enters Arizona, about halfway across the top of the state, the Engineers, over the protests of conservationists, have built Glen Canyon Dam. Behind it, backed up into Utah, is Lake Powell, named for the first man to travel the Grand Canyon by boat (and a man who would have detested the idea of the dam and the lake). The Engineers like to call it "Powell Reservoir," but it is no more a reservoir than is the mud puddle in your backyard; it's just backed-up water.

Below Glen Canyon, the river flows south for 60 miles or so, through Marble Canyon and past the Vermilion Cliffs. Then it flows generally west, to become Arizona's border with Nevada, and turns south again to separate the state from California and ultimately to flow—or, more accurately, to struggle—into the Gulf of California in Mexico.

Just below its southward turn, between Arizona and Nevada, the Engineers have built Hoover Dam. Backed up behind Hoover Dam, of course, is Lake Mead, and surrounding it is the Lake Mead Recreational Area.

All of the river between Glen Canyon and Lake Mead can be, and should be, called the Grand Canyon. While it still flows south below Glen Canyon, however, it is unprotected, except that its eastern bank is a Navajo reservation. Where it turns westward, it flows into a small protected area, less than 60 miles long on a straight line; *that* is Grand Canyon National Park. The remaining area between the park and Lake Mead was designated by President Hoover as the Grand Canyon National Monument—a designation that does not carry the protections that national park status carries—except for a short stretch on the south bank that is part of a Hualapai Reservation.

The Engineers want to put one of their absolutely unnecessary dams in Marble Gorge, and back water 55 miles to the foot of Glen Canyon Dam. The backed-up water in the gorge would be more than 300 feet deep. The other dam would be at Bridge Canyon, near the Hualapai Reservation, and would back its "reservoir" (that's the word they keep using) entirely through the Grand Canyon National Monument and 13 miles into the Grand Canyon National Park—a total length of 93 miles. It would be more than 600 feet deep in spots.

The Engineers don't like to talk about it, but that backed-up water would also affect the level of the channel upstream, causing immediate silt deposits for another 15 miles or so above the head of the "reservoir"; so they'd be messing up the Grand Canyon through the entire national monument and for 30 miles into the national park. Incidentally, Los Angeles has suggested that Bridge Canyon Dam be a pump storage project, something like Storm King. It's not clear how this would work, since there are no detailed plans available for study, but you can be sure it won't do the Grand Canyon any good.

The dams are intended to generate "peaking" power, which is to say that the water will be released as the demand for power dictates. This means, of course, that the water level (not the "river level"; there won't be any river) behind the dam will rise and fall every day—probably as much as 15 feet. You may still want to go boating on a "river" that may rise or fall 15 feet a day, even if, when it's down, the "shore" will be 15 feet of mud; but you may be certain that it isn't going to do much for the ecology of either the river or its banks. In fact, *none* of the Colorado River anywhere in Arizona would be left in its natural state because of changes in its level and the overwhelming effect on its ecology.

What's the point of these dams? Well, Engineers and politicians keep muttering vague phrases so that the citizens of the Southwest will think they have something to do with bringing water to the area, or with completing the Central Arizona Project, or with providing much-needed electric power. But when you pin them down in Congressional committees or similar places in which somebody knows something about the facts, it turns out that at the moment, or in the immediate future, nobody needs the power; and Arizona isn't going to get any of the water.

In fact, in that water-hungry part of the world, which has fought for decades over the division of the Colorado's flow, the dams will cause the absolute waste of about 100,000 acre-feet of water. That's what will disappear every year by evaporation—and that is enough, by the way, to serve the annual needs of Phoenix. Lake Powell (which is much bigger than the two proposed lakes would be) already wastes 750,000 acre-feet of water a year through evaporation, and Lake Mead (which is bigger yet) loses 1,000,-000.

Besides that, when you hold the water still and backed up like that, some of it is lost through percolation—that is, it sinks down into the porous bed of the river. In 1965, 25% of the water that flowed into Lake Powell disappeared into the walls and floor of its basin (the Engineers had estimated a 15% maximum). At Marble Gorge, there is cavernous limestone that would probably take even more. Certainly that conserves water, in a sense, but it seems like the hard way.

Whenever water evaporates, it leaves solid matter behind it—which is another way of saying that the more backed-up water you have, the more impurities there are in the water below the dam. If two gallons of water each contain 1% magnesium (which is pretty unlikely, but let's use it as an illustration), and if you put the two gallons together and then evaporate one gallon away, the remaining gallon will contain 2% magnesium. So what you pour out of the container will be twice as impure as what you put in it. This is what's happening in Lake Powell and Lake Mead—and in Lake Havasu, behind Parker Dam on the Arizona-California border. By the time the Colorado reaches Mexico, it's already so impure that it's no good for agricultural use—which makes Mexico rather unhappy, by the way.

So if it's water the Southwest is interested in, they are going about it rather foolishly. But nobody pretends it's the water (except in vaguely worded propaganda to keep Arizona citizens in line and to confuse the rest of us). They say it's the power, and the whole point of building the dams is economic. The idea, we are told, is that the two dams will generate power, which will then be sold (somewhere; not in Arizona). The money from selling the power will then be used to help finance the Central Arizona Project, which has nothing to do with the Grand Canyon.

In other words, these two atrocities against mankind are simply massive fund-raisers.

Actually, even that roundabout reason, which is the official one, is probably a little too straightforward for the Engineers and their allies among the politicians. The questions about the dams in the Grand Canyon seem really to be—sordidly enough—simple questions about who gets rich. But first, there are more things to say about the dams themselves.

There is in California a considerably less impressive, though quite pretty, river, the Santa Ynez, which has provided water for the city of Santa Barbara. To create a reservoir (a real reservoir), Santa Barbara built a dam. Alas, they found that the reservoir quickly built up silt behind the dam, until they faced the imminent possibility of a flat plain of silt over which the Santa Ynez would flow to turn the dam into a waterfall. So Santa Barbara built another dam. Same problem. Now they have built a third dam. If we are spared death by nuclear war or by the depredations of Engineers, some future explorer will locate a strange river flowing to the sea in California, over an odd series of flat alluvial plains, one above the other. They will probably grow vegetation eventually, but they will probably never be as pretty as the original Santa Ynez River bed.

A series of flat alluvial plains where the deepest gorges of the Grand Canyon used to be hardly seems worth paying $1.5 billion for. That's a low figure, several years old, for what the dams will cost. It's a Bureau of Reclamation figure, so you can assume they didn't guess high. And it is also, if anybody cares, slightly more than the cost estimate for the waterworks of the entire Central Arizona Project itself.

But a series of flat alluvial plains where the deepest gorges of the Grand Canyon are is exactly what we will get if these dams are built: Providing that silt retention dams are built, as suggested, on the Paria and Little Colorado Rivers, and providing that there are no abnormal floods (which would speed things up), it should take a little over a hundred years for the four new dams to silt up. Your grandchildren will be able to see the alluvial plains where your children can now see the archeozoic age exposed to view. Glen Canyon Dam will probably take longer—about two hundred years—before the "magnificent recreational opportunities" of Lake Powell will require jeeps instead of boats.

There is simply no way around this. In fact, building the dams also builds up the amount of silt *below* them. The water, heavily laden with sediment, deposits all its silt behind Glen Canyon Dam, comes pouring out (when it's allowed out) relatively clean and picks up a great deal more sediment on its way to Marble Gorge than it ever did before. Another dam at Marble Gorge will repeat that process, and so on. There will be—in addition to those stupid "reservoirs," which are in fact not reservoirs at all but just bodies of standing water—a lot more erosion of the streamsides and the streamside habitats. Habitats are places where living things live. Where the water is backed up, of course, those habitats (which at the side of the Colorado in the Grand Canyon are ecologically unique) will be destroyed anyway.

Can you imagine *filling in the Grand Canyon?* That's what they're doing. And they're going to charge us for doing it.

And even then—in case you haven't had enough—the Engineers may not be through. They have another little plan up their sleeves: a tunnel from Marble Gorge (water level about 2,800 feet) to

Kanab Creek (water level about 2,000 feet), which is at the head of the Bridge Canyon water backup. This would leave only a sort of token flow of water in Grand Canyon National Park, which the tunnel would go around, and make possible still another hydroelectric plant that nobody needs. The fact that Kanab Creek meets the Colorado inside the national park bothers the Engineers not at all.

The Bureau of Reclamation, by the way, says that the Kanab Diversion and Bridge Canyon Dam are incompatible. Either they're telling a blatant lie or they're such poor engineers that they can't measure water levels.

I can attempt to explain the ecological or other issues involved in the Great Smokies or the Great Cascades or the Everglades; and of course the Grand Canyon, in addition to its uniqueness of beauty and wonder, is an unequaled living laboratory not only for ecologists but for scientists of many other kinds. But I cannot convince myself that I have to do any arguing about saving the Grand Canyon. It is so atrocious an idea that the horror of it, my mind insists, simply must be self-evident.

The Engineers are not doing this, as noted, to bring any water to anybody. The Central Arizona Project (CAP) will bring water to central Arizona, but it will come from Lake Havasu, which is hundreds of miles below the Grand Canyon and already exists. They say they're doing it to sell the power, to pay for the CAP.

But the man in charge of all these Engineers—Commissioner of Reclamation Floyd E. Dominy—testified before Congress that if the CAP were built *without either dam,* the project would still pay for itself and, at the end of its fifty-year "payout period," it would have a surplus of $100 million. Other witnesses said the surplus might be as high as $800 million. No witnesses said the project would lose money, even if the dams weren't built.

What hurts—aside from the pain that comes with contemplating the whole idea to begin with—is that if the Secretary of the Interior approves this madness (he has to, if they're going to back water into the park), he is going to be in clear violation of the law that created the park in the first place. That law says

that whenever consistent with the primary purposes of said park, the

Secretary of the Interior is authorized to permit the utilization of areas therein which may be necessary for the development and maintenance of a Government reclamation project.

But first of all, a "reclamation project" isn't whatever the Engineers of the Bureau of Reclamation want to do. Neither of these dams is a reclamation project by any stretch of the meaning of the word. And anyway, the dams are not "consistent with the primary purposes of" the park. That phrase is in the law because a previous Secretary insisted on it, just to keep this sort of atrocity from taking place. The "primary purposes" of the park, set out in the law, are

to conserve the scenery and the natural and historic objects and the wild life therein and to provide for the enjoyment of the same in such manner and by such means *as will leave them unimpaired* for the enjoyment of future generations [my emphasis].

As a matter of fact, you would be justified in asking, as a citizen, what the Bureau of Reclamation is doing in this operation anyway. It is supposed to be concerned with "reclaiming land," which means in practice that when they build dams—while they may be hydroelectric dams in order to meet their own cost—the purpose is supposed to be irrigation. Possibly building dams in order to make money in order to pay for irrigation with some other water in some other place may be legal (like the TVA condemning land to give away to the National Park Service), but it certainly ought to be examined at least as closely as the courts examined what happened in 1943 on the Little Tennessee.

Not that it matters, in practice. Catch-22 again; they've got a right to do whatever you can't stop them from doing. Like the Corps of Engineers' flood-control dams, the Bureau's irrigation dams always turn out to be hydroelectric dams. Considering the power of the two agencies, though, it is interesting that neither can have any stake in any kind of power plant except a hydroelectric power plant. They *have* to build dams, as Wallace Stegner among others notes, in order to survive. The dams (and the Engineers' agencies) get bigger and bigger, and the agricultural surpluses grow and grow.

Actually, the Engineers of the Bureau of Reclamation are, if possible, even worse than the Engineers of the Army. James A. Crutchfield, who is probably the nation's leading economist in the natural resources field, says that of all Federal water agencies, "the Bureau has the least defensible record in terms of the accuracy of its economic appraisals of water projects, the soundness of its evaluation procedures, and its efficiency in project construction and operation." Considering what we already know about the Corps of Engineers, that's quite a statement.

Another economist, Kenneth Boulding, says the Bureau should have been abolished twenty years ago, and that

we also ought to abolish the subsidization of agriculture and water. This is nonsense. Somewhere somebody ought to come up and do some real cost-benefit analysis of all this imaginary stuff. . . .

The only way you could explain the water policy in this country was the religious explanation that we worship the water goddess, and hence had to build all these pyramids—all these dams and temples. There is no other conceivable rational explanation.

. . . The domination of almost all resources policy by engineers and people of this kind is utterly disastrous.

Precisely.

Had Dr. Boulding attended a different panel at the same conference at which he made those remarks, he would have heard that a serious analysis of the economics of "all this imaginary stuff," and specifically of the use of hydroelectric power, *was* done—in Scotland. E. M. Nicholson reported that with new and clear criteria set up as a result of that study, "they found that there wasn't a single hydroelectric project that could be put forward which would match these perfectly objective criteria. Yet the schemes had been going forward as if they were an addition to the national wealth."

In the United States, they still are. And—if the Engineers have their way—they'll go forward in the Grand Canyon, to the accompaniment of a massive propaganda campaign.

Still another economist, R. B. DuBoff of Bryn Mawr College, has provided me with a copy of *The Household Gazette,* which he describes as "a free newspaper circulated to customers of Sealtest Foods in this area." I don't know what Sealtest Foods has to do with the Grand Canyon, but the story Dr. DuBoff sent me has to be the most blatant piece of propaganda this side of a Chinese wall poster. I pick on it as an outstanding, but by no means isolated, example.

Under the headline MORE OF COLORADO RIVER'S SHORELINE BEAUTY TO BE REVEALED (by drowning it?), a long "feature story" relates the wonders of Lake Powell, on which everyone can now get close to the walls of the Grand Canyon where only a few could go before. More dams would thus make more canyon wall available to more people—while nowadays they are available only to the hardy. In fact, one man, the story says, "piloted small parties of daredevils down the turbulent stream for dangerous thrills."

"Daredevils," "turbulent," "dangerous" and "thrills" all in one sentence. You'd never guess that six-year-old kids frequently make that trip with their families, would you?

Most of the story simply goes on about how more dams in the Grand Canyon would "enable all Americans to enjoy their scenic heritage . . . a treasure now isolated in forbidding wilderness"—which is a lot of nonsense—but perhaps the two closing paragraphs, by now, will sound familiar:

Basic need for developing the Colorado River is economic. Households, factories, irrigators and hydropower users need the development. But they are meeting resistance from a fraction of the recreationist group.

Opening Colorado River wilderness areas to hundreds of thousands of owners of trailers or camper vehicles, to boaters and swimmers and fishing parties, is opposed by a relatively small but influential group of outdoor aristocrats who do not want their isolated preserves invaded by crowds.

"Development": a word left over from Theodore Roosevelt and dragged up whenever the Engineers want to despoil something. "Households, factories, irrigators and hydropower users": at least one lie and two half-truths; some households and factories may *be* hydropower users, but that's the only way they'll get anything out of the dams—and no irrigators will get anything from them at all. And the hydropower users will be nowhere near the Grand Canyon. "Opening" any precious and unique area to "hundreds of thousands of owners of trailers or camper vehicles" is, as we have seen, a pretty dangerous idea; but aside from that, we have seen this attack on the backpack snob before. You couldn't tell from that paragraph that there is any difference between drowning 600 feet of the Grand Canyon and building an access road to a park somewhere.

Commissioner Dominy has been on this public relations kick, too, and talks about how Lake Powell makes possible "peace" and "oneness with the world and God." I suggest that such peace and oneness are possible without the intervention of a hydroelectric dam. And I agree with Wallace Stegner that

. . . though Lake Powell is indeed beautiful, it will not be half so beautiful once the drawdown has left the gulches and walls slimed with silt and quicksand; and it is not nearly so beautiful as it was before the water filled it. Any drawdown reservoir may be handsome enough when full; it is invariably uglified when low, for nothing grows below high-water mark, and the shores are mudflats or stained cliffs.

That goes for the dams and lakes they have not built yet as well as the ones they have.

So the plan is ugly, it's illegal, they don't need the water, they don't need the power, and they don't need the money. But surely, if Arizona continues to grow (and it probably will, if CAP is built), they'll need the power eventually?

Well, yes—but just to get power you don't have to dam the Grand Canyon. In fact, it's not even a good idea economically.

The dams in the Grand Canyon will (the Engineers say) produce their "peaking power" at a cost of 6 mills—six-tenths of a cent—per kilowatt-hour. TVA has already contracted for a nuclear power plant that will produce power at 2.37 mills per kilowatt-hour (it will also produce solid wastes, of course, but at least it won't produce them in the middle of the Grand Canyon).

More important, economically, is the recent development of technology for building coal-burning power plants at the coal source. Such a plant is being built on the Kaiparowitz Plateau of southern Utah, just north of Lake Powell; it will generate two and a half times as much power as both the Engineers' proposed Grand Canyon atrocities put together.

There is coal around, including a good supply recently found on the Navajo Reservation east of Marble Gorge. One reason the Engineers avoid *that* subject is that the Navajo tribe is a tough bunch of bargainers and would insist on a fair price for the coal, unlike some more cowed or more pliable tribes.

The Navajos oppose the dams, by the way—which raises some interesting questions about putting a dam on *their* land against their will (the Bureau of Indian Affairs is also in Interior; the Secretary must have fun keeping all those balls in the air). They are a feisty bunch, these Navajos, and they persist in thinking of themselves as a nation with whom the United States signed a treaty. The more malleable downstream Hualapais are all for the projects (the Sealtest paper mentioned that, but said nothing about the far more numerous Navajos), and the Navajo opposition, in all honesty, is probably not bothering either the Engineers or the great white politicians. Catch-22, chief.

Of course Congress has never authorized a steam generating plant outside the TVA area; Congressmen seem to be married to the idea of hydroelectric power, just as the Engineers have to be. But Congress is not usually given to totally uneconomical investments either, and this project would be throwing money away even if it were not being spent to fill in the Grand Canyon, and even if no one had ever done any studies in Scotland. Aside from all the other considerations given so far, the generating capacity of these two proposed dams is so small that it would supply growth needs for the Southwest for only about five years anyway.

The whole idea is so fantastically unthinkable—except to Engineers—that not even journalistic training is needed to know that there is more to it than the feeble reasons you hear in public—especially when men like Congressman Morris Udall, a vigorous and distinguished fighter for conservation in the past, are ardently advocating the dams (A conversation between Representative Udall and an Assistant Secretary of the Treasury is said to have led to the decision by the Internal Revenue Service to cancel the tax-exempt status of the Sierra Club, which vehemently opposes the dams.).

The original bill authorizing both dams was defeated in 1968, as was a "compromise" calling for only one (Asks the Sierra Club,

"If someone threatened to put two bullets through your heart, would you consider one bullet an acceptable compromise?"). They are far from forever dead, however; one dam or two, other provisions of the bills were the same, and, while technical in language, they were pretty clear in intent.

First of all, the Colorado basin states are required by law to share the Colorado's water with Mexico. The legislation would relieve those states of that burden and shift it to the whole nation—so that if compensation had to be paid, for instance, we would all have to pay it.

Second, the bills contained other technical provisions intended to set the stage for a massive transfer of water from the headwaters of the Columbia to the headwaters of the Colorado. This sounds more difficult than it is, as a glance at a map of Wyoming, where the Green and Snake Rivers are not far apart, will show. In simple terms, the land promoters, the real estate operators, the bankers and the savings and loan magnates of the Southwest are setting themselves up to get rich at the ultimate expense of Washington, Oregon and Idaho. This explains the unusual alliance on the dam proposal between Southwestern and Californian legislators, usually bitter enemies on water questions; the more water the basin states can get into the Colorado River, the better for California, which takes it out at the other end.

California's Director of Water Resources is already insisting that "interstate water controversies" have to be straightened out so that Californians (meaning, in this case, *southern* Californians and the big landowners of the San Joaquin Valley) can get all the water they need—because the flow from the Colorado has to be augmented. Governor Ronald Reagan says the extra water will have to come from—you'll never guess—the Columbia.

Now the Columbia *could* spare it—if the water was taken from the lower part of the river. There will be extra water in the lower Columbia fifty years from now, even if we play the Engineers' growth-rate games. But hold that for a minute while we look at some more politicians.

Governor John A. Love of Colorado told a Senate subcommittee in 1967 that his state can't support the Central Arizona Project unless (1) *five* Colorado projects are authorized at the same time (always take a tough position when you start your bargaining), (2) Bridge Canyon Dam is built, and (3) an immediate start is made on bringing additional water into the Colorado basin. At the same hearing, Governor Daniel J. Evans of Washington and Governor Tom McCall of Oregon opposed such an immediate start, saying that their states were still studying their own needs.

What's going on here? To what have the Engineers and their political and profiteering cohorts committed themselves? Evans and McCall know perfectly well that they can spare a lot of Columbia River water (and Reagan knows it, too). Love has no use for Bridge Canyon Dam—except to see the bill passed that authorizes it. But he'll back it and the Central Arizona Project *if* a Northwest water switch is begun immediately. And Love's state, lest we forget, is also Wayne Aspinall's.

We turn now, once again, to Dr. Crutchfield:

If the Southwest states really mean that they would divert only from the lower Columbia, it seems virtually certain that the costs of the project would be far in excess of the benefits created, and that it could only be made to appear feasible by gross overstatement of benefits, understatement of costs, or both. Only the possibility of a concealed subsidy of truly massive proportions gives life to the proposal; if the Southwest states could not play the federal subsidy game, there is little doubt that they would turn first to cheaper sources of water, and to measures that would promote more economic use of the water they already have.

In other words, if everybody in the country pays for it, then "the possibility of *regional* economic gain is enormous." Dr. Crutchfield, meet Dr. Boulding. But that's not all, says Crutchfield:

The economic facts of life about the cost of moving water southward from the lower reaches of the Columbia raise serious doubts that this is, in fact, the target area. It would be far cheaper to shift water from the Snake River to the Colorado River basin, thus using natural water courses to cover much of the distance to the areas of use. But if this were done, the threat of economic damage to the Northwest states would become a reality. Operation of the multiple-purpose dams on the Columbia River involves a complicated set of interlocking procedures. Diversions that would hardly be noted in the lower Columbia would, if taken from the Snake, cause major losses throughout the system. We tend to think immediately of losses of hydroelectric power, but irrigation, fisheries, and the general level of water quality in the Snake would also be critically affected. Regardless of where the diversion might take place, the possibility of siphoning off small amounts of water to support local irrigation projects en route is being dangled before both Oregon and Idaho as bait, and there are influential nibblers.

That, friends, is what it's really about. The massive fund-raisers in the Grand Canyon, huge as they are, are only the visible part of an economic iceberg. It is an old, old pattern, though it isn't usually conducted on so grandiose a scale. In California, Los Angeles is famous for it; a water-poor area, it has successfully conned water out of first the Owens Valley, then the Colorado, and most recently—through a fantastic and fantastically expensive Engineers' dream that covers the whole huge state—out of water-rich northern California. The fortunes that have been made in Los Angeles are legend—and the legends have been heard in the Colorado basin.

What Arizona would do in a rational world may be an idle speculation, but agricultural chemist Firman E. Bear once tried it, suggesting that "the tendency might be to discourage the use of any more water for agricultural purposes—or to reduce it." To which geographer Gilbert White immediately replied:

This isn't to say that this is what the State of Arizona is now trying to do. Quite the contrary. Its policy is to get as much from the Federal Treasury for further water development as it can, while the policy still permits this.

The point is that Arizona makes $500 million a year from agriculture, and that 70 percent of all the water it uses is not imported or diverted from rivers but pumped from underground wells. This ground water is being used twice as fast as it is being replaced—dropping by 2.5 million acre-feet a year.

The easiest explanation is that there are simply too many people for the water—but Los Angeles beat that one, and Arizona figures it can too. Before you start feeling sorry for all those thirsty babies in Tucson, though, Dr. Crutchfield suggests that your sympathy might wane "once it becomes obvious that water at

$3 per acre-foot is being used to produce surplus cotton . . . while municipalities and industries are begging for water priced at five to ten times that amount."

Make no mistake [Crutchfield writes], the need is not for municipal and industrial water—the marginal user of water throughout the Southwest is agriculture. To continue expansion of irrigated acreage on the basis of water priced at one-third or less of the actual cost of production and delivery, while maintaining that the area is incapable of providing water for its expanding urban population, is sheer sophistry.

The real question behind those fantastic fund-raisers in the Grand Canyon is simple: Do the rest of us support the growth of Arizona and southern California and Colorado beyond the natural limits imposed by the ecological facts of life in the area? If people want to go there, knowing that water is scarce and therefore expensive, all right; but do we all pay so they can have it more cheaply, when they could go somewhere (like Seattle) where there is plenty of water in the first place? It's not only an ecologist's question but—to quote Dr. Crutchfield one last time—an economist's as well:

True, the arid states may then find it impossible to raise crops for which their general environment is otherwise suitable; but we do not build automobiles in the Northwest for exactly the same reason. If somebody were willing to pay all of the freight charges on raw materials and finished products, we could expect a thriving automobile industry in the Puget Sound basin.

Washington's Senator Henry Jackson succeeded, late in 1968, in heading off the Southwesterners' raid for a time. Into a piece of enabling legislation for the Central Arizona Project, he inserted a clause providing that there will be no water transfer from the Northwest for ten years.

But Congress can change its mind; there is tricky technical language in any bill; and at best, ten years is but a momentary setback for the slick promoters of the Southwest.

Of course, they want to get rich at the expense of all of us; that is a pattern one quickly gets used to finding behind the rapine of the Engineers. But increasingly, the pattern finds the few (the major landowners and bankers of Phoenix and the rest of Arizona, for example) getting rich at the expense of some other few (the major beneficiaries of upper Columbia "development," for instance).

In Florida's Everglades, I was taken across an expanse of the astonishing saw grass in an airboat, a curious flat-bottomed craft with an airplane engine and propellor mounted on the back—the only way (except for a half-track) that you can travel at will over that sea of grass. Miles from the nearest structure, we stopped to look around at the wondrous aquatic system, a plain stretching for miles in every direction, interrupted only occasionally by the higher hammocks with their dry land and tree and shrub growth. It looks as if you could plow it—until you look down, over the side of the boat, or drop your arm over to find your hand in water.

Just south of Lake Okeechobee, however, there is no more water. The Engineers, in their fantastic remaking of Florida, have completely drained a large portion of Hendry and Palm Beach Counties, "reclaiming" it for agriculture. To the south and west, Collier County eagerly awaits similar development. To the south and east, Aerojet General waits to make just that much more money on the cheap barge transport that canal C-111 will provide.

But in the meantime, as described in Chapter III, the Engineers have so distorted the normal water patterns in southern Florida that the level of salinity in the southern part of Everglades National Park, and particularly in Florida Bay, is certain to change, possibly to the "brine basin" that Superintendent Allin fears. And we have already noted that such changes in salinity are lethal to the eggs and the young of most aquatic species.

Researchers at the Marine Institute in Miami are busily tracing the life pattern of the Tortugas shrimp, and they have it pretty well figured out by now. Mostly floating on existing currents, the enormous schools of shrimp travel in a great oval, spawning and growing to maturity in the Florida Bay area, then circling generally southwestward to the Tortugas, then circling back again into the estuarine waters to begin the cycle over again. The Tortugas shrimp industry is worth $3 million a year to Florida. Again, the Engineers are making some people rich at the expense of others. The agriculturalists to the north of the park, and developers like the Gulf American Land Corporation, will profit mightily from the Engineers' meddling; the vitally important shrimp industry may very well go broke.

And yet the shrimp fishermen do not complain, do not go as an organized bloc to Congress to demand that the Engineers' foolishness be stopped. Nor do the businessmen and politicians of the Miami area—which lives on tourism—seem to understand what the Engineers are doing to their future livelihood.

The Department of Commerce estimates, for instance, that if a community is visited throughout the year by a couple of dozen visitors a day, the value to that community is as great as would be an industrial payroll of $100,000. The Everglades National Park alone was visited in 1965 by more than a million people—an average of about 2,600 a day. The Park is worth $11 million a year to southern Florida at that rate, and the annual increase in the number of visitors is about 11 percent. This is aside from the park's payroll—80 permanent staff members and 20 seasonal employees—and the payroll of 125 people employed by concessionaires. Nor does it include the 164 man-years of contractual labor hired by the park.

Tourism is Florida's top source of income. Yet Florida's Representative Charles Bennett—an exception to the generalization above about short-sighted politicians—says with anguish that in Florida "all lands not protected by conservation-minded people are destined to become fifty-foot lots." Unless the Engineers are stopped, those lands will become 50-foot lots bearing houses that in turn bear unpayable mortgages. And while Florida's state legislature makes it possible for local governments to save the precious estuaries, the local governments hurry as fast as they can to fill them in.

Politicians and businessmen, bemused by the dreams of the Engineers, remain blind not only to esthetics but to economics. The John Buchanans continue to oppose a Wilderness Act that would interfere, even marginally, with their right to get rich by cutting down trees. Gus Norwood, executive secretary of the Northwest Public Power Association, opposed Senator Nelson's ecological research bill on the ground that "we know from experience that irrigation disrupts the desert life, what life there is, and makes the desert bloom"—so who needs ecology? Who cares about "what life there is"?

But in the meantime, sulfur goes up in smoke, fisheries disappear, land booms in newly popular regions destroy the reasons for the popularity. The number of oysters taken from Chesapeake Bay drops to a tenth of what it was a few years ago. Pollution alone—gnawing at metals and stone and fabrics, ruining crops, killing wildlife—costs the nation at least $11 billion a year, not counting any effect of pollution on real estate values. Edmund Faltermayer wrote in *Fortune* that "an expenditure of less than one-half of one per cent of the gross national product—probably about $3 billion a year—would reduce air pollution by at least two-thirds. By drastically reducing that $11 billion a year of property damage, the expenditure would easily pay for itself."

But pay *whom?* Nobody would get rich, and nobody seriously considers the expenditure. Instead, thousands of dollars are spent in debating—as though it were a possibility to be considered by rational men—whether we will spend $1.5 billion, or possibly twice that much, to fill in the Grand Canyon. There is indeed no animal so stupid as a human fool.

XI · THE RUBBER JETPORT

SECRETARY OF THE INTERIOR Stewart Udall begins his book *The Quiet Crisis* like this:

There are, today, a few wilderness reaches on the North American continent—in Alaska, in Canada, and on the high places of the Rocky Mountains—where the early-morning mantle of primeval America can be seen in its pristine glory, where one can gaze with wonder on the land as it was when the Indians first came.

If you will allow for the barest touch of man, largely invisible from within the area itself, and for the existence of a little second-growth timber, there is such a wilderness reach 30 miles from Times Square. If it is not precisely in its pristine glory, it still contains vegetation that was there not only when the Indians came but when the dinosaurs walked.

Forty thousand years ago the Wisconsin Glacier carried gravel and boulders southward until the gradually changing climate stopped it at what is now Morris County, New Jersey. As it receded, it dropped its till, and then its melting formed a lake behind the natural dam it had created. Thirty miles long and ten miles wide, the lake sat patiently for years, slowly working to escape, and finally found an outlet at what is now Little Falls Gap. Lake Passaic became today's Passaic River, and left behind it the Great Swamp of New Jersey.

On what should have been an unfriendly winter day, I was shown the Great Swamp by a woman who loves it—Mrs. James Hand of Green Village, a research chemist's wife who, like her husband, is an active member of the North Jersey Conservation Foundation. Blue-eyed, gray-haired and fiftyish, Mrs. Hand donned no-nonsense trousers and boots for the tour and eyed suspiciously—though she politely did not mention—my polished city shoes.

"It's too bad that it's called a swamp," she said as we walked around a nature trail at the area's eastern end. "It's such an unfriendly word. Actually there are forests—different kinds with different trees of different ages—and brooks, and springs." She paused at a sound, identified it as "the first titmouse I've heard this year," and went on. "There's some open land, and there's cattail marsh—that's where the waterfowl live. It's been dry this year, and there's woody brush in with the cattails, but it will be cleaned out. Normally it would burn out, but there are too many homes near the swamp now, and too many animals in it. Part of the area, of course, is real flooded bog."

She interrupted herself to point out a tulip tree and seemed surprised to learn that I knew it is also called, in other areas, a yellow poplar (I was a little surprised myself). Fallen gray birches along the trail, in the shadow of harder and stronger oaks, marked the progress of ecological succession: the birches come first into an open area, slowly to give way to the larger oaks that over-shadow them and block the vital sunshine.

"There are oaks in the swamp that two people can't put their arms around," Mrs. Hand said. "Of course they're well back in the wood, away from the trail. And not very long ago we found one of the largest beech trees ever discovered. It must be very old."

It is. Probably, I learned later, it is about five hundred years old; its girth is about 14 feet. Some of the white oak in the Great Swamp run larger than 4½ feet in diameter, and up to 95 feet high.

Before the day had ended, we had by car and on foot moved from one to another of the constantly varying environments of the Great Swamp—a shallow, bowl-shaped depression seven miles long and three miles wide. Mrs. Hand pointed out an even row of blueberry vines—"It's an old fence line," she explained—and, standing on a boardwalk laid over a bog, explained some of the ecological importance of the swamp to the entire area.

"It's a natural water retention basin," she pointed out, "and by holding water and allowing it to rise and fall naturally, it's a natural flood control device. The two brooks that drain it flow into the Passaic River. Do you know that the Army Engineers have a plan for draining it?"

I said, as quietly as I could, that I didn't doubt it.

"Some of the swamp areas in the rest of the county and nearby have been filled in," she went on. "People found out that not only did the wildlife disappear, but the water tables dropped, and floods became far more frequent. We were terrified that the swamp would be filled in a few years ago."

The "we" referred to a group of individuals, most of them from the immediate area, who became alarmed in the late 1950s at the growing development of the region and at the almost certain fate of the Great Swamp: the spread of the filling and residential "development" that was already nibbling at the edges of its 8,000 acres. The group became the Great Swamp Committee of the North American Wildlife Foundation and began to investigate the purchase of the swamp area.

In 1959, the Port Authority of New York and New Jersey, one of the world's great collections of Engineers, decided that the Great Swamp would be an ideal place for a fourth New York airport, and in 1961 the Authority issued a report recommending that the swamp be acquired for that purpose.

The jetport threat proved to be the spur that the committee needed. They contacted the Secretary of the Interior, advised him that the Great Swamp is a resting place for migratory waterfowl on the Atlantic Flyway, acquainted him with its 150 species of birds and its populations of deer, grouse, raccoons, opossums, squirrels, foxes, muskrat, weasels, otter and mink, told him about its unique vegetation, and persuaded him to accept a portion of it—if they could raise the money to buy it—as a national wildlife refuge.

And raise the money they did. In May, 1964, Secretary Udall was present for the formal dedication. The Great Swamp Committee proudly turned over 2,700 acres—for the purchase of which they had raised more than a million dollars from 6,100 individuals and 462 industries, organizations and foundations, located in 286 towns and 29 states. The Secretary promptly directed the Bureau of Sport Fisheries and Wildlife to acquire another 3,264 acres; the acquisition is still going on.

Later, the Interior Department recommended that 2,400 acres at the eastern end of the refuge be designated as the M. Hartley Dodge Wilderness Area (it's a "roadless island" within the meaning of the Wilderness Act). It would be, the Department pointed out, the only wilderness area anywhere near New York City, and the only one in all of New Jersey.

After Mrs. Hand taught me to distinguish among the four varieties of club moss that can be found at one spot, and confessed that she has a special affection for the red maple, which in spring carpets the floor of its forest home with its brilliant flowers, I left her and drove across the swamp, on one of the two roads that have been built through it, to talk with Refuge Director Tom McAndrew at the refuge headquarters in Meyersville.

On the way I passed some of the private holdings that still exist in the swamp (all of which belonged to William Penn in the late seventeenth century, when it was inhabited by the Delawares). Mostly, they are individual homes on small filled areas; the Bureau has options on many, and will tear the homes down and allow the area to revert to its natural swamp condition. On the other side of the road, a little way in the distance, I could see young forest, marking areas that were logged until the early 1900s; the lumber supported a hub and felly factory during the Revolutionary War. Beyond, I knew, were areas of virgin forest that began to grow when Passaic Lake drained away, before man ever saw the area; inaccessible by nineteenth-century methods, they have never been logged.

McAndrew, a mild and serious young man, was advising some local residents on the restocking of a nearby fishing pond when I arrived. When he had finished, he showed me—after a few friendly questions had convinced him that I was really a reporter and not a land speculator—a large map on which were marked the acreage already acquired by the Bureau, the lands optioned, and the remaining private holdings.

"This is the only extensive swamp and forest habitat left in this area," McAndrew told me. "It has an amazing variety of ecosystems. You can walk from a climax hardwood forest to a completely aquatic environment, and you can see all the stages of ecological succession. It's an 8,000-acre laboratory for ecologists. But it's much more than that." His young, serious face soft-ened into a smile. "All the schoolchildren around here use it for nature study. They're very fortunate—they can grow up seeing a large part of the land as it is naturally. If we can keep it like this, at least some people won't feel that drive to get away to the Adirondacks or the Great Smokies all the time."

I found myself thinking of children I have seen on other assign-ments—on the streets of Harlem, for instance, 40 miles away or less—who have never seen a horse or cow, much less a deer living in the wild. I thought of the population density of New Jersey, which at the moment is 833 persons per square mile. I thought of the bumper-to-bumper traffic on U.S. 441 in the Great Smokies, the jammed-together campers in Yosemite, and the Wilderness Society's Stewart Brandborg, insisting in his Washington office that the answer to the growing outdoor recreation problem is more, smaller recreation areas, in locations nearer the population centers.

And I thought of the Engineers of the Port Authority of New York and New Jersey, who in December, 1966, issued another "comprehensive" report on its search for a site for a fourth New York area jetport. After discussing 22 possible sites, the Authority came back, as it had done in 1961 and again in 1963, 1964 and 1965, to the Great Swamp of New Jersey. "The engi-neering and physical facts," the report said, "and the fundamental economic interest of all the people of this great and growing metropolitan area, preclude any other recommendation." What, I wondered, is a "physical fact"? What is a "fundamental eco-nomic interest"?

The Great Swamp Committee has in the meantime evolved into the North Jersey Conservation Foundation, which now exists independently of any other organization and in fact, besides continuing to defend the Great Swamp, devotes much of its time to helping smaller citizen groups elsewhere in New Jersey to save small pieces of their natural environment. The Foundation's dy-namic director, Helen Fenske, left no doubt in 1967 about her feelings on the subject of building the jetport in the swamp: "We simply won't let them, that's all."

And they didn't. Secretary Udall came out on the side of the swamp, and so, reluctantly, did Governor Richard J. Hughes. A couple of years ago, spurred by the conservationists (when you can raise a million bucks like that, people pay attention), the New Jersey Legislature passed a law forbidding the construction of an interstate or overseas airport anywhere in a seven-county area surrounding the Great Swamp. Hughes found it a little too sweeping and vetoed it—but in his reelection campaign, he promised not to allow a Great Swamp jetport during his tenure. After the Port Authority's December report, he said he regretted the pledge but would stick to it.

The airport cannot be built anywhere in New Jersey unless the legislatures of both states agree to it and it gets the approval of both governors. To obtain necessary Federal aid, of course, it also needs the approval of the Federal Aviation Administration, which has its own Engineers. They have decreed that to avoid interference with existing traffic, the airport should be in the "northwest quadrant"—that is, somewhere northwest of Manhattan.

The Port Authority used this argument to rule out a number of sites, in Suffolk County on Long Island and elsewhere, and then used cost or distance to rule out most others (Solberg Airport in Hunterdon County, of which more later, was ruled out for distance). Six sites were rejected because they would necessitate closing down New Jersey's McGuire Air Force Base, which I confess bothers the FAA more than it bothers me.

The Port Authority's report, however, can have been written only by Engineers, for only Engineers can make a jetport out of rubber.

Referring back to its first report, the Authority says that at that time, "the airport was estimated to require an aggregate of 10,000 acres of land for all purposes. Studies made since 1961 substantiate the prototype airport plan described above." Elsewhere in the report, the Authority's Engineers deal with public concern about the wildlife refuge by pointing out that the Jamaica Bay Bird Sanctuary is only 3,000 feet from the boundary of Kennedy Airport ("and a damned poor refuge it is, too," Refuge Director McAndrew told me irreverently; William Vogt of The Conservation Foundation says flatly that "Kennedy Airport de-

stroyed one of the finest salt-marsh habitats in the Northeast").
"It would appear," the Engineers go on, "that much of the land on
or near an airport on the Great Swamp site could continue to
serve as a wildlife preserve."

Leaving aside the preposition "on"—can you imagine the deer
or the American egret living happily between the runways?—it
remains true that the entire Great Swamp, including the private
holdings and Somerset County's Passaic River Park at the western
end, consists of 8,000 acres. Somewhere on these 8,000 acres,
the Engineers of the Port Authority claim to be able to build a
10,000-acre jetport and leave room for a wildlife refuge that
today takes up nearly 6,000 acres. Obviously, the plan calls not
only for a rubber jetport but for an elastic swamp.

As it happens, I have obtained a copy of a rare document little
seen since the conservationists turned the swamp into a wildlife
refuge and demonstrated their political power. It is a map, drawn
for the Port Authority in 1960, showing precisely where the jetport would go. It is titled: "Proposed New Jetport Site in Morris
County, New Jersey; Possible Runway Pattern for Smooth
Operational Procedure with Associated Noise Levels and Excavation."

I have not bothered to work out the noise levels; the "excavation" is interesting enough. Along the southern boundary of the
Great Swamp is a road, variously called the North Long Hill
Road and Fairmount Avenue, which goes through the town of
Meyersville. South of the road is a ridge of hills—the natural side
of the bowl that is the swamp itself. They are nice hills; people
live in them. South of the ridge is Long Hill Road. The map clearly
shows that in order to have a jetport on the swamp, it would be
necessary to flatten the top of the entire ridge, and not just a
little; the proposed runway pattern has the planes coming in over
the ridge, which is simply too high. North of the swamp, too, in
the area of New Vernon, the tops would have to be taken off a
number of hills; some of them would have to be sheared off quite
drastically.

But most important is that the boundaries of the proposed
jetport not only include the entire Great Swamp (except for the
Somerset County park); to the north they extend past the present

edge of the swamp and include part if not all of the community of Green Village. If I read the map correctly, the airport boundary (never mind the noise level just outside the boundary) would be a few hundred yards from a school in New Vernon. And there would be, of course, absolutely no Great Swamp at all. The variety of ecosystems we need to preserve in order to learn what we are and where we are going, our precious custody of the dwindling genetic information of our planet, the guarded stopping place for waterfowl on the Atlantic Flyway, the vital water retention basin for the Passaic River—all would disappear.

Yes, there has to be a new jetport; the Authority's Engineers make that quite clear. "Air passenger demand" in the New Jersey-New York area in 1965 is given as 25.8 million air travelers, which, the report says, will go up to 53.5 million in 1975 and 65 million in 1980. The report adds a lot of scare words about airplanes crashing into each other (which has happened twice within the past decade in the New York area—two times too many), and lengthy descriptions of Kennedy's two "Black Fridays" in 1963 and 1965 when delays of up to four hours were experienced. A delay in an airport is not particularly unusual, much less is it the end of the world, but you wouldn't know that from reading the report.

Finally, the Authority provides a further persuasive, if unprovable, argument: "Recent decisions by several large manufacturers to remain in the New York-New Jersey metropolitan area have been based in part on the continuance of the high level of fast and convenient air service to which they have become accustomed here."

I can testify, as an itinerant reporter, that air service is just as fast and convenient in every other metropolitan area of the nation —which is not saying much—and is rather better in some. The Authority goes on, however, to add that "location within hours of any place in the nation for purposes of selling or shipping is one major reason for plant location in this area"—which is a good reason for an airport in St. Louis but hardly in New York.

In any case, the pressure is clear. Senator Jacob Javits says that the fourth jetport may be needed to avert "economic disaster." The FAA, too, is clearly on the side of the Authority (its "northwest quadrant" requirement may simply be intended to boost the Authority's arguments for what the Engineers want to do anyway). Oscar Bakke, who directs its Eastern region for the FAA, menacingly waved the headsman's ax right after the Authority issued its report:

Since Kennedy Airport is by far the most important United States port of entry, accounting for 45.5 percent of all foreign arrivals, the adequacy of international service at New York is of vital national significance.

In the likelihood of further deterioration of international air service at Kennedy, because of traffic congestion, it has become necessary for the FAA to consider whether the public interest requires the designation of a port of entry and the development of required international service facilities for customs, immigration, public health, agriculture and the like at some other strategic location in the northeast.

We can look whimsically on the difference between Bakke's deteriorated and congested conditions and the Authority's "fast and convenient service," and can even point out that the facilities Bakke describes already exist at other airports, and would have to be duplicated at a fourth jetport in any case. We can go further and note that 45.5% of foreign arrivals land at Kennedy because that's where the planes land; try taking a nonstop flight from the U.S. to Manchester in England or Tours in France—or, for that matter, from London or Paris to St. Louis.

But the point of Mr. Bakke's disputatiousness is that the pressure is on. He wrote to Senator Javits that "the alternatives are serious and, for New York, should be frightening."

It depends on what frightens you. No doubt it frightens some New Yorkers to think that the increasing crowding of the city may not increase quite so fast. But those New Yorkers, one suspects, are driven through the crowds by chauffeurs. And of course the Port Authority may be expected to feel fear at the idea that its empire may not grow quite so large quite so soon.

But it won't really hurt New York all that much. Based in San Francisco, I can choose today from more than a dozen nonstop flights to New York, most of which will have at least some empty seats. Within limits, I can as easily take one flight as another, go on Wednesday instead of Tuesday, even fly to Washington or Boston and shuttle to New York, all without the demands of my work being seriously affected; and certainly this is true of many, probably most, air travelers—whether they themselves know it or not. After all, they manage if they have to get to a place to which there's only one flight a day, and that one with two stops.

In fact—although I confess that because of deadline demands and similar pressures, I probably *would* fly nonstop to New York whenever I had to go there (and of course I would go there just as often in any case)—if there were decent trains to take I'd just as soon return home on one. I could do some writing en route, I would be less crowded, and I'd see more of this still beautiful and always interesting land. Theodore Edison suggested something of the kind in a statement he submitted to the hearings on turning part of the Great Swamp into a wilderness area:

As certain problems of traffic congestion, noise and smog production can probably best be solved by reviving and improving mass rail transportation, there would seem to be good reason to eliminate subsidies to at least the more dubious airports and highways that are helping to defeat the railroads. If rail services are allowed to deteriorate to the point of abandonment, revivals may become almost prohibitively difficult and expensive.

Then, too, as any air traveler knows (and it's worth remembering for the rest of this chapter—especially when the subject of public money comes up—that the overwhelming majority of Americans do not fly at all), Eastern Air Lines doesn't need a jetport for its Boston and Washington shuttles, Mohawk doesn't need one to fly to Albany, Allegheny and Piedmont and a number of other short-haul lines don't need one for their operations. A lot of those planes at Kennedy and LaGuardia and Newark could land in any one of a dozen other airports, or could with relatively minor changes in their operations. So you would have to redesign the flight patterns. At least that would give the Engineers something to keep them off the streets—and out of the swamps.

And beyond that, what about noncommercial aircraft? Between 75 and 80% of the flights into the three major airports of the New

York area are noncommercial. Why not smaller noncommercial airports in the area to divert this traffic?

Questions like these are obviously too far afield for the Engineers. Temporarily balked in one straight-line solution, they look for the next best. Governor Hughes, like the Port Authority, wants a jetport, and if he can't have it in the Great Swamp, he'll settle for it somewhere else.

Happily, he can't have it in the Great Swamp. As one of its last acts in 1968, Congress designated not the 2,400 acres Secretary Udall had asked for, but 3,750 acres of the Great Swamp as a wilderness area. Meyersville Road is to be blocked at both ends and allowed to return to nature. But the Engineers were ready for that one.

Shortly after my article on the Great Swamp appeared in *Ramparts,* I received a half-angry, half-pleading letter from a lady in Califon, New Jersey. "WE NEED HELP," she ended the letter, complete with capitals. After investigating, however, I am not so sure that she and her neighbors need any help at all; they seem to be doing quite well by themselves.

Her, and their, concern arose from the realization by officials in Hunterdon and Somerset Counties that state officials had about decided to avoid the Great Swamp controversy by persuading the Port Authority to locate the fourth jetport at Solberg Airport, the now tiny airport in Hunterdon County, just over the Somerset County line. If you look at a big enough map, you can find the spot by locating the township of Readington, which is smack in the middle of where the jetport would be.

By March, 1967, *The Hunterdon County Democrat* was conducting a poll on the jetport (10–1 against), the Readington Township Committee had voted 5–0 against the idea, and the Clinton Junior Woman's Club were passing out petitions in Flemington, Clinton and Whitehouse (they wore five-inch-wide pins shaped like jet planes and bearing the single word "NO!"). The Somerset County Board of Freeholders got into the act with a resolution opposing a jetport anywhere in central New Jersey.

On March 31, the Department of Transportation of the state of New Jersey held a conference in Trenton on jetport location, with Mr. Bakke in attendance. Also there were a representative of the Metropolitan Airlines Association (which is what it sounds like), one from the Airline Pilots Union, and several from Morris and Burlington Counties. Nobody from Hunterdon or Somerset was invited, but several—including members of the local press in that area and a lady from the League of Women Voters— showed up anyway.

What happened at the conference, in effect, was that the con- ferees talked about, and eliminated, a lot of New Jersey sites, including—because of Hughes's pledge—the Great Swamp (the Port Authority wasn't there, and it isn't clear whether eliminating the site was actually a decision or merely a charade to await the election of Hughes's successor). When they had eliminated sev- eral, only one that was mentioned at all still remained: Solberg- Hunterdon.

The Port Authority, of course, had originally said that Solberg- Hunterdon was too far away (Mr. Bakke said in Trenton that the FAA has no objection to the site). The press pointed out, however, that if Hughes asks for Solberg, the Authority will pretty well have to reconsider.

It was a few more days before the full story broke, not in a country weekly but in an Associated Press dispatch from the wire service's sharp bureau at the state capitol. Somebody had figured out a way to make a buck:

New Jersey's search for a fourth metropolitan jetport site focused sharply today on Solberg Airport in rural Hunterdon County, with the Central Railroad of New Jersey playing an important role in influenc- ing the choice. . . .

The Metropolitan Airlines Committee, which represents the major air carriers serving Kennedy, LaGuardia and Newark, is conducting a study of its own. But airline sources said the big carriers anticipate the selection of Solberg. . . .

. . . the Jersey Central Railroad's tracks run along the boundaries of the jetport site. Under the so-called Aldene Plan scheduled to take effect April 30, the Jersey Central would have a direct rail link with midtown Manhattan. . . .

Furthermore, [sources] said, the Jersey Central tracks could be con- verted into a high speed rail system, providing speedy transit to and from Manhattan.

They viewed a Solberg Jetport as a boon to the Jersey Central, which recently announced its bankruptcy because of heavy commuter and freight losses.

Besides hauling air travelers to and from the airport, the Jersey Central would stand to gain considerably from air cargo shipments. FAA figures show that air freight business has been rising at an astronomical rate in the metropolitan area.

All in all, a pretty fair piece of reporting.

Good enough, at any rate, to fire up the local citizens. A day later, the press was able to report that teachers at Hunterdon Central High School were calling an anti-jetport meeting, students were passing out bumper stickers with bright red lettering (PEOPLE, NOT PLANES—BAN THE JETPORT), and the Clinton Junior Woman's Club—which had obtained 4,000 signatures on its petitions—was organizing a march on Trenton.

The lady who wrote to me called it "the most beautiful, quiet, mountainous, dairy-farming area of the state—the last retreat from megalopolis in New Jersey." Apparently the people who live around there don't want a jetport. And they have some reason, aside from the noise and the intrusion of the megalopolis. For instance, H. Mat Adams, who used to be Commissioner of Conservation and Economic Development for New Jersey, says that a jetport at Solberg would pollute the state's enormous Round Valley-Spruce Run reservoir system, which is nearby. Jet exhausts, says Adams, will lay down a cover of waste materials that no one knows how to remove from the water.

In any case, the Hunterdon-Somerset resistance movement, which seems almost as strong as the one that developed around the Great Swamp, must have had some effect, because no official announcement was ever made, and in June, the governor had come up with still another idea.

Some time before all this, President Johnson had appointed a commission to investigate airport needs on a nationwide basis; at the head of the group were Secretary of Transportation Alan S. Boyd and Chairman Charles S. Murphy of the Civil Aeronautics Board. Hughes got in touch with Boyd and asked him to review the idea of putting the jetport in the Pine Barrens, farther south.

No ecologist is going to be particularly happy about that idea, either—but the request and Boyd's response to it are interesting in themselves. Boyd said he would order a study of the possibility of altering air patterns over Burlington and Ocean Counties. The point is that the FAA's "northwest quadrant" argument and the Port Authority's rejection of several sites were based on interference with present air patterns. Neither agency, as far as can be told from any public document or statement, has ever even considered—in the face of all the professed urgency with which they shriek about a new jetport—the possibility of changing those patterns.

Nor should it be overlooked that the Port Authority rejected two Long Island sites because, it said, New Jersey passengers would not use them. But what *would* they use, then? And what does that have to do with an *international* airport? Clearly, the Port Authority at least, and probably the FAA and the Metropolitan Airlines Association and Governor Hughes, *want* an airport in northern or central New Jersey; and to get one, they are determined to convince people that there *must* be an airport in northern or central New Jersey.

The whole situation is not without irony. In 1964, the Public Service Electricity and Gas Company—New Jersey's version of Con Ed—sent picture postcards, in sets, all over the country, inviting business to locate in New Jersey. Besides the state's allegedly wondrous port facilities and other industrial conveniences, the postcards showed some lovely farm country and wild areas. "New Jersey," the message said, "is a beautiful state and one that offers the industrialist and his employees and visitors many opportunities to enjoy the great outdoors." And that's not all: "Few other states can boast of such a desirable diversification and balance in land utilization."

I hate to say it about a utility company, but that's all true. Still, it is obvious that industrialization can do for a state exactly what visitors can do for Yosemite: ruin the reason they came to the locality in the first place.

What's happening now in New Jersey will happen soon—if you aren't already in the middle of it—wherever you live, too. Jetports are the newest toys for Engineers who are still too little to play with dams in Grand Canyon or gouges in the Great Cascades. Towns like Oakland, California, have built enormous airports that most airlines have no use for (to take a helicopter from the Berkeley heliport to the Oakland airport a few miles away, you have to go by way of the San Francisco airport, across the Bay and back, and in some cases switch helicopters). And Los Angeles—always in the lead with a fresh idea, especially if it fouls up the environment—is now actively studying an airport five miles out in Santa Monica Bay. "To many," says a San Francisco newspaper, airports in the ocean appear "to be the only way to meet the problems of longer runways and additional terminals and maintenance facilities, because land is at a premium—or totally unavailable." And then, too, there's nobody out there but us fish to be bothered by all that noise—although you can bet that nobody has done any studies on the effect of all this on, say, commercial fishermen, much less offshore ecology.

Believe it or not, though, there was a conference on ocean airports in San Francisco. John Thomas O'Brien, of the Navy's civil engineering laboratory at Port Hueneme, California, said that floating airports are best. Myles K. Mashburn, of New Orleans' J. Ray McDermott and Company, said they should be anchored to the ocean floor. Neither of them, nor any other conferees, had any idea how you get the passengers to and from the airport, but they were willing to talk cheerfully about tunnels, causeways and floating bridges (the boat as a method of traveling across water is obviously not to be considered by Engineers, since it requires building nothing but a simple dock). In the case of San Francisco, where the offshore shelf is shallow, they would probably agree on an island—and maybe they could get together with those two bright supervisors and build the airport on a pile of garbage.

These are truly Engineers at their most innocently rapacious. We've got airplanes, so we've gotta have airports. We're getting bigger airplanes, so we've gotta have bigger airports. And we've gotta have bigger airplanes, and therefore bigger airports, because the number of air travelers is going up, because the airlines are advertising wildly to fill their bigger airplanes. And Boeing turns out a 707 every 2.3 days.

It would be bad enough if a 707 every 2.3 days were all we had to worry about. But now we have to worry about the supersonic transport (SST) as well.

I will not dwell on the ridiculous politics and the even more ridiculous economics of the proposed supersonic transport plane. Let it be said simply that it is a plane nobody needs—and indeed, a plane that, except for a few who will profit, nobody wants. It will probably bankrupt airlines and cost American taxpayers billions.

The SST—like the Grand Canyon dams or Storm King—is an Engineers' fantasy, the sort of problem-solution that can be dreamed up only by men whose normal approach to their work begins with donning blinders. The problem, in this case, was the British economy. To give it a boost, somebody thought of a bigger airplane. The French got into the game. They designed the plane—the *Concorde*—to fly at perhaps 1,800 miles an hour. Pan American ordered six. American aircraft executives, and their handful of marionettes in both houses of Congress, panicked— and now America has an SST program. Boeing, having won a race with Lockheed, is building two prototypes (with engines by General Electric).

Who wants to go anywhere that fast?

Nobody, really. The human body already gets pretty confused on a jet flight across the country, and more so on a flight across an ocean. Pan Am, presumably, can get you from New York City to Quito, or BOAC can fly you from Lagos to London, without running into this problem—but such flights do not account for a very significant percentage of world air travel.

That doesn't matter, though. The Engineers will build the supersonic plane anyway, because, as the man said about the mountain, it's there. It's the next fastest plane you can build. Writing in *The Nation,* Karl Ruppenthal—who is an airline pilot, an attorney *and* a teacher at Stanford—explains that to an airline buying planes, or a manufacturer developing them, the relationship between speed and cost has so far been linear:

Thus an airline could decide whether to increase its investment in aircraft, say, 10 percent, in order to achieve a 5 percent increase in speed. But when we enter the supersonic age, the old cost-speed equation will no longer apply. It will become entangled in a variety of complex physical laws and the airline industry will have much more difficult choices to make.

Basic to the problem is the fact that present jets now cruise at speeds slightly less than the speed of sound—usually in the range between Mach .80 and Mach .86. Because of the nature of the turbulence (and other phenomena) associated with flying at and near the speed of Mach 1, it is not practical to think in terms of small increases in speed. And since it is similarly impractical to think in terms of Mach 1.2 or Mach 1.5, the only real question is whether the next generation of jets should cruise at speeds on the order of Mach 2 or Mach 3—that is, at twice or three times the speed of sound.

So they build it, and what happens?

What happens (besides a need in every major city for a still bigger jetport) is that it makes one hell of a noise.

It is called a sonic boom. It happens because, when an aircraft "breaks the sound barrier," it creates, at that point, a pressure wave that is also a sound wave—and from then on it goes on creating it. Like the bow wave of a boat, which continues to exist but not with the same water, the sonic-boom wave is actually being re-created all the time as the aircraft proceeds through the air.

Unlike the bow wave of a boat, however, a sonic boom doesn't always diminish; and when it does, it doesn't diminish fast enough. The ecological point here is that sound—like the salt marsh, the California condor, the ebony spleenwort, the Grand Canyon and lima beans—is part of our environment. Too much, or the wrong kind, and you can't function temporarily—and sometimes permanently. It can make you irritable, drive you insane or kill you. Tests at Edwards Air Force Base, which is in a California desert, have shown that the impact of a sonic boom generated at 65,000 feet—which is up around where the SST will fly—is about like living 1,000 feet from the end of one of today's jetport runways. They won't let you live 1,000 feet from the end of one of today's jetport runways. Even the birds at the Jamaica Bay sanctuary live three times farther away than that.

Military planes, which already fly at supersonic speeds and which cause the relatively few sonic booms we have heard so far, have also demonstrated some other effects. The sonic boom from one of them, for instance, dislodged with its vibrations 80 tons of rock which poured down onto prehistoric cliff dwellings in Colorado's Mesa Verde National Park. They are forbidden to fly there now—and Secretary Udall would just as soon stop them from flying over any national parks at all.

What will happen, then, when SSTs are flying across the country?

They tried creating a few sonic booms on purpose over Oklahoma City in 1964 (no one seems to have asked the people of Oklahoma City whether they wanted to be tested), and got 15,-000 complaints and 4,000 claims for damages. Since most people wouldn't know whom to complain to, or that damages are recoverable (much less how to go about filing claims), that's a pretty impressive figure.

"A boom has a startle effect," says Major General Jewell C. Maxwell of the Air Force, who heads the SST program for the FAA, "especially if you've never heard it before. The first time, you might jump. But the thousandth time, you don't do anything."

Major General Jewell C. Maxwell of the Air Force is talking through his gold-braided flyboy cap, and he knows it. The 4,000 damage claims in Oklahoma City weren't for people jumping, and those 80 tons of rock in Mesa Verde didn't fall down because of a startle effect. In Oklahoma City—leaving out the mink grower who said that his breeding mink were so disturbed they ate their young, which is entirely possible and not at all funny—animals were frightened, tiny babies were seriously disturbed, and some of the people who got that little ol' startle effect were cardiac patients.

Early in 1967, Donald F. Hornig, a White House science adviser, told a Congressional committee that if an SST flies across the United States (creating a "sonic boom corridor" *65 miles wide*), everyone in an area of 100,000 square miles—possibly ten million people—"would be likely to hear and react." Another source makes it 20,000,000 people. But even 10,000,000 is one out of every 20 people in the United States, including Hawaii and Alaska. And there is nothing whatever that can be done about it.

Anything traveling at that speed will make that wave, and nobody has the beginning of a glimmer of an idea how it might be damped.

That kind of noise as a regular part of your life is a far more serious disruption than you might think—ask any psychiatrist. At least two countries—West Germany and Switzerland—have indicated that they may ban supersonic transport flights over their air space if the noise is as bad as it seems it will be. But it isn't just the noise (and ecology or not, I'm skipping over the possible effect on wildlife; even today aircraft are recognized as a factor in the scarcity of the California condor, because they can't nest comfortably and undisturbed in their high eyries). It's the potential damage.

Ruppenthal doesn't think cities like Athens, Florence, Paris or Rome will let SSTs fly over, because of potential damage to art treasures, architectural wonders like Notre Dame or the Parthenon, and just plain urban damage. "Historic cities," he goes on, "such as Antwerp, Nuremberg and Vienna will never permit supersonic planes to approach within 100 miles." The FAA says the SST is a good investment even if it only flies over water and "sparsely populated land areas," but who needs to travel from Attu to Society Island at 1,800 miles an hour?

In case you don't think the Engineers are in control, the FAA, when it started on the SST program, set up sonic boom "standards." Neither Boeing nor Lockheed could meet them. Says Major General Jewell C. Maxwell of the Air Force, "We decided we were not correct in specifying the limits the way we did." So now the FAA specifies the limits no way at all. There aren't any.

In 1966, some FAA types were ready to run more tests (using supersonic B-58s) over Midwestern cities—again without asking anybody. FAA Administrator William F. McKee (known to his subordinates as "Bozo") killed the plan, because "it might cause the defeat of some marginal Democrats in the fall elections." You bet. What it actually might have caused is the defeat of the SST.

The Engineers, if they don't succeed in killing us all by completely destroying the environment, are determined at least to drive us nuts.

Still, what are you going to do? There's the demand: Britain and France need the money; Arizona needs the water; New York

City needs the power; there will be 65 million air travelers into and out of the New York-New Jersey area in 1980.

Of course airports by their nature are unbeautiful. But I am no more ready to give up air travel than I am ready to give up phonograph records or typewriters or automobiles—and it wouldn't matter much to anyone else if I were. A lack of beauty, though, is not the point (and who knows whether airports might not be the next generation's standard of beauty?). If you have ever landed at the new airport in Oakland and watched the newly homeless ducks try to compete with a DC-8 or seen a rabbit scurry across the runway in front of an Electra; if you have ever flown into Kennedy, looking down at the fantastic estuarine shoreline and then, on the ground, looking around at what you are standing on; if you have ever arrived by day at San Francisco, convinced until the last second that you are landing in the water only to see with relief the sharp, clean line of the runway's end marking the point to which the Bay was filled; if ever, in fact, you have landed at a major jetport and thought of what the jetport displaced, then the relevance of all this has not escaped you.

It even seems at times as though ecological problems have their own ecological, everything-comes-together logic. The Audubon Society is concerned once more about the Everglades, because the Engineers now want to build an SST jetport just north of the Tamiami Trail, connected to Miami by a new superhighway.

There is not a Great Swamp or a unique ecosystem under every jetport, any more than there is a destructive ecological upheaval associated with every dam or power plant. But like dams and power plants, jetports are, by and large, constructed without any real thought about what may be involved in the process.

Before I had read anything about the SST and when Solberg was just another name in the Port Authority report, I sat in my rented car parked beside a road in the Great Swamp, where I could see the woody shrubs encroaching on the cattail marsh, with a shining birch on the other side of the marsh sunnily defying the winter afternoon, and I pondered my notes on the need for a jetport. Tentatively, I decided to write that it would be worth the extra cost, whatever it might be, to build the jetport somewhere else and save the swamp from the rapacious Engineers. A short time later, I was back in Manhattan, in the office of attorney David Sive, who fought the Storm King case before the Federal Power Commission. After rehashing the Storm King story, we fell to talking of other matters, and I found myself blurting out my enthusiasm for the beauty and wonder I had found in the Great Swamp.

Sive is a quiet man with sandy hair that manages to look unruly even when it's combed; he hunches forward over his desk when he speaks, and his voice is so quiet that full attention is necessary to hear it. In a movie he would be cast not as a dynamic attorney but, perhaps, as a shy accountant. When I mentioned my tentative decision, he hunched forward characteristically and softly smiled.

"Did you ever think," he asked me curiously, "that you might be asking the wrong questions? I mean—suppose we simply didn't build the airport?"

Not build the airport? "But . . . by 1980," I said instead of stopping to think, "there will be 65 million air travelers in and out of the area."

"Who says so?" Sive smiled.

And suddenly I understood what he was driving at.

XII · KILL A BABY THIS WEEK

THERE'S A LITTLE ISLAND in the Pacific, not far from Guadalcanal of World War II fame, where they've got the biggest problem in the world all figured out.

By our standards, Tikopia isn't very big. You can stand there and look around and see that there's just so much land and that there are a certain number of people. The people who live there have a pretty strict patriarchal society: what the old man says, goes. And the old man controls all the land that the family has.

He is responsible, however, for making sure that everybody eats. So what he does is very simple: after a couple of his older sons have married and become fathers, he forbids the younger sons to marry. They still get to enjoy the island girls without anybody caring much about it, but impregnating them is strictly out. If somebody goofs, there's an abortion. And if a pregnancy somehow slips by, they simply kill the baby.

Westerners find this revolting. The restrictions on marriage they understand; the abortions many of them are willing to accept; but the cruelty of the calmly effected and cold-blooded infanticides, however rarely they occur, turns Western stomachs.

Possibly that is because Western stomachs are full.

This is the difference between the island you live on and the island of Tikopia: On your island the younger sons may marry and breed. Abortion is possible but generally frowned upon. And —even more cold-bloodedly than the Tikopians—on your island the *only* control is to kill the babies.

Of course we do not kill our babies as directly, or as quickly and mercifully, as the Tikopians do. We starve them to death—10,-000 of them every day. It is true that some of them struggle, half-starved, into their twenties or even their thirties before they die. And it is true that we sometimes keep a few more babies alive for a while by killing older people instead. But the total is 10,000 people a day all the same. For, also unlike Tikopia, we have not solved our problem. Having omitted from our practice the essential factor of theirs, we have to kill more babies every day, and even so we can't keep up.

Yes, you have heard the population story before. They have it tough over there in India and down there in Latin America. We ought to give them all pills or something. And I guess we ought to cool it a little ourselves. I'll have to be sure to teach the kids about that.

Do. Please do.

Back in Chapter II, we mentioned the "greenhouse effect" —the possible problem for our planet arising from the fact that we are turning loose too much carbon dioxide, so that by the year 2000 we might be faced with melting ice caps and drowned coastlines. If I were a Martian Engineer with interplanetary imperialist tendencies, I might at first glance find that a salutary development, because it would obviously kill off a lot of people, and by 2000 there are going to be too many of them. Unfortunately, even as a Martian Engineer I would have to take a second look at that solution, because it would also reduce the amount of room, and a lot of good arable land would go under water.

Mentioning greenhouses is not too bad an association, though, because our problem is with a weed—with, in fact, the worst, most persistent, most ubiquitous weed in the history of the planet: you. You, and me, and the rest of the human race—at least if a weed is a form of life that crowds out others by moving in and taking over the room and the nutrients.

A weed, of course, doesn't know what it's doing. Neither, by definition, does an Engineer. But a lot of you do. You may not want to think about it, but that's not the same thing. *They* do not have it tough in India and Latin America; *we* have it tough in India and Latin America. *You* are killing those babies as surely as any Tikopian—at least you are if you have more than two children —and if you can't think of it any other way you can at least realize that, like human groups everywhere throughout the history of man, when they get too crowded they will sooner or later move somewhere where it is less crowded. Think about that next time you watch your kids playing in the park.

If you really don't understand the population problem generally, read *Moment in the Sun* by Robert and Leona Train Rienow (the second chapter alone will do it for you). I will say only that by 2000, if the ice caps don't melt and World War III or bubonic plague or something doesn't decimate the population and the Engineers don't come up with some new and awe-inspiring way of killing us all off like they almost did with DDT, the population of the world will be 6.6 billion people (at the present rate of growth) where it is now 3.3 billion people. Or, if it helps: the population of the world will double in the next thirty years or so. Which, Wallace Stegner points out, will mean

two New Yorks instead of one, two Londons, two Tokyos, two Calcuttas, two Hong Kongs, one more of every existing human congregation. There will be double the highways and freeways to link them, double the consumption of oxygen by human and industrial and automotive combustion, double the air and water pollution, half the elbow room, a shrunken area of cropland that will have to be more and more intensively mined, a limited amount of parkland and open space trampled flat by the millions wanting to smell mown grass or show the kids a squirrel. This will be in the lifetime of some of us, in the lifetime of all our children, but it is difficult for the imagination to grasp it.

I will spare you Mr. Stegner's description of life—given a continuation of growth at the present rate—in 2150 A.D., except to note that there is something about this being the last century in the millennium that makes the future seem farther away; in 1868, 1900 cannot have seemed so far in the future as 2000 does to us. At any rate, 2150 is but three average American lifetimes into the future; and the world population, if we have done nothing about it by then, will be *fifty times* what it is now. Maybe you can picture it for yourself. I hope so.

One of the leading demographers of America is Dr. Philip M. Hauser, and you may get some comfort from his statement that "anyone who claims to know what the future population of this nation, or any area, is going to be is either a fool or a charlatan." There is a third possibility: he might be, like Mr. Stegner, a writer trying to warn us of something. For instance, even a 100%

increase in population need not, as I hope to show, mean a 100% increase in highways and freeways, oxygen consumption, or air and water pollution; and Mr. Stegner of course knows that. But Dr. Hauser goes on like this:

Nevertheless, such projections are much more than exercises in arithmetic. They indicate the implications of observed rates of growth. The fact that man is able to consider their consequences is one reason the projected numbers will never come to pass. For in recognizing the implications of his birth rate, mankind will proceed to modify it.

We'll see.

In the meantime, Dr. Hauser has a projection of his own which is more than an exercise in arithmetic. It says that even if there is "a reasonable decline in the birth rate, of the type assumed by the Social Security Administration in its population projections" (the birth rate did drop startlingly in 1967), there will still be more than 300 million people in the United States by 2000. There are right now, as I write, somewhere between 200 and 210 million. Which means that for every two people in Yosemite, or on the Chicago lakefront, or in the Great Smokies, or in Central Park, there will be three by the time your kids are established adult members of their communities.

Perhaps we can handle three for two, if we work at it a little and don't make it any worse. We can even make it a little better, if enough of us are willing to consume enough Enovid and if as a society we are willing to do a little something about spreading the birth-control word among the people who don't have the affluence to read polemic books by worried reporters.

And a lot of good it will do us. Stanford biologist Paul Ehrlich has a nice phrase. He says that to say "that the population explosion is a problem of the underdeveloped countries is like telling a fellow passenger, 'Your end of the boat is sinking.'" Less graphically but more directly, bioclimatologist Paul Waggoner puts it this way:

I don't think that the people of Connecticut would long live on the produce of their rocky acres alone while the people in Iowa grew fat. And I don't think that in the period of, say, the rest of this century that North America is going to be permitted the luxury of great quantities of idle fertile land while two or three billion people starve elsewhere. . . .

Since the population will increase by a billion people in the next fifteen years [Dr. Waggoner was speaking in 1965], and I don't know how any significant birth-control measures can be effected before that, it is going to take 300 million tons of grain [a year] to feed these people, and 300 million tons of grain are approximately the present production of North America and Western Europe together. I think we are indeed living in a very brief period of affluence for land.

So what's all this nonsense about wilderness areas, and saving the California condor, and preserving the salt marshes? Can we really speak meaningfully about saving the upper Selway when people are starving and we could be growing food there? Can we waste time with the natural habitat of the moose when the moose is good to eat?

You're right. You're absolutely right. Even zoos and pet dogs will probably have to disappear very soon.

The chances really are, I guess, that as an island in space we will not achieve the wisdom that the Tikopians have achieved on their island in the Pacific. The chances are that we will not make it in time to Africa and Asia and Latin America with our pills and our intrauterine devices and our imperfect methods of persuasion and education. The chances are that the human race will overrun every conceivable square yard of land, at least of arable land, until the entire earth is no more "natural" than the mountain terraces of Japan.

The chances are that if that doesn't happen, it will be because the blind fiddling around of the Engineers will kill us first, by wiping out our nitrogen or our potassium or our phosphorus. Or perhaps our oxygen: because while we are filling the air with carbon dioxide faster than the ecology of the earth can keep up with it, we are also, by the same process, tying up oxygen. The same oxygen that combines with the carbon from the coal we burn would otherwise be free in the atmosphere. The oxygen produced by plants is not produced if we pave over the plants.

Most oxygen—perhaps 70 percent—is produced by planktonic diatoms in the oceans. And it happens, as Dr. LaMont Cole points out, that we are dumping into the oceans vast quantities of pollutants consisting, according to one estimate by the U. S. Food and Drug Administration, of as many as a half million substances, many of which are of recent origin and biologically active materials such as pesticides, radioisotopes, and detergents, and to which the earth's living forms have never before had to try to adapt. No more than a minute fraction of these substances and combinations of them has been tested for toxicity to marine diatoms or, for that matter, to the equally vital forms involved in the cycles of nitrogen and other essential elements.

If we don't eliminate all the oxygen too quickly, the process could serve as a population control in the meantime. The effect would be the same as moving everybody to a higher altitude, and the death rate would go up. But then the Engineers may find a more spectacular way—such as by using hydrogen explosions for construction purposes, thereby releasing tritium (the radioactive isotope of hydrogen), which even the Atomic Energy Commission suggests may cause "ground water contamination or ventilation problems."

The chances are that even if none of this happens, our population will finally be held in check by the horrible planet-wide wars that overcrowding must inevitably bring, or by the spread of some mutant form of *bilharzia* from the Nile Valley through the jammed-together of the world in an epidemic that will make the Black Death look like a mild day in a children's ward.

Possibly, if each of us had to strangle a baby every week with our own hands, we would get the idea.

On the other hand, there is just a chance. More and more people, not only in relatively well-educated North America but at least in leadership circles in other countries, *are* getting the the idea. The leaders of new nations have the unique opportunity to spread death control and birth control simultaneously. Our children may see some things strange to our minds—astonishingly different social attitudes toward sex and marriage, legally *required* abortions in some cases, licenses to have children, international birth-rate treaties—but population control *could* happen.

But we can't wait to find out. If the planet is saved from the explosion of the population bomb, then its population should have—and in fact will badly need, and forever—the California condor and the Everglades, the peregrine falcon and the Great Swamp. It will, in fact, need all the genetic information we can save and all the ecological sense we can bequeath.

On this continent of all continents, we must—even as we pray for the survival of our species—prepare its legacy. For if ours is the greatest problem of industrialization, with its attendant pollution and waste, it is also the least problem of *Lebensraum*. When British reporter Ian Nairn toured the United States in 1967, he wrote for *The Observer* of London a scathing denunciation of the deterioration of the American landscape, then added:

It is a crazy situation, and I think it has some crazy human consequences. But the first thing that ought to be said about this disintegrated landscape is that it is not due to the pressure of population.

In Western European terms the U.S. has no suburban problem at all; at the density of England and Wales—which still allows us some of the world's greatest rural landscape and a large area of mountain—the whole population of the U.S. could comfortably be fitted into Texas.

So it is not the numbers of people but the way they are distributed that has caused this mess.

And so it is we who have the chance to do something for the world, just in case by some crazy chance it should survive, in case we are able to prevent the weed from choking the garden entirely. "What America does," Wallace Stegner has written, "to curb its waste, control its population, husband its resources, decontaminate its polluted air and waters, and reserve open space for the refreshment and relaxation of its industrially punch-drunk citizens is a favor done the whole world."

Of course our own national population problems bring with them other problems, problems that are not in the narrow sense ecological; and we have problems, too, related to the distribution not merely of people but of wealth. We, too, have starvation—not because we have too many people for the food we produce (on the contrary) but simply because we are too busy with our own lives to know or care that black children in Mississippi quite often starve to death. We do not, as a nation, *really* understand that we have very, very hungry people. I personally know at least two dozen people who go to work every day in midtown Manhattan, three or four miles from starving children, and who don't know it.

Those drastic problems aside, we can read—and write—of wilderness and open space and rarely think of the fact that most Americans can see such space, if they can ever see it at all, for two or three weeks a year. This, says Raymond Dasmann, is

when they are free to visit the old "wide open spaces," the national parks and national forests of the West.

But it is only necessary to count the percentage of Negro faces among the national park visitors in the Western United States to realize that this freedom is not truly available to all.

And even if it were, there are problems behind the problems. Dr. Seymour Farber is an expert on stress, and he spoke once in a discussion about the meaning behind that two- or three-week vacation, that partial denial of freedom:

I don't think you can take people from the city streets or children or anyone who may not have ever seen a cow, and suddenly put them in a forest away from the blare of the truck horns, the noises of factory whistles, and all the other city things that we consider. They feel insecure—they feel lost. That is why you see millions of people on the floor of the Yosemite Valley. And if you just walk a mile or two miles up above there to May Lake or anywhere else, there are very few people.

The wilderness does not automatically renew, and too many American adults, as well as American children, have no sense of their heritage from the land. But that, too, can be solved. What has to be broken in the United States is the profound conviction—held by few conservationists but, I'm afraid, by most Americans—that they don't really have any choice, that things are simply the way they are and that there's nothing that can be done, about birth control or wilderness, war or peace.

And it is no surprise that they think that way—because that is how an Engineer thinks, and the biggest problem America faces from within is that Engineers do its thinking.

Perhaps it is time to say again that "Engineers" does not (necessarily) mean "engineers," that the rape of America is being perpetrated not merely by men with hard hats and surveying instruments (though such men are by no means excluded), but by men in a number of professions who have in common an "engineering mentality," the capacity to approach problems only in the way that the least imaginative and most robotic of engineers would approach them. The identifying characteristic of the Engineer is that, if you show him two sections of road with a gully between them, he will build a bridge without ever looking down into the gully to see whether it might be, in fact, a river teeming with life and vital to the well-being of a dozen communities. Tell an Engineer that his dam will destroy a salmon run and he will meet *that* problem with a fish ladder. Tell him that his fish ladder will create another problem, and he will deal with *that*—but never by abandoning the fish ladder and certainly never by questioning the existence of the dam. What he will not do is look at the totality of what he is doing. He cannot, any more than a raven can fly backward.

The Engineer is fascinated with figures. There will be 65 million air travelers in and out of New York by 1980; therefore there must be another airport. The population of the world by the year 2000 will be 6.6 billion people. No Engineer makes even the cautious disclaimer voiced by Dr. Hauser. Even less does it occur to him that the very citing of the figure can hasten the future event described.

Conservationists do it too, so pervasive a part of our life is the engineering mentality. The North American Wildlife Foundation, for example, in its pre-acquisition brochure on the Great Swamp, says that in Morris County, New Jersey, "every home, every factory and every human facility will be duplicated in the next 40 years." But of course it won't, if Morris County doesn't let it happen. The problem is that Engineers take the projection for the fact.

The most carefully logical exposition I have found of what happens when the Engineers are in control is in a paper by Dr. Sanford S. Farness of the School of Urban Planning and Landscape Architecture at Michigan State University. "The entire history of American government policy, federal, state and local," he says, "has been based upon the notion of growth indefinitely extended." We are all used to that—which perhaps explains our response to a slogan like "the New Frontier." Anything that sounds as though it might get in the way of "growth" becomes a kind of threat.

But we get so hung up on the idea of "growth" that whenever we start to *plan*—and of course planning is the whole key to saving what we must save while continuing to make use of the resources our land provides—we make policy decisions without realizing that we make them. We project growth rates and then take them as absolute facts of the future for which we have to prepare—and we don't realize that we've made a decision: a decision to let the growth happen.

How often have you heard a politician say it, or a utilities executive, or some other power-structure version of the Engineer: unless such-and-such a service is provided, unless this dam is built, unless that power plant is constructed, we can't meet the problems of growth. Dr. Farness puts it like this (except for the emphasis, which is mine):

We must assume in any absolute growth forecast . . . that *a decision has been made* to provide the public capital and urban facilities necessary to service the forecasted growth, otherwise the growth could not occur. But this is precisely the critical policy action that is ignored or glossed over. . . .

We have to build the expressway because we have to get the cars from here to there. Why? Well, because by next year there will be more cars, and still more the year after that. But when you decide to build the expressway, you are *not* meeting a need created by the cars. You are saying that you *want* the cars; you are making a policy decision that having more cars next year, and still more the year after that, is what you want. If you don't build the expressway, don't provide the parking space, don't let anybody put a gas station in the area, you won't get the cars next year and the year after. That's what Dr. Farness is saying:

. . . trends are derived . . . producing a future growth estimate, which then becomes a bench mark for scaling plans and defining "future needs." Instead of treating these "needs" as results of self-generated policy, present methodology implies that they are the result of automatic, impersonal, socioeconomic technological "forces" playing over the region with relentless effects. The hidden policy decision is never brought to awareness and made explicit.

The Engineers, in other words, because they can't think straight, succeed in convincing Americans that there is some sort of determinism about the way things grow—when in fact we can control automobiles, and even populations, far more easily than we can control rivers or estuaries. And that, of course, was what David Sive was trying to suggest to me that day in his midtown office. "Suppose we didn't build the airport?"

The American assumption—that growth is somehow built into the system, that "automatic forces" mean that we "have to" meet certain needs, that the "growth rate" is handed down, chiseled in stone, from on high—has always been, as Dr. Farness suggests, a wrong assumption. It has always been, in our planning, a policy disguised as an inevitability.

Today it is more than that. It is a downright danger. We cannot continue blindly to plan for an automatically assumed "growth rate" when we do not dare continue to grow at the same rate. We cannot prepare the legacy we owe to the world's tomorrow unless we are prepared to make a startling—to an American almost an unthinkable—decision.

It is time to stop.

XIII · WHO NEEDS INTERSTATE 20?

CONSIDER—now that we have reached this point—the frightening depredations that the Engineers are wreaking on the land.

Consider the rape of southern Florida, which, if it is not stopped, will destroy not only the beauty and the life and the economy but the vital ecology of that lovely area. Consider the insistence of the Engineers who, if they are not stopped, will literally fill in the lower gorges of the Grand Canyon. Consider the callous murder of the striped bass of the Hudson by the Consolidated Edison Company. Consider the attempt to wipe out the Great Swamp of New Jersey with no concern for the consequences, the ravaging of literally everything that is natural in California for its water transfer plan, the rape of the Great Smokies, the pit mining in the Cascades for two days' copper, the sickening destruction of the Long Island wetlands, the heartless drowning of Alaska. Consider the literally hundreds of projects by Engineers and developers and short-range private profiteers all over America, projects large and small, and the continuing rape of the environments and ecosystems on which we all depend by the forces of what they insist on calling progress.

And consider how feeble, though noble, are our responses.

Wisconsin—a state far in advance of most—added a cent a pack to its cigarette tax and earmarked it for recreational purchases: $50 million over a ten-year period. California passed an $85-million bond issue for park purchases (and blew about $10 million of it through procrastination). In Huntington, New York —on Long Island—a citizens' committee rallied after a defeat to get a $2.5-million bond issue passed for parks. In Sacramento, California, a group called the Save the American River Association saved 23 miles of shoreline from urban sprawl. In East Concord, New Hampshire, citizens, through a volunteer clean-up effort, shamed the city council into development of a 12-acre park area. In New Jersey, a private developer was going to build 35 houses on 77 previously untouched acres in Mendham Township; the North Jersey Conservation Foundation, moving to help local residents, dug up $115,000 and bought the land, which will become a town park.

Sometimes you even find more or less conscientious Engineers. When 20th Century-Fox was making movies in Culver City, they imported and maintained about 25 varieties of trees, most of them, of course, unique to southern California—they were there primarily for movie backgrounds. When the 260-acre property was sold to Zeckendorf Properties and the Aluminum Company of America, the 1,200 trees, worth perhaps a million dollars, went with the sale. Century City—an office-hotel-apartment complex that would be ugly anywhere except in Los Angeles County (where it looks normal)—rose on the site, but their Engineers, at a cost of nearly $150,000, saved the trees, by digging them up, boxing them and later replanting them.

And there are Mr. and Mrs. George Heinzman of the Florida Audubon Society, who worried about the bald eagle. They went to 80 ranches, ranging from 4,000 to 200,000 acres, and persuaded the owners to protect eagles from hunters, to be careful of nest trees (and to be sure to leave some trees standing) and in general to care about the eagles. Now the 80 ranches, besides being ranches, are the Kissimmee Prairie Cooperative Bald Eagle Sanctuary.

But America can't be saved from the Engineers in 77-acre batches bought by enthusiastic private citizens; there are not 80 private ranches that can save the roseate spoonbill; we can't buy the Grand Canyon or the Long Island wetlands (in fact, we already own, in company with the Navajo tribe, the portion of the Grand Canyon in question).

But we *can* just *not build* the dam. Or the power plant. Or the jetport. Not every dam or power plant or jetport, but every one whose only excuse for being is a blindly projected "need" that is really a want.

North of New York City, ecologist Ron Dagon drove me on a tour of the western part of suburban Westchester County, pointing here to the wise use of land by men, there to some fruit of our fantastic talent for fouling things up. From the encompassing point of view of the ecologist, he showed me how a sacrifice here can make possible an accomplishment there, how even the demands of population can be accommodated to the basic need we do not yet, as a nation, realize: the need to live as part of an environment we can defile only so far.

But underlying his explanations was a running tone of despair: there are too many people, too many demands on a land that can accommodate only so much. I was reminded of an editor, years ago, who advised me to move to Los Angeles because "that's where the money is." When I asked why the money should be there, he replied with a grin that it is because "that's where the people go." Is the spiral unstoppable?

If a fourth jetport is not built in the New York-New Jersey area, perhaps some factories will move. Some are moving, anyway; Revlon, the cosmetics firm which operates three plants in New Jersey, has opened a fourth—in Arizona. There will be fewer jobs. But in the long run, the people will go where the jobs are. Certainly some human families will suffer; but no more—in fact, far less—than human families will suffer if we go ahead and build all the jetports and the canals and the freeways and fill in the swamps and dam the canyons.

Some international travelers may have to leave from, or arrive in, Boston or Baltimore or somewhere else. But why not Boston or Baltimore? Why not Richmond, Virginia? Or Charleston, South Carolina? If I were to fly from San Francisco to Paris via the East Coast, it would hardly matter whether I stopped to change planes at New York or Brunswick, Georgia. A German scientist on his way to an international conference in Chicago could as easily enter the country at Portland, Maine. Obviously the immigration and other facilities would have to be duplicated in any case.

"Economic disaster," Senator Javits said—but where is the disaster? Lack of air travel facilities is not what drove factories from New York to South Carolina. Where are the studies of *who* flies, and how important is arrival at 6 P.M. instead of 7? No one who spends any part of his life in airports can seriously believe that, in 99 out of 100 cases, an hour or two matters one way or the other; in most cases, even a day or two doesn't matter that much.

Just stop. It is an idea that is beginning to occur to a lot of people. After the Trenton conference on a possible fourth jetport site, Mrs. Robert Tatton of Readington Township—who crashed the conference—returned to say, "I seriously question whether we would not be doing New York a favor by standing in the way of some of its commercial growth at this time."

Of course you would, Mrs. Tatton. New York City is, God and Mayor Lindsay know, quite big enough already.

As a citizen of California, I have long opposed the massive California Water Plan, which in its final form will alter the distribution of water from every river in the state. Even the bond issue of $1.75 billion passed by the voters of California in 1960 was not nearly enough to pay for it (as a number of us warned at the time and as has proved, only recently, to be true). In addition it requires northern Californians to pay as much per capita for giving up their water as southern Californians will pay for receiving it.

Primarily, though, my opposition was political and social, based on the fact that—while it was touted as a plan to supply water to arid Los Angeles—it is actually as much a scheme to enrich a few of the state's feudal landholders in the southern San Joaquin Valley; it is also, of course, as massive an ecological rape as an eager group of Engineers has ever successfully sold.

Recently I learned of another negative argument: that according to geologists, the construction of the plan may make earthquakes in California far worse—a dramatic example of the unplanned ecological result. Clay deposits that underlie large areas, it is feared, may become unstable through the application of large quantities of water to the soil through irrigation and reservoir seepage. The fresh water can flush out salt water which now acts as a kind of electrolytic "glue" holding the clay together; the result is what geologists call a "quick clay," which can trigger landslides.

But there is still another question: Suppose Los Angeles simply doesn't get any more water—from the water plan, from the Colorado, from anywhere? Ask the question, and you will be answered with either panic or derision, answered not only by Engineers but by intellectual liberal editorial writers and otherwise sober and intelligent citizens, with projections of population growth: we *must* have the water, they insist, because we will have the people, and we must provide for their needs. Look at these figures.

But if there is not a fourth jetport, then New York will *not* have 65 million air travelers in 1980. And if there is not a California Water Plan, and water shortage becomes a serious problem, then the people will not go to Los Angeles, and some of the people who are there will leave.

Is that bad?

For a few whose profit is based on that population growth, yes, of course. But for the rest of us, and for the nation as a whole, what is lost? Does it matter to the black citizen in Bedford-Stuyvesant whether there is a fourth jetport—to the Mexican-American on the east side of Los Angeles whether there is a water plan?

The economy will decline, the Engineers reply, and *all* the citizens will suffer. An Engineer's answer indeed—because for many citizens, a further decline in the economy is an ungraspable abstraction. For the rest of us, we will suffer, at worst, a temporary dislocation as the population adjusts to the situation (and intelligent planning can even provide for various forms of cushioning against the dislocation). Inconvenience for a short time, yes. But *suffering?*

Not build a fourth jetport? Not construct the California Water Plan? The whole idea is incredibly reactionary (it is, in fact, a thought for California's simplistic Governor Ronald Reagan, if he really wants to save money as much as he says he does). Surely nobody would take such an approach seriously.

But there are people who do.

Around San Francisco Bay, for instance. The Bay is now 40 percent filled in, and threatened by a dozen more plans. An investment group headed by New York's David Rockefeller has proposed an enormous, 3,000-acre development just south of San Francisco, to be constructed on filled land opposite Millbrae,

San Mateo and Burlingame. The local officials of those towns seem able to worry only about the "tax base," the possible (money) cost to their citizens, the enchanting vistas of "growth" and "progress" offered by the plan.

And of course, we have to have the space: look at these figures.

The newest addition to this particular catalogue of nonsense is provided by the Santa Fe Railway, which, unfortunately, owns eight miles of mud flats and tidelands along the east shore of the Bay, between the San Francisco-Oakland Bay Bridge and a spot on the edge of the city of Richmond. Santa Fe has decided that it wants to fill in 1,000 acres of the Bay along this stretch, mostly for apartment towers—to give the East Bay a Chinese wall like Miami's—and shopping centers. Another 1,500 acres will be offered to shoreline cities (Oakland, Emeryville, Berkeley, Albany and Richmond) to develop or not, as they choose.

The proposal, prepared by the planning firm of Victor Gruen Associates, includes an optional "recreation island" for Berkeley, which extends all the way to the "bulkhead line"—an imaginary line a mile and a half offshore which the Corps of Engineers has set, for navigational reasons, as the limit for filling in this area. In this case, as in the case of David Rockefeller's "City in the Bay," the Engineers of the Army turn up wearing white hats for a change. The Corps has announced that there is enough suitable land *not* in the Bay to take care of 14,000,000 people in the Bay Area where 4,000,000 now live—and still leave 30 percent of the land undeveloped.

In the midst of all this, there is now an official organization called the Bay Conservation and Development Commission, a temporary group set up by the state legislature with instructions to come up with a comprehensive plan for the Bay by 1969. The Commission hired a team of young architects and planners, Rai Okamoto and William Liskamm, who studied the values of the Bay for months. They recommended that the entire San Francisco Bay be made a national park before the rest of us idiots ruin it.

In other words: It is time simply to stop.

If we have to stop David Rockefeller, who's going to suffer? Millbrae and San Mateo and Burlingame will survive—and the citizens of those towns who live there mostly because of the marvelous peninsular climate (which depends on the Bay) and the proximity of the Bay's breathtaking beauty will still be there ten or a hundred years from now.

If it is difficult to conceive of an Engineers' horror more massive than the California Water Plan or a pair of dams in the Grand Canyon, come with me to a symposium in Montreal, where Dr. Raymond Nace—a research hydrologist with the Interior Department's Geological Survey—reported with barely disguised anguish on the proposed North American Water and Power Alliance (NAWAPA).

NAWAPA would cost $100 billion. It is a proposal to divert water which now flows to the North Pacific, to the Bering Sea, to the Arctic Ocean and to Hudson Bay. The water would be redistributed to water-short areas in the United States, Canada and Mexico. It would do for all of the northern rivers of the continent what the California Water Plan will do for the rivers of that state. If the plan were completed, Dr. Nace asked, would another $100 billion be needed "to combat unwanted and unforeseen sideeffect phenomena that were not included in the original plan?"

And if you think *that's* bad, hold on. There are proposals for a sea-level canal across Central America, and the plan being pushed by the Corps of Engineers, which wants to build it, calls for using nuclear explosives to "dig" it with. The description is too much for me; listen instead to the renowned ecologist, LaMont Cole:

In that latitude the Pacific Ocean stands higher than the Atlantic by a disputed amount which I believe to average six feet. The tides are out of phase on the two sides of the Isthmus of Panama so the maximum difference in level can be as great as 18 feet. Also, the Pacific is much colder than the Atlantic as a result of current patterns and the upwelling of cold water. If the new canal should move a mass of very cold water into the Caribbean, what might this do to climates, or to sea food industries? Nobody has the information to render an authoritative decision but I have heard suggestions of a new hurricane center, or even diversion of the Gulf Stream with a resultant drastic effect on the climates of all regions bordering the North Atlantic.

After noting that the Suez Canal permitted an interchange of species between the Red Sea and the Mediterranean, and that the Welland Canal let sea lampreys into the upper Great Lakes and thereby ruined fisheries, Dr. Cole goes on to note that the Corps of Engineers figures on using 170 megatons of nuclear charges. That, he notes, would release enough cesium-137 to give everyone on earth, if it were evenly distributed, 26½ times today's maximum permissible whole body dose. Cesium, he continues,

behaves as a gas in a cratering explosion and prevailing winds in the region are from east to west, so the Pacific would presumably be contaminated first. And cesium behaves like potassium in biological food chains so we could anticipate its rapid dissemination among living things.

Especially since, in the meantime, the potassium is disappearing.

This is not just a bad idea. It is a valid, if dramatic, demonstration of the fact that it is time to stop before it's too late, time to insist on stopping the whole Engineers' approach to raping the earth.

The principle applies to virtually everything this book has so far discussed. Bertram C. Raynes, vice president of the Rand Development Corporation (not to be confused with the think-factory RAND Corporation of southern California), insisted at a Congressional hearing in 1966 that the way to stop pollution is to stop pollution. Although he did not use this example, his argument was that if we chose to make it illegal to sell an internal combustion engine after, say, 1972, you can bet that General Motors would come up with another way to power an automobile; but until we do, they won't. On October 1, 1966, *The Milwaukee Journal* made substantially the same point as it expressed the growing popular impatience with pollution: "There have been enough 'studies.' The major polluters are known. The job now is to get them to stop polluting."

"The major sources of polluted waters, ugly refuse heaps, and of a substantial part of the pollution in the atmosphere," Raynes told Congress, "are in the management offices of industrial and municipal plants of all descriptions. It simply is so much cheaper and so much less trouble to dump stuff or vent stuff than it is to take care of it, that production management will dump and vent just so long as it can get away with doing it." You can try to make them want to stop, Raynes said, but we have been doing that and it hasn't worked. What is left is to

force them to take care of their wastes properly. Simply to require that the water they dump be pure, regardless of its condition when they receive it. That the gases they vent be free of pollution. That their spoil doesn't in turn despoil other property or remain ugly, regardless of how poor the area might have been when they undertook their operations. . . . Instead of comforting the public with statements to the effect that "there is no evidence that these pollutants have unfavorable effects upon humans," let's see some evidence that they are definitely not harmful.

When Congressmen brought up the inadequacy of technology to combat pollution in some cases, and asked Raynes whether he thought the laws should be passed anyway, he answered simply, "Necessity has always been the father of technology."

Not long ago, having visited the great ecologist, Eugene Odum, at the University of Georgia, I drove south through the gentle, rolling country of northeast Georgia, renewing a sentimental attachment from previous visits to the area, and then turned west toward Atlanta on U.S. 278. The highway runs from Atlanta to Augusta, across the state; on a beautifully sunny Saturday afternoon, it was probably carrying as much traffic as it ever needs to handle.

But as a driver, I had no problem. I held the car exactly at the speed limit (a Georgia habit left over from the days of the civil rights movement), passed a few cars, was passed by a few. I could without hindrance have driven 10 miles an hour faster. Traffic in the other direction was no heavier. For part of its distance 278 is only two-laned, but it does not wind; the land is flat and vision is clear, and even Saturday afternoon traffic presented no problem. There are few towns on the route, none large enough so that local traffic crowds the highway; you stop at a couple of stop signs, perhaps, and you're on your way. Only at the outskirts of burgeoning Atlanta did the traffic become heavy enough to demand freeway conditions if speed was to be maintained.

But the freeway started long before the traffic needed it. Alongside U.S. 278, the land is being torn to construct Interstate 20 all the way to Augusta: three and four lanes in each direction, with a 70-mile-an-hour speed limit instead of 60, a snap for the Engineers. It is perhaps the most absolutely unnecessary highway I have ever seen.

I tried, driving those uncrowded miles through country I happen to love, to understand why the Engineers are building that highway, where no traffic demands it. One of the official reasons for the interstate system, I know, is "national defense"; I thought of the Chinese hordes swarming up the Savannah River, and caught myself grinning. Congress had voted the system, and Georgia had to have its piece of the pie, whether anybody needed the highway or not. That was all.

The interstate highway system—leaving out all the freeways and thruways and expressways and byways built before it—will, when complete, consist of enough concrete so that, as a parking lot, it could accommodate two-thirds of the automobiles in the United States (it would be 20 miles square). It will take up 1.5 million acres of *new* right of way (the right of way, as opposed to just the concrete, would cover an area one and a half times the size of Rhode Island). It will use up 30 million tons of iron ore to make its steel, plus 18 million tons of coal (from strip mines?) and 6.5 million tons of limestone. The coal, of course, will be combined with oxygen while the concrete covers photosynthetic plants. Its lumber requirements would take all the trees from a 400-square-mile forest.

Who needs it?

The highway program would not, of course, be all that easy to stop; it would, for example, require some changes in the law. Once a highway construction agreement is signed by the Federal highway administrator and a state highway department, the Federal funds must be paid out within two years. If it isn't done by then, the Federal share—which is 90 percent for interstate roads—lapses and is doled out to other states.

That means, in turn, that state highway departments simply cannot get involved in long arguments about routes—it's build it now, or build it never. And the Bureau of Public Roads is putting on all possible pressure to complete the interstate system by 1973; *it's* under fiscal pressure to prefer the cheapest route, and nobody has money left over for beauty or public good or human concern, much less for ecosystems (in May, 1967, Engineers building a four-lane approach road to the Poughkeepsie Mid-Hudson Bridge forcibly evicted Mrs. Elizabeth Collier, then aged eighty-three, from a 148-year-old house; what kind of values does our society have when we can allow that to happen?).

But at least, as I proceeded westward through Georgia and approached Atlanta, I could take some comfort in knowing that Atlanta has had it. A much smaller city, it is already as thoroughly dominated by freeways as Los Angeles. Now the citizens have begun to revolt, as they have in New Orleans and Philadelphia and elsewhere. The Engineers aimed Interstate 485 through the middle of Atlanta's Morningside-Lenox Park area—a middle-class residential section in which many of the present residents still live in the houses they grew up in. Faced with repeated defeat in their attempts to block the highway administratively, the citizens have taken the matter to court.

Al Kuettner, president of the neighborhood group conducting the fight, says, "We haven't been fighting this just as a little neighborhood obstruction thing, but as a means of saving close-in communities in general. If this is not stopped, a large part of Atlanta is going to be ripped up by highways. It's just got to stop somewhere."

The citizens of Atlanta have even recognized that freeways force their own growth patterns on cities, and serve all too often as the walls of ghettos. But mostly, they have simply come to see that there is a time to stop.

In San Francisco, I encountered at a cocktail party a county supervisor who had alienated some supporters and friends by espousing a freeway route that would cut off a corner of Golden Gate Park, ruin the park's Panhandle area, and incidentally wall off a currently integrated area as a ghetto. When I insisted that the freeway should not be built, he answered, "Of course it's bad. But I've looked at the alternatives and we can't afford any of them. We have to move the cars from south of the city to the Golden Gate Bridge."

But we don't. If San Francisco is too crowded for them to drive through, let them take some other route—or leave their cars at home. An aerial photograph of San Francisco shows dramatically the invasion of that world-famous city by freeways to date; it will take little more before the unique beauty that lures thousands of visitors every year will be buried under the concrete tentacles of the freeway system. It is time to stop.

Local columnist Harold Gilliam, among others, has made a number of suggestions for San Francisco, some of which he related to a statement by the San Francisco Department of City Planning that ought to give even an Engineer a reason to think about stopping:

It has been estimated that each additional automobile entering the downtown during the rush hour requires an additional investment in street and parking space amounting to $25,000. The carrying charges on this investment work out to about four dollars per round trip per automobile.

So, Gilliam suggests, if a second deck is to be built on the Golden Gate Bridge as some idiots have suggested, then every car should be charged the bridge toll plus two dollars every time it crosses. That, of course, would not pay for the noise and smog and disruption, as Gilliam notes.

More seriously, he is one of the few critics who recognize that the only way to keep too many automobiles out of downtown San Francisco is to refuse to provide a way for them to get in (although Gilliam has a tendency not to go beyond the sacred growth-rate figures). The city of Fresno, California, has gone further and rebuilt its downtown area so that there is nowhere for automobiles to go. Unfortunately, in that case city planner Victor Gruen, the same man who wants to fill in San Francisco Bay for Santa Fe, has so set up the plan as to concentrate, just outside the area, whatever air pollution Fresno's automobiles might create; but it should also be noted that Fresno is not a "metropolitan area" in the sense that San Francisco is.

The even larger city of New York has increasingly made it more and more difficult for automobiles to operate in central Manhattan, to the point that today you can't park there at all.

Still, according to the city's Transportation Administrator, Arthur E. Palmer, it doesn't seem to hurt "progress": "In 1907, it was found that the average speed of horse-drawn vehicles through the city's streets was 11.5 miles per hour. In 1966 the average speed of motor vehicles through the central business district was 8.5 miles per hour—and during the midday crushes slower still."

Now the cities, still pursuing the phantom values of growth, are talking about air rights over the freeways—another Engineer's idea that ignores, as Engineers could be expected to do, the fact that the area of maximum air pollution from automobile exhausts is the air immediately over a freeway. But instead of simply banning cars from downtown cities, we keep relying on hope. We will add buses. We will build rapid transit systems. We will build monorails or subways or high-rise parking lots.

Leon Moses and Harold Williamson did a study of auto commuters in Chicago. They found out that the city would have to pay drivers 40 or 50 cents a trip to get them to take an "el" or a subway. If public transportation were free, they found, fewer than one-fifth of the drivers would leave their cars home and use it. But they would damned well use it—and demand that it be made adequate—if it were illegal to bring a car into downtown Chicago.

Stopping—just stopping—would not be easy; and in some cases it's expensive and complicated enough to refute any charge that it is a simplistic notion. We have already mentioned both the phosphorus-removal process in use at Lake Tahoe—which costs about $100 for every acre-foot of water treated—and Kimberly-Clark's $2 million pollution treatment installation at their Mount Shasta mill. The whole idea would, in fact, demand the best brains that our legislatures and public administrators can command; it would mean whole new sets of plans for every city, every region, every state. It would mean—in some cases it would force—wholesale rechannelings of wealth. It would mean that every real estate speculator, every labor union leader, every department store magnate, even every taxicab owner would have to reevaluate his future and the future of whatever organization he might direct.

It may even be that an attorney friend of mine was right.

He is about my age, a bright attorney employed by a major corporation; active in politics and civic affairs, to which he unselfishly gives an astonishing amount of time and effort; genuinely dedicated to a better life for his fellow citizens. At a meeting of a civic organization in 1967, I spoke to the group about some of the ideas in the articles that preceded this book and mentioned my conviction that the only viable answer is simply to stop. After the meeting, my attorney friend greeted me with a sardonic grin and a remark something like, "Okay—so now the rest of us have to go out and work on those little things that can *really* be accomplished."

I know the feeling; I, too, have played on the political fields. And if I sometimes believe, for example, that the frustration of our ghettos is so strong that no liberal palliatives can quiet it, that doesn't keep me from wanting a rat control bill so that black babies won't be gnawed in the meantime.

But just as the pressures in the ghetto cannot be relieved by well-meaning people who devote all of their efforts to rat control or house-painting projects, so, too, there is a fuse on that population bomb, and it simply will not do to shrug off the difficult as impossible and to devote ourselves to this year's candidacy or next month's Heart Fund drive. We not only *should* stop; we *must* stop.

And some of the "costs" are not costs at all. What New York would lose through not building its rubber jetport, or any other, some other community would gain. What Los Angeles would lose if the California Water Plan were not pursued, some other community would gain. There is enough that needs to be done—schools and hospitals are the usual examples, and they will serve to make the point—to provide work for the building trades.

Stopping, of course, does not mean freezing. To stop the Engineers, to stop the nonsense of building always from a projected and totally mythical growth rate, is simultaneously to provide the opportunity for fantastic strides in new directions. "Progress" in so overcrowded a world may be a word-magic luxury we have to forego; but opportunity opens before us as never before.

XIV · CHILDREN OF SUN
AND GRASS

ON WASHINGTON'S BIRTHDAY in 1967, Secretary of Agriculture
Orville Freeman joined the rest of us reactionaries who think it's
about time to put the wagons into a circle and fight. The growth
of urban masses, he said, and the concentration of industry into
metropolitan areas, are "national idiocy."

"Seventy percent of our population live on . . . one percent
of the continental land mass," he said, and "insuperable problems,
including riots and waste disposal problems, have been created."

What to do? With the increasing mechanization of agriculture,
he said, and with the increasing amount of farmland now passing
out of agricultural use, the sensible thing is for industries to move
back into the areas that once were the hearts of farm belts. Defense contracts ought to be shifted, at least to some extent, out
of California—including contracts for food supplies.

Freeman used San Francisco as an example of a city which,
like virtually all others, spends much of its money and energy
trying to attract new industry when in fact it would be better off
without it, and wouldn't suffer economically if it existed primarily
as a service industry center. "You have problems," he told San
Franciscans, "of waste disposal . . . crime . . . smog . . . these
things have been caused by overcrowded urban conditions."

Shifting the defense contracts would probably appeal to Raymond Dasmann, who, ignoring mythical growth-rate projections,
took the problem to the state level:

Immigrants [to California] could be discouraged, or guided to areas
where their presence would not create new problems. This could be
done without infringing upon any human freedoms, through a process
of not planning to accommodate them, through not encouraging the

growth of industry or the expansion of other employment opportunities.

Throughout this book, I have pleaded for an ecological sense of what we are, of how we are tied to, are inherently *a part of,* the planet on which we live. I have posited against such a sense the "engineering mentality," the straight-line problem solver—and for most of the book, I have tried to portray some of the more idiotic results of leaving the United States to the rapine of the Engineers. But there is a danger, perhaps, that in emphasizing the ecological conscience and the crucial need to conserve genetic information, I may leave the impression that the endangered egret is more important than the hungry child, that the rocky crag under which we spend an idyllic weekend is more important than the city in which we spend the bulk of our lives.

Perhaps it is a failing of ecologists, which I have somehow absorbed along with the details of their work. At least one economist, Kenneth Boulding, thinks it is, and said so to a group of ecologists; but his criticism was that the ecological sense of which I write is more important than many ecologists recognize:

It seems to me the ideal of ecologists is a world of ghosts who just won't leave any trace, who won't make any paths, won't even disturb the air. This is so idiotic.

Here we have man, by far the most interesting species on this planet. If you develop the ecological idea, as I suggested, and start studying social species, criminals, the role structure, the degradation of urban environments as well as natural environments, you have a key to enormous numbers of these problems; and you are just not using it.

I am mad at you. I am really mad at you!

Of course I want to save the Grand Canyon from the Engineers. Anyone with any sense at all, ecological or otherwise, wants that. But beyond that I am convinced that we will not save the Grand Canyon or the roseate spoonbill or anything else worth saving unless we can save our cities, and our entire way of living together. For ours is the world's best chance to do it, and if we fail, we will become not man but some other creature adapted to two square feet of space and an anthill life—if, indeed, we survive at all.

Already, most Americans do not like large cities, so there is a place to start—to start stopping, if the phrase can be allowed —that may at least be popular. "It will take some doing," says political scientist Robert Dahl, "but we do not have to end up all jammed together in the asphalt desert of the large metropolis."

A 1966 Gallup Poll says that in cities of more than 500,000 people, the majority of residents would rather live in a smaller town, or in a suburb, or on a farm. In the suburbs and smaller towns, however, few people want to move to the city. And on being told that their own community will probably double in population, three out of four Americans expressed distress.

With a little imagination, we could exploit this feeling and make important other gains as well. Dr. Athelstan Spilhaus of the Institute of Technology at the University of Minnesota has seriously suggested that we build, from scratch, an "experimental city" of some 250,000 people or so, deliberately trying to incorporate every advance of technology we know about, in order to attempt to discover what actions, however drastic, might help to solve the problems of the cities that already exist. Other scientists have expressed enthusiasm at the idea, and Spilhaus points out that we build the equivalent of twelve cities that size every year anyway—except that we do it haphazardly, through additions to existing metropolitan areas.

Spilhaus' experimental city ought to be built (and really built, not "built" in a computer which can't, because we can't, anticipate the myriad "ecological" reactions of the city and the citizens), if only to demonstrate once and for all that we *can* do all the things the Engineers and industrialists and private utility companies insist we *can't* do—including exist without freeways, without most pollution, without motor vehicles in our central cities, and without completely tearing apart our ecologies.

The planning for the Spilhaus city, in fact, is already under way at the University of Minnesota, backed—although meagerly —by several Federal agencies. If we can shake the engineering mentality, we can build it virtually overnight; it will cost millions— but it costs millions every year to jam more and more people into the cities we have.

London has already, in fact, decided to stop. A five-mile green belt around the city has been declared inviolate, and the British Government has built eight new towns outside the belt—not suburbs, but towns. Theodore Osmundson, president at the time of the American Society of Landscape Architects, visited one of them, the town of Harlow:

This completely new city houses 80,000 people and is planned to be self-sufficient economically and socially. It provides employment for 80 percent of its working population, schools, hospitals, parks and has over 100 social or recreational organizations.

There is no major commute highway or rail connection with London, as none is needed. There are no significant number [*sic*] of commuters to demand them.

Can you imagine the Engineers of the United States allowing a population center of 80,000 people to exist that close to so large a city without a major highway or rail connection?

Other, related planning in Europe has led to similar towns like Tapiola in Finland, to the virtual elimination of slums in Madrid, to a new residential community at Mantes in France. "There seemed to be," Osmundson wrote, "a far greater interest in building livable communities for people than in worrying about who was going to earn a profit or what kind of unpopular political label could be placed on a program."

Another San Francisco Bay Area planner, Daniel C. Cook, is writing a book about his proposed planned community, Cosmopolitas, which he says can be duplicated and put down in 100 sites. His design is for a circular city, and as it happens I think it looks a little too much like another Engineers' dream; but Cook is thinking, and thinking in concepts outside the engineering mentality. Harold Gilliam writes, for instance: "Recalling the Homestead Act of 1870, which offered 160 acres to anyone who would settle and cultivate the land, Cook hit upon the idea of an Urban Homestead Act to attract settlers to the new cities by offering free homesites. Tax advantages would provide further inducements to both residents and industries."

The idea, of course, would apply to any new city, not only to Cook's (and must—as some planners forget—be implemented in such a way as to assure a genuine lack of racial discrimination).

Cosmopolitas would hold 1,000,000 people, and that may be too many. Ask a contented dweller in a large city why he likes living there, and you are apt to get answers relating to cultural matters. But, says Dahl, that may be an illusion:

On the basis of his research on American cities, [Otis Dudley] Duncan estimates that the requisite population base for a library of "desirable minimum professional standards" is 50,000–75,000, for an art museum, 100,000, "with a somewhat higher figure for science and historical museums." Yet, even though larger cities have larger libraries, the circulation of library books per capita markedly decreases with size of city. There is also a negative correlation between city size and per capita museum attendance.

The implication is clear that the advantages of the large library and the large museum are to a small proportion of the urban population. Wilbur Thompson has a way to deal with that. Build the American Harlows or Spilhaus cities close enough together, he suggests, so that—while they will be independent cities and have space between them—they could co-sponsor, in groups, such things as large museums, major hospitals and professional athletic teams.

I am not a city planner—and I don't particularly want to be. I don't know, for example, whether any of these proposals, or any combination of them, would provide the cultural *diversity* that is a part of the pleasure I derive from living in a city. Although I live across the Bay at the moment, I prefer San Francisco with its evolving history of Irish, Italian, Greek, Latin, Portuguese and black American subcultures. This is, perhaps, not a problem for the Finns of Tapiola, but I would fear for it in Cosmopolitas, and I find in the preservation of cultural information an analogy to the conservation of genetic information.

I can foresee, too, a racist misuse of the entire concept. Little will be gained from an ecological viewpoint if a predominantly white community decides to turn to deliberate limits on its own growth—just as black immigration starts to rise.

And those who most enthusiastically hail Cosmopolitas or the Spilhaus city are apt to forget that to be viable—and ecologically meaningful—those cities must include and provide for the unemployed as well as the employed, the poorly educated as well as the highly trained, the poverty-stricken as well as the affluent, and the black and brown as well as the white. Otherwise they are—as they are often made to seem in the writings of some architects and planners—creatures of the unconscious racism that, not long ago, so frightened a Presidential commission. They will be not American cities far closer to an ecological ideal but merely well-planned white suburbs, farther away.

It would be as silly—if the ecological point of view is going to be applied to problems other than saving the ebony spleenwort— to build a Cosmopolitas without planning for *racial* ecology as it would be to overlook problems of water supply or air pollution. It would be ecologically as well as socially criminal to seize on the idea of being free from growth-rate planning, and to begin to think of limits on population crowding in a given area, and then to use that concept as a high-sounding excuse for discrimination against a racial minority. It is a point easy for whites in America to overlook in such a discussion as this one, but it is one that should never be far from our minds as long as racism is the deepest illness of American society.

These plans, though, are not here because I endorse them, but because they prove that not all Americans are Engineers. There is plenty of idea material around; the opportunities to shake off the weight of the projected growth rate and to plan intelligently for the use of our land are open. And only when we have so spread our population—and thus its recreation—can we have any hope of retaining whatever ecological conscience we possess.

That won't be easy, either—as is evident from a letter written by James Rouse of Community Research and Development, Inc., of Baltimore, builders of the planned new town of Columbia, Maryland:

We are building a new city midway between Washington and Baltimore. . . . It has been one of our goals to respect and dignify the land in the course of planning and development and thus to enhance the enrichment of the new city. . . . We have provided for the preservation of the stream valleys; the building of five lakes; the proper forestation of natural wooded areas, and the building of parks and bridle paths.

All of this has been done . . . with insufficient information regarding the ecological conditions which would be affected. It would be wonderful, for example, to have really substantial knowledge as to the role of water in the environment. The process of building the many lakes which we propose in Columbia is a difficult and tedious one. We are confident that the creation of lakes is a worthwhile effort; but because of the lack of general knowledge as to their broader values to the environment, we seem to have few allies in the process. The same general problem pervades the entire city-building process.

You can be sure that no such problems concern the Engineers who are proposing to build David Rockefeller's "City in the Bay" near San Francisco, or most of the Engineers constructing most of the projects across America.

Our planning has a long way to go; we have a lot yet to learn; and unless we stop the Engineers, we will never have a chance. We talk of food for the exploding population of the world, for example—and only within the last few years have we found that the Nile basin, one of the world's most fertile areas and one about which our knowledge goes back for centuries, is apparently not fertilized in the way men have assumed for all these ages.

We talk of preserving some contact with our natural heritage—and Russell Train tells us that pesticides have wiped out butterflies in most of Europe. "I wonder," he asks, "if your grandchildren will ever see a butterfly?" And he adds, "Does it make any difference?"

In the meantime, we have to take the problems away from the Engineers. They will never solve the problem of our wastes, because to them it *is* a waste problem, not a problem of recovering the content of the pile for reuse—which we *must* learn to do, as another part of our legacy to the world that may yet, despite our past follies, survive.

Nor can we make the mistake of turning over to them the new problems that a halt to progress creates. We cannot get from them a way to make ecologically sensible use of our land and what it bears. We can, however, do some other things. For one, we can borrow a concept from the local treatment of land use. "Everyone agrees," says Eugene Odum, "on the principle of zoning in cities, since a given piece of land cannot serve as both factory and residential sites. Why not then zone paper mills so as to place them on the part of the landscape where water and airflows provide the best waste disposal possibilities?"

Ecologist John Buckley of the Interior Department suggested it for estuarine lands like the southern shore of Long Island:

We may need to come around soon to a kind of landscaping zoning, a decision that for the estuaries the principle of multiple use won't work. An estuary can be used either for this purpose or for something else. Carrying it to an extreme, clearly if one dredges and builds industrial sites, this is one valuable use for an estuary. At the same time, you can't expect the shallow waters along the edge of it to serve as a nursery ground for shrimp and other aquatic resources. This is a choice that you have to make, and it seems to me that a zoning concept is the way to make it.

Industrialist Bertram Raynes goes further, and suggests that if we really want to save America, we could in effect zone it all:

Zoning controls should include ecological considerations as well as the tax duplicate. As an example, homes or businesses should not be allowed to be built on flood plains, flooded out, and then to use their plight to push for the damming of free-flowing rivers. Natural drainage areas should not be automatically assigned as fill areas or garbage dumps and so forth. Whole riverfronts or lakefronts should not be given over to industry and commerce without the respite of green areas. Natural areas should not be abandoned to indiscriminate abuse of their land, water and air—and simply thereafter be called the heavy industrial zone.

Actually, it is time now to go even beyond that concept—to put paper mills not "where water and air flows provide the best waste disposal possibilities" but where it will be easiest for them, with due regard to other ecological situations, to conduct their operation without any waste disposal which is not subject to reclamation before it becomes a pollutant.

We take it for granted that we can control the waters of the earth and master the height of its mountains—and we take it equally for granted that we can do nothing about the number or location of our automobiles, our factories or our populations.

We insist that we dare not interfere with whatever will make a few people richer—and we insist that we dare not use our power to make all of our people better able to live decent lives.

If, for most of this book, I have avoided the word "conservation," it is because what I am concerned with is what Raymond Dasmann calls "land use and population planning in the widest sense," and because, as he proceeds to point out, that sense "goes far beyond the scope of what the older, traditional conservation movement has encompassed. It is, however, an integral part of modern conservation [which must include] a rational, ecologically-oriented national policy on land use and population."

Dr. Eugene Odum, in Athens, Georgia, sat back in a comfortable chair after we had finished luncheon in the state university's Center for Continuing Education, and mused about the engineering mentality in broad, metaphorical terms.

"We still think of ourselves," he said to me, "as waging a war against nature, conquering the land. But the war is over. We've won. We know that nature is defeated now before the advance of man—we have the weapons to fight the forest and flood, the storm and the heat. We are even conquering space."

He leaned forward, suddenly serious. "But when we defeat an enemy in battle—when we defeated Germany and Japan in World War II—do we simply go on killing and slaughtering? Of course not. We have defeated nature. We must do as we do with a defeated nation—help nature, and recognize that we must live with nature, from now on, forever. The war is over."

The war against nature is over. But it is time for the war against the Engineers. It is time to remind them of who we are: creatures, as Stegner says,

made of water and chemicals but the children of sun and grass, and cousin by warm blood to birds and mammals. Though it is necessary for our survival to husband resources, it is necessary for our emotional health to husband natural things, and places where they may be known.

We must teach them, too, what we mean when we speak of the ecological conscience—no longer merely a sense of responsibility toward the land and the rivers and the trees, but a whole way of thinking constantly in environmental terms, a way of thinking that embraces cities as well as mountains, hungry and emotionally stunted black children as well as the roseate spoonbill. It is all one—we are all one—and if there is anything to be learned from standing on Glacier Peak without an open-pit mine in the foreground or from watching a wary anhinga in the Everglades, it is that.

We must learn—even if it is beyond the Engineers to learn—that we *must* save our ecosystems, not only because they may be pretty or because man may have a need to get away for recreation or meditation or the simple inhalation of fresh air, but because we may, someday, vitally need what they contain—and we cannot preserve even a single life form in its true manifestation if we take it from its natural home. Biologist Julian Huxley, for instance, writes that

animals do not reveal the higher possibilities of their nature and behavior, nor the full range of their individual diversity, except in such conditions of freedom. Captivity cages minds as well as bodies, and rigid experimental procedure limits the range of performance; while freedom liberates the creatures' capacities and permits the observer to study their fullest developments.

And still we persist and allow our servants to persist—as we allow the Navy, for example, to continue to use San Miguel Island, off the coast of California, as a missile target, although we know it is one of the last homes of the rare sea elephant. We must, somehow, pound it into the heads of the Engineers that we *need* the sea elephant. Dr. John Cantlon of the National Science Foundation calls it "the purely practical argument that these arrays of organisms harbor vast amounts of potentially useful information," and goes on:

It would be utterly repugnant to all except the hard-core anti-intellectual to encourage a madman to tour world libraries randomly destroying books. Such a practice permitted to continue unabated would surely result in the total loss of some works and the disappearance of the local translations of others. The genetic information contained in species populations as well as the ecological information content of the total functioning array of organisms in an ecological system represents an irreplaceable resource.

Or, as Theodore Edison charmingly put it in a communication he sent to me, "Would it not be a tragedy to banish *all* classical music from the metropolitan area, *without possibility of recall,* just because rock and roll now seems to be more popular?"

Finally, for those few Congressmen and other legislators who are beginning to gain some understanding of the harm that Engineers can do, we need not only to provide support, but to make sure that they do not confuse the understanding of ecological relationships with mere systems engineering, the simple measuring in quantitative terms of various items and relationships.

"Such approaches," Dr. Odum wrote recently, "will undoubtedly be increasingly useful, since they are particularly applicable to computer programming, but they are still only technics. We have so little basic understanding of environmental interaction that we do not yet know how to set up units or compartments so as to take advantage of computer technology."

And so we must take the time to learn. If the world is to survive, then let it say that we—the momentary inhabitants of the only remaining continent where it can be done—preserved and enhanced its legacy. If it is not to survive, then at least let us perish in an activity more dignified than surrender.

The freedom of the pike, Tawney said, is the death of the minnow. The freedom of the builder of projects, the growth-rate planner, the rapacious Engineer, is the certain death of man.

NOTES

BECAUSE of frequent use, three sources are referred to in the notes by shorthand designation.

Senate Hearings refers to hearings in April, 1966, before the Committee on Interior and Insular Affairs of the United States Senate. The hearings were on a bill by Senator Gaylord Nelson to create an ecological research program within the Department of the Interior; as I write, the bill is still pending. It is potentially one of the most civilized and important pieces of legislation ever proposed.

House Hearings refers to a series of 1966 hearings by the Subcommittee on Science, Research and Development of the Committee on Science and Astronautics of the United States House of Representatives. These hearings dealt generally with questions of pollution and waste, but occasionally ventured beyond those limits.

"Darling and Milton" refers to F. Fraser Darling and John P. Milton, eds., *Future Environments of North America* (Garden City, New York: Natural History Press, 1966). This is one of those invaluable symposia that bring together summaries of the major work currently being done in a particular field, with participation by most of the leaders in that field. In addition to a number of formal papers, the book includes transcriptions of several extemporaneous discussions by many of the world's leading ecologists. I have used it as the treasure-house of examples it is.

Reference in the notes for Chapter III to "C-111" is to a statement, so headed, issued by the National Park Service, Department of the Interior, on September 30, 1966.

Portions of Chapter V concerning the Cascades can be supplemented by two excellent articles by Paul Brooks. "The Fight for America's Alps" (*The Atlantic Monthly,* February, 1967) is on the Cascades generally, and "A Copper Company vs. the North Cascades" (*Harper's,* September, 1967) deals with the specific question of the proposed Kennecott mine. I did not use either article in preparing the chapter, but only because I found them too late.

Material in Chapter VII not otherwise annotated is from *House Hearings,* from publications of the Federal Water Pollution Control Administration, or from a superb article by John Bird, "Our Dying Waters," in the April 23, 1966, *Saturday Evening Post.*

The historical section beginning Chapter VIII is based on information provided by the Wilderness Society (see *The Living Wilderness,* Spring, 1966), but checked directly with the Interior Department. In the notes for Chapter VIII, reference to *The Living Wilderness,* unless otherwise specified, is to that Spring, 1966, issue–a special issue on the Great Smoky Mountains.

Chapter X relies heavily on *The Sierra Club Bulletin,* July–August 1966 ("Why Grand Canyon Should Not Be Dammed"), and on Crutchfield (see first note for p. 124). I went over the *Bulletin* article with its author, Hugh Nash, who kindly allowed access to his sources, and where there might have been any question I checked other sources. In a few cases I have different figures–always in the direction of least damage (*e.g.,* the *Bulletin* gives the maximum depth of the Bridge Canyon Lake as 650 feet; I used 600, the most conservative figure I found).

Information relating directly to the dams, if not otherwise supported, is from the *Bulletin;* other information, especially about proposed water switches from northwest to southwest, is from Crutchfield, from whom I also borrowed a couple of arguments I hadn't thought of.

Facts in Chapter XI about the Great Swamp of New Jersey, its history and its wildlife, are taken unless otherwise indicated from "The Great Swamp," a pre-acquisition brochure published by the North American Wildlife Foundation (but undated), and from the Interior Department's 1966 proposal for the M. Hartley Dodge Wilderness Area.

I: WHO NEEDS A SWAMP?

Page 13

Georgia-Pacific: On the Passamaquoddys, see David Welsh, "Brothers of Passamaquodia," *Ramparts,* March, 1967. On Little Stony Point, *The New York Times,* January 12 and 13, 1967. On eagle studies, Michael Frome, "The Politics of Conservation," *Holiday,* February, 1967, and *The San Francisco Sunday Examiner and Chronicle,* November 12, 1967. On the California coast, the Sierra Club and the Save-the-Redwoods League have mountains of data too extensive to cite; see for example *The San Francisco Sunday Examiner and Chronicle,* November 26, 1967.

Page 14

"*. . . a periodical devoted to*

. . .": It's called *Water Control News* and is officially published by Commerce Clearing House.

Pages 14–15

salt marshes: The Odum quotation is from Claire L. Schelske and Eugene P. Odum, "Mechanisms Maintaining High Productivity in Georgia Estuaries," *Proceedings of the Gulf and Caribbean Fisheries Institute, 14th Annual Session,* November, 1961. The value of the salt marshes is described, in a publication both easier to read and easier to obtain, by Dr. Odum in "The Role of Tidal Marshes in Estuarine Production," published and distributed by the New York State Conservation Department.

Page 15

"*What good is a salt marsh?*":

Senator Gaylord Nelson, during the *Senate Hearings*, remarked: "I have a lawyer friend who had a scientist friend who spent all of his time studying the spider, and one day the lawyer asked him, 'What good are spiders?' and he said, 'They are interesting, and may I ask, what good are you?' "

"*. . . the biological world . . .*": The quotation is from Ian Mc-Taggart Cowan, "Management, Response and Variety," in Darling and Milton. Dr. Cowan is a leading animal ecologist.

land classifications: The quotation is from the minutes of the March 3, 1967, regular meeting of the Resources Agency, Department of Water Resources, California Water Commission. The meeting was held in Napa, California.

goats and flowers: The quotation is from a personal communication to the author from Ken Turner of Sacramento, a civil engineer specializing in the development of water resources.

good engineers: William Hammond Hall, first state engineer of California, was one of the founders of the Sierra Club. Those were the days. Hall was also one of the men responsible for the creation of Golden Gate Park in San Francisco, which the state's Engineers now want to tear up for a freeway.

Mild conflict among engineers about whether they should be concerned even with pollution is manifested in Ed Seiler's column in *Air Conditioning, Heating and Ventilating* for August, 1968. Mr. Seiler, on the side of social concern, goes so far as to list in detail, with dates, 35 technical courses on air pollution being given during 1968 and 1969 by the Public Health Service, and to urge engineers to participate.

Page 16

"the engineering of consent": The phrase was used many years ago as the title of a *Reporter* article by Robert Bendiner, who said that a public relations firm had so defined its own function.

the "engineering mentality": This is what some writers mean by "the computer mentality," but that's much too narrow a phrase and makes the whole thing seem too recent a development. For a fuller exposition in a startlingly different context, see this author's "Think Factory De Luxe" in *The Nation*, February 14, 1959. As will be seen in the late chapters of the book, I mean to include all planners who start by taking projected growth rates as unalterable, given facts; all economists and/or industrialists who assume given economic limits on any venture; and anyone in a position of any power who thinks that "bigger" means "richer" or "better" or both.

Page 17

Halprin: The quotation is from an interview in *Science and Technology*, November, 1967, in which Halprin describes the Engineer as "a unipurpose kind of animal," and adds that Engineers "don't understand the impact of what they are doing—or aren't interested in the impact." The entire interview is interesting, and I am grateful to Tom Crowe, who called my attention to it.

deer: See first of all Lorus and

Margery Milne, *The Balance of Nature* (New York: Alfred A. Knopf, 1960)—incidentally a delightful book for an adult or for any bright high school student. Some of Chapter II is based on it. Cougars are now protected in Florida (where they are called panthers) and South Dakota; the three West Coast states and British Columbia have removed bounties. As recently as September, 1967, however, Wallace McGregor of the California Department of Fish and Game said that proposed legislation in that state will make the cougar a "game animal" and will create cougar tags. Outdoor columnist Bud Boyd of *The San Francisco Chronicle* noted (September 19, 1967) that "whenever the State offers tags, tickets or special permits to shoot anything with hair on it, the hunters get in line." McGregor was quoted as saying that California has between 600 and 1,000 cougar; the state is notoriously overpopulated with deer.

On the predators mentioned, see Victor H. Calahane's *Cougar, Grizzly and Wolf in North America,* published in 1964 by the New York Zoological Society.

The quotation about dividing the world is from Durward L. Allen, professor of wildlife ecology at Purdue University. From his paper, "The Preservation of Endangered Habitats and Vertebrates of North America" (in Darling and Milton), a fuller quotation may be helpful. Noting that the gray wolf (*Canis lupus*) is in good enough shape in Canada, Dr. Allen goes on: ". . . the several hundred wolves now found in northern Minnesota constitute our only breeding population.

There the situation appears precarious, since Minnesota still pays a bounty. . . . The famed Boundary Waters Canoe Area might logically function as a retreat of the wolf, but this country has experienced a rapidly growing influx of snow mobiles which traverse lakes and portages far to the interior, contributing to a build-up of bounty hunting. While this situation exists in the Superior National Forest, it is notable that on the Canadian side, in Quetico Provincial Park, the only legal wolf hunting is by Indians, and no bounty is paid. . . . Biologically, the wolf can only help to preserve deer range and other features of the canoe country in a naturally productive condition . . . [but the maintenance of such a condition] could come about only if a portion of the area, at least, were under a 'wilderness' classification."

Page 18

". . . *what they think is Pinchot*": The correct quotation, according to Michael Frome (in the *Holiday* article cited above), is "Conservation means the wise use of the earth and its resources for the lasting good of men. Conservation is the foresighted utilization, preservation and/or renewal of forests, waters, lands and minerals, for the greatest good of the greatest number for the longest time."

Muir and Pinchot: Raymond Dasmann's *The Destruction of California* (New York: The Macmillan Company, 1965) contains a brief description of the actual clash between Muir and Pinchot over construction of Hetch Hetchy Dam in Yosemite National Park.

II: THE BUG OF BERMUDA

Page 20

American industrialist: The story of the Bermuda businessman is from Lorus and Margery Milne, *The Balance of Nature* (cited in note for p. 17).

Page 21

Bermuda's imported bananas: And according to an Associated Press dispatch from Johannesburg, published in *The San Francisco Examiner* for May 28, 1967, South Africa now imports lions—from Britain and Continental Europe.

crocodiles: The effects of crocodile hunting in Africa are from *The Balance of Nature,* mentioned above.

Page 22

learning a little ecology: See *The Bulletin of the Atomic Scientists* for most of the 1950s; Ralph Lapp's *The Voyage of the Lucky Dragon* (New York: Harper and Brothers, 1958); and Eugene P. Odum, "The New Ecology," *BioScience,* Vol. 14, No. 7, 1964.

Also among people who quickly learn a little ecology are keepers of aquaria. In his *King Solomon's Ring* (New York: Thomas Y. Crowell Company, 1952)—another book which any bright high school student can enjoy and perhaps the best book for conveying what we will later call a "sense" of ecology—Konrad Lorenz notes what happens when "children and adults alike are unable to resist the temptation of slipping just one more fish into the container, the capacity of whose green plants is already overburdened with animals.

And just this one more fish may be the final straw that breaks the camel's back. With too many animals in the aquarium, a lack of oxygen ensues. Sooner or later some organism will succumb to this and its death may easily pass unnoticed. The decomposing corpse causes an enormous multiplication of bacteria in the aquarium, the water becomes turbid, the oxygen content decreases rapidly, then further animals die and, through this vicious circle, the whole of our carefully tended little world is doomed" [Marjorie Kerr Wilson translation from German]. Not because of one extra fish, but for other, related reasons, the same thing can happen in much larger bodies of water; see Chapter VII.

DDT in Clear Lake: Details are in a Senate speech by Senator Gaylord Nelson, *Congressional Record,* July 12, 1966.

concentration: It isn't necessarily biological, either; an oenophile, for instance, may decide to "concentrate" out of his environment and into his cellar all the Château D'Issan 1962 he can afford. It's pretty much the same thing, except that biologically it's usually not so voluntary a practice. The radioactive clams I just happen to know about; the radiologists in question were in San Francisco. Wesley Marx, however, mentions the incident in *The Frail Ocean* (New York: Coward-McCann, 1967), and Marx also mentions one of the best-known examples of similar concentration: the fact that the harvesting of mussels, clams and other shellfish is prohibited in California between May and September—because they concentrate toxins which come from certain Pacific Coast dinoflagellates.

Page 23

Strontium 90: The Sr⁹⁰ cycle was widely publicized in the 1950s. See for example Lapp (cited in first note, p. 22).

wild geese: The example is from Dr. Eugene Odum's *Ecology,* cited in the Foreword. So is the quotation a few lines further on.

Pages 23–24

The Office of Science and Technology: The quotation is from the prepared statement by OST Deputy Director Colin M. MacLeod in *Senate Hearings.*

Page 24

amounts spent on research: Dr. Galler's statement is from *Senate Hearings.*

gravid rose aphids: Dr. Fosberg's spontaneous statement is quoted from Darling and Milton. There's a familiar dirty joke about alligators that makes the same point.

hawks and owls: This example is from Robert and Leona Train Rienow, *Moment in the Sun* (New York: Dial Press, 1967), a book that makes a good companion for this one.

elk in Yellowstone: The example is from Peter Farb's "National Parks: Noisy, Crowded Crisis," in *Call of the Vanishing Wild,* a collection of articles written for *The Christian Science Monitor* in 1966 and published in booklet form in 1967.

Page 25

Long Island oysters: Odum's *Ecology* again.

mussels: Odum again, but a different work: "Relationships between Structure and Function in the Ecosystem," *Japanese Journal of Ecology,* August, 1962.

niches: Back to Odum's *Ecology.* The italics are his.

Page 26

medical research and niches: Dr. Stanley A. Cain, "Biotope and Habitat," in Darling and Milton. Dr. Hans Zinsser (in *Rats, Lice and History;* Boston: Little, Brown and Company, 1935) pointed out with regard to the control of diphtheria that "we are just beginning to observe the return of excessively toxic and deadly cases, reported in increasing numbers from Central Europe. It is not at all unlikely that the successful control of an epidemic disease through several generations may interfere with the more permanently effective, though far more cruel, processes by which nature gradually immunizes a race." Which does *not* mean that we shouldn't control diphtheria—only that it's nice to know what we're doing.

Dr. Zinsser, by the way, makes an interesting medico-ecological point about another feared ailment: "It has often been claimed that since so many brilliant men have had syphilis, much of the world's greatest achievement was evidently formulated in brains stimulated by the cerebral irritation of an early general paresis." There must be an easier way.

DDT: Rachel Carson, of course,

wrote *Silent Spring* (Boston: Houghton Mifflin Company, 1962). Information on Antarctic penguins is in *House Hearings* and in Marx (cited above).

nitrogen: Dr. LaMont Cole of Cornell explained the nitrogen problem to Congress; see *Senate Hearings*. In an address ("Can the World Be Saved?") to a symposium on human ecology and environmental pollution during the 1967 convention of the American Association for the Advancement of Science (New York City, December 27, 1967), Dr. Cole noted that many other elements are necessary to life, "and a few, notably phosphorus and potassium, are gradually washing into the oceans to remain there in sediments until major geologic upheavals, or possibly human ingenuity, can retrieve them and so perpetuate life on earth." Dr. Odum's *Ecology* also describes the gradual disappearance of phosphorus.

In the same address, Dr. Cole noted, with regard to carbon dioxide (see p. 28 *et seq.*), that every Boeing 707 in flight releases about 1.3 tons of water and 2.6 tons of CO_2 every two minutes. Other jets are comparable. See page 190, add in 720s, 727s and the products of the other aircraft manufacturers, and do your own calculating. The non-jet airplane's contamination, by the way, may be a little worse per ton because it flies at lower altitudes.

Page 27

limiting factors: Odum's *Ecology* provided the trout example. I haven't made any attempt to describe fully the ramifications of the concept, nor the many ways—some of them not so obvious—in which it works. But there's a library in your town. In Darling and Milton, Pierre Danserau ("Ecological Impact and Human Ecology") credits E. Huguet del Villan with formulation of what Danserau calls ecology's "law of factorial control."

Ovington: Dr. Ovington, of the Australian National University at Canberra, made these remarks during an informal colloquy at the North American Habitats Study Conference, which is the meeting recorded in Darling and Milton.

Page 28

carbon dioxide: The insurance executive is Dr. Thomas F. Malone, vice president and director of research of the Travelers Insurance Company. His testimony, including the description of Dr. Manabe's work, is in *House Hearings*. In Darling and Milton, bioclimatologist Paul Waggoner, of the Connecticut Agricultural Experiment Station, adds this wry comment in a conversation: "The presence of pollution in the air does decrease the amount of light reaching the earth and does conserve water. This is a pretty tough way to conserve water." And in the same conference, Firman E. Bear, in his paper, "Highly Productive Lands of North America," points out that a CO_2 increase may make some plants, including food plants, "grow more luxuriantly."

Page 29

ecosystems: A carefully described example of an unusual and complex ecosystem is Chapter Four of Wesley Marx's *The Frail Ocean* (cited above), which deals with kelp forests off the California coast.

Page 29

space capsule: I first had all this pointed out to me by Dr. Odum in conversation; it was set forth a few days later by Dr. Wallace O. Fenn in a newspaper feature distributed by the World Book Encyclopedia Science Service; I tore it out of *The Miami Herald* for February 5, 1967. The propellants aren't the safest things around, either; an official Air Force chart, "Air Quality Criteria for Liquid Propellants," says of oxygen difluoride: "The extreme toxicity and insidious character of OF_2 makes it imperative to exclude its inhalation by personnel"—an excellent example also of governmental prose.

For a full discussion of how the engineering and bureaucratic mentalities combined to bring about the Apollo tragedy—covering much more than the full-oxygen ecosystem —see James A. Skardon, "The Apollo Story," in *The Columbia Journalism Review,* Fall and Winter, 1967, and discussion by other writers in subsequent issues.

Page 30

Central America: Dr. Budowski's paper, "Middle America: The Human Factor," is in Darling and Milton.

Page 31

Santo Domingo and the Bay of Pigs: The "engineering mentality" is not, of course, a phenomenon whose effects are limited to the environment in an ecological sense. For a splendid discussion of how the engineering mentality functions among non-engineers on a political level, see John McDermott, "Crisis Mana-

ger," *The New York Review of Books,* September 14, 1967.

Page 31

Water Resources Research Seminar: Dr. Cain's paper, published by the Interior Department, is titled "Ecological Impacts of Water Resources Development."

endangered species: The figure is from the Bureau's Circular No. 223, 1965.

Page 32

hybrid corn: See an address by Dr. Cain to an environmental quality conference at Boulder, Colorado, on January 31, 1967. I don't know *how* you can see it, but the Interior Department probably has some copies.

zoos and greenhouses: Don't misunderstand me—I love zoos and we certainly should have them.

bison: The example is from Durward L. Allen, "The Preservation of Endangered Habitats and Vertebrates of North America," in Darling and Milton. "There are no criteria for selection," Dr. Allen writes, "which will remove annually the same individuals in the same age groups which would have been eliminated from a wild herd on the plains. . . . The long-term biological problem probably requires a large Great Plains park confined to accommodate an unmanaged bison herd and a population of wolves."

ring-necked pheasant: Dr. Leopold's suggestion was in extemporaneous remarks recorded in Darling and Milton.

"our most valuable resource": Dr. Darnell's testimony is in *Senate*

Hearings. In Darling and Milton, Pierre Danserau (mentioned above) writes: "We have been slow to realize that ecology is not a purely biological science since it must account for the whole environment and trace the origin and the effect of the resources which the plant and animal bodies are instrumental in cycling."

Page 33

tomorrow's wonder drug: Wesley Marx writes in *The Frail Ocean* (cited above), "Scientists are fascinated by the way in which a marine organism . . . can immobilize creatures ten times its size by excreting a toxin. A study of this constant chemical warfare promises to produce a rich source of pharmaceuticals. Dr. Ross Nigrelli of the New York Aquarium injected poison from a sea cucumber into cancers induced in mice. The cancer tumor stopped growing." And noting that Representative Edward A. Garmatz of Maryland has proposed a $10-million program to eliminate stinging jellyfish "and other similar pests," Marx writes: "Dr. Frank Johnson of Princeton now finds that the bather's stinging pest contains a rare substance that glows green in the presence of calcium. This luminous property can determine calcium levels in the human bloodstream, a prime indicator of parathyroid disorders."

III: ALGAE AND AEROJET

Page 34

ecologists: Ronald R. Dagon is the nation's only city ecologist; the city is Croton-on-Hudson, New York, and it doesn't always take his advice. John P. Milton (the Milton of Darling and Milton, cited frequently herein) is with the Conservation Foundation. The others are identified elsewhere.

Page 35

Scammon Lagoon: Assistant Secretary of the Interior Stanley Cain, "Ecological Impacts of Water Resources Development" (see p. 31). A more thorough (and less optimistic) treatment of the gray whales' problem in the lagoon can be found in Wesley Marx, *The Frail Ocean* (third note for p. 22).

Page 36

the Everglades water cycle: There are many descriptions of the unique ecosystem we call the Everglades, including at least two in Darling and Milton.

productivity: Both quotations, and the shrimp example, are from "C-111."

Saylor Pond: The study by Kahl is "Food Ecology of the Wood Stork (*Mycteria americana*) in Florida," published in *Ecological Monographs*, Spring, 1964.

Page 37

grope feeders: See Odum's *Ecology*, cited in the Foreword, or the paper by Kahl cited immediately above.

C&SFFCD: The Coordinating Committee of South Florida, a group consisting mostly of sportsmen, supplied much of this information.

Page 38

alligators: The count is from "C-111." The quotation is from *The New York Times*, June 7, 1967, as is the item in the next paragraph.

Dr. Ian Cowan, in "Management, Response and Variety," in Darling and Milton, has proposed blasting "alligator holes" to hold water during drought periods, enabling alligators and other animals to survive and to recover more rapidly. Of course Florida could import alligators, as Bermuda does bananas—but from where? Incidentally, those "baby alligators" you can buy in Miami to send to your friends *are* imported—but they aren't alligators. You can't ship alligators out of Florida. The babies are caimans (bonier above the eyes and firmer of body) imported from South America to sell to tourists. Another illusion shot to hell.

more on endangered species: Durward Allen, "The Preservation of Endangered Habitats and Vertebrates of North America," in Darling and Milton.

Page 39

". . . *eliminating the biotypes*": . . . Dr. Stanley A. Cain, "Biotype and Habitat," in Darling and Milton.

"*Simple life forms*": Superintendent Allin's quotation is from an address to the Historical Association of Southern Florida, given on March 16, 1966.

disappearing and dwindling birds: From "C-111."

Pages 39–40

wood stork: M. Philip Kahl, Jr. See second note for p. 36. The relationship between breeding and water level is from "C-111," in which the bird is called the wood ibis. Of course the wood stork doesn't *know* anything, but every writer is allowed one anthropomorphization per book.

nutrients, etc.: From "C-111" and Allen (cited above).

Page 40

fire: The acreage figure is from *The New York Times*, June 7, 1967. On the important role of fire in ecology, see Odum's *Ecology*. For specific examples, see John McPhee, "The Pine Barrens" (*The New Yorker*, November 25 and December 2, 1967) and Cain's paper (first note for p. 39). Cain—who as Assistant Secretary is the immediate superior of the head of the National Park Service—points out that in Isle Royale National Park, moose are thinning out because the balsam trees are growing out of their reach and there has been no fire to clear the forest for young growth (but see p. 148 on Isle Royale). Odum notes that without occasional fires, deer can't survive in California chaparral —and goes on to note that in Los Angeles County fire *prevention* in chaparral has allowed larger fires that have destroyed many valuable homes.

Raymond Dasmann, in *The Destruction of California* (cited in second note for p. 18), tells how early redwood loggers in California, with nothing on their minds but fast profit, demonstrated the value of fire, which they "used freely, to clear the land before logging, and to destroy the slash afterward. Burned-over slopes were left in a barren, blackened condition. But, surprisingly, they recovered. Some of the worst areas produced excellent stands of second growth. The once-barren slopes around Humboldt Bay are now covered with tall new redwoods, some of them being logged now for a second crop. Through luck the logging and burning treatment that these lands received encouraged sprouting from redwood stumps and roots, so that where one giant tree once grew, a ring of its young descendants now stands."

There is also a theory that big enough fires bring rain. The late Senator Robert Kerr, in *Land, Wood, and Water* (New York: Fleet Publishing Corporation, 1960), wrote that "a cross-country series of fires was proposed in 1841 to test the theory, but nothing came of the suggestion." Be thankful; the Engineers would be restaging the bombing of Hamburg at every dry spell.

Page 41

the National Audubon Society: See the letter by Charles H. Callison of the Society in *Ramparts*, May, 1967.

salt water in the canal: See "C-111" for a detailed version of all this. I'm aware that this is a Park Service document and may therefore be said to be on "one side" of the controversy. As a colleague once retorted when charged with subjectivity, sometimes the facts are biased.

Aerojet: See the Florida press from 1966 on.

Page 42

the Everglades kite: See Odum's *Ecology* for the snail, and the Bureau of Sport Fisheries and Wildlife's handout on "Wildlife Refuges"

for the 20 holdouts in Loxahatchee. Twenty is probably not a viable breeding population, but you never know.

a study made in 1964: The report is called "Summary of the Evidence Supporting the Contention that Everglades National Park Depends on Supplies of Fresh Water for Its Existence." It's by Dr. Clarence P. Idyll of the Marine Institute of Science, University of Miami, and Dr. Durbin C. Tabb was in on it too. It's dated October, 1964, and you may be able to get it from the Institute. Nancy Maynard gave me the copy I have.

aquatic birds: Dr. Idyll writes: "As one example of the complete dependence of one species of bird on aquatic food, a nesting colony of 5,000 pairs of wood storks requires over 1,000,000 pounds of small live fish per nesting season to raise 10,-000 young. This enormous amount of food must be provided within a flight radius of about 15 miles from the rookery or nest site." Kahl (in the study cited above) has similar data. When you add this to our previous information about the wood stork—that it won't nest until the water gets *down* to a certain level— you can see that a pretty delicate ecological balance is involved in survival for poor old *Mycteria americana*. The wood stork is a grope feeder; it walks through the water with its open bill below the surface, and snaps it shut when it touches a fish (the snap takes about 25 milliseconds!).

The ecological balance is demonstrated further when you see in figures what low water means to a grope feeder. Near the Corkscrew Sanctuary in October, 1962, when the water level was 15½ inches, there were 50 fish per cubic meter of water. In March, 1963, when the level was 3 inches, the average per cubic meter of water was 2,248 fish, some of which are pretty small. This is also from Kahl.

aquatic mammals: Included, along with the deer, are the purely aquatic manatee, the otter, and the water rat.

invertebrates: This includes, of course, the shrimp, crab and oyster population. Some swimming worms and barnacles are important fish food. Some small varieties of shrimp and clam, along with snails and dragonfly young, are major food items for ducks and coots.

vegetation: Everglades soil is also dependent on fresh water. Peat soil is formed only under virtually permanent surface water. Coastal marl soil is produced by blue-green algae when the water and temperature factors are right.

diluting effects: The quotation is from "C-111."

fish and salinity: From Dr. Idyll's study (mentioned above). So is the quotation that follows.

Page 43

menhaden, mullet, etc.: Also from Idyll.

water supply: From Odum's *Ecology*. He would be quick to point out that it would probably take a lot of drainage; but he brought it up, I didn't.

Atlantic City: From McPhee (cited above). Geographer Robert E. Dickinson ("The Process of Urbanization," in Darling and Milton)

notes that despite the salty tap water, the citizens of Atlantic City not long ago voted down funds for a new storage reservoir.

"hydrologic change": The figures are from "C-111."

"rare and endangered" species: You can get a list of these from the Bureau of Sport Fisheries and Wildlife. It doesn't pretend to be complete, concerning itself mostly with vertebrates.

"We'll pull the plug": "C-111" attributes the quotation to the Corps, and provides the reply quoted.

Page 44

Shark River, etc.: Details are in "Threats to Everglades National Park," an address by Superintendent Allin to the annual meeting of the Monroe County Audubon Society at Key West on April 29, 1966. Allin also mentions—besides the things we've talked about—a threat to the park from rapid development of Collier County (resulting in drainage and consequent salinity intrusion), and a further threat from just plain too many people. The first would require a separate investigation. The second we'll get to in a later chapter.

IV: THE GOLDEN SAND DUNE

Page 45

dredge-and-fill projects: Figures in this and the next paragraph are from an address by Assistant Secretary Cain to the annual meeting of the Salt Pond Areas Bird Sanctuary, Inc., at Falmouth, Massachusetts, August 11, 1966.

Page 46

Dr. Cain's essay: "Ecological Impacts of Water Resources Development" (see pp. 30–31). Cain also notes that even present coordination requirements have severe practical limits ". . . the Bureau of Sport Fisheries and Wildlife . . . can do little more than make quick field reconnaissances of the possible consequences of a proposed water resources development project of the Bureau of Reclamation or the Corps of Engineers. And even this has to be done in a limited time, usually all too short for adequate appraisal."

legislation in Congress: My thanks to Frank Kieliger, of the office of Representative Phillip Burton of California, for helping me out with this information.

the depredations of the Engineers: Gathright Dam and the Mill Creek proposal are described in bulletins from the Wilderness Society. Details on the St. Joe dams are in *The St. Maries Gazette Record* for April 20, 1967.

Pages 46–47

more depredations: The Puget Sound project was described to me by Rod Pegues of the Sierra Club in Seattle; material sent to me by Theodore Edison of New Jersey (one of the good engineers) describes the Cross-Florida Barge Canal. The Big Walnut Creek proposal is described by Cain in the essay mentioned above.

Page 47

red tides: Wesley Marx, in *The Frail Ocean* (cited in third note for p. 22), has a long and fascinating

section on the complex problems posed by *Gymnodinium breve.*

the Long Island dune: Information is from the files of the Hempstead Town Lands Resources Council (which include statements by the Corps of Engineers) and from *The Long Island Press.*

Page 48

shoreline generally: Again, Marx (mentioned above) has an excellent and eminently readable description of the whole beach problem. Marx also provides the quotation from the President's Panel and the item about the San Diego beaches.

Page 49

testimony: The testimony was on June 22, 1966, before the Subcommittee on Fisheries and Wildlife Conservation of the House Committee on Merchant Marine and Fisheries.

"that's only Long Island": Stanley Cain (cited above) covers the entire question of wetlands, potholes and estuaries across America. In his essay, "Earth's Wrecking Crew at Work" (in *Call of the Vanishing Wild,* cited in fourth note for p. 24), Roger Tory Peterson writes of a decline in the number of ducks, which, he says, "is not due primarily to gun pressure. Virtually every day new plans are made somewhere to drain another pond or swamp or marsh, until more than 50 million acres of the original 127 million acres of wetland in the United States have disappeared, and millions of other acres are crisscrossed with mosquito-control ditches." Peterson goes on

to condemn Federal subsidies for draining land to grow "crops we don't need," and to kill off ducks we *do* need, even for hunting.

Congressmen: Some members of Congress are adept at making pork sound like pheasant under glass. The late Senator Robert Kerr, in *Land, Wood, and Water* (cited in note for p. 40), did it with a not-too-subtle alteration in the meaning of the word "conservation": "The success in our region is pointing the way for a national program of conservation, basin by basin. The need for such an effort has been written in the dusty soil of our denuded areas, our silted watercourses, our barren hills and mountains. I have been in the thick of the fight for broadened and accelerated conservation, serving as Chairman of the Senate Public Works Subcommittee for Flood Control and Rivers and Harbors, and an ex-officio member of the Appropriations Committee for such projects. We are shaping a national program with the river basin as the unit of development, both upstream and downstream."

"Conservation" thus becomes a matter of building levees and dams.

parking lot: There is already more *paved* land area in the United States than there is *total* land area in the state of Georgia.

Page 50

more depredations: The TVA and Duke Power projects are described in Wilderness Society bulletins, and details on the Duke project are in Cain (cited above). The Florida projects were described to me in various private conversations in the Miami area.

Page 51

Rampart Dam: Dr. Goodwin reports on the dam in *Senate Hearings.* Other information is from Paul Brooks, "The Plot to Drown Alaska," *The Atlantic Monthly,* May, 1965. See pages 149–152.

highways: Since April, 1967, the Secretary of Transportation may not approve projects if they bisect valuable public lands—unless no feasible alternative exists, or unless the projects take steps to protect the lands. This is a pretty vague protection (it's an amendment introduced into the Federal Highway Act of 1966 by Senator Ralph Yarborough of Texas), but it's at least a handle for pressure. The Secretary of the Interior used it to urge the Secretary of Transportation to go along with the city of San Francisco in a recent routing dispute with the California Highway Commission (*San Francisco Examiner,* April 14, 1967).

Masochistic conservationists might be interested in looking up a two-page, full-color ad in *Business Week* for May 20, 1967, a copy of which was sent to me by Dr. John Dockery of the Illinois Institute of Technology. The photo—with lovely pines in the background—is of three bulldozers, abreast. The caption reads, "Here comes your new road to the mountains—at 40 tons per push." The advertised International bulldozers, according to the copy, "cut straight through the hill. They bowl over trees, gouge out stumps and rip up the rocky footing." The "precision earthmovers reshape the land to exact specifications." The result? "The scenery is preserved. And your view is better."

Examples in the first paragraph on highways are from the Wilderness Society, except for the New Jersey item, which is from *Footprints* (published by the North Jersey Conservation Foundation) for October, 1966. The February, 1967, issue of the same publication quotes a New Jersey Highway Department booklet, "Development of the State Highway System," as saying that by 1975, 821 additional miles of freeways will be necessary (1967 figure: 1,930 existing miles), and 900 miles of the present system will have to be widened or turned into dual roadways. It has to be done because the Engineers say so.

New York Thruway: This route was shown me privately, and Congressman Saylor told me in an interview about stopping the highway in Pennsylvania. The California redwood dispute has been continually reported in *The San Francisco Chronicle* (reporter Scott Thurber is a redwoods expert), and inspired Governor Ronald Reagan's now famous comment, "When you've seen one tree, you've seen 'em all." He has since said he was kidding. There's a short (pre-Reagan) account of the battle in Dasmann, *The Destruction of California* (cited in second note for p. 18), but he fails to note that the Highway Commission itself favored the state park route.

Mammoth Cave: The 14-building Great Onyx Job Corps Center in Mammoth Cave National Park is described in a Wilderness Society bulletin.

the Missouri River: Author A. B. Guthrie told me about these two proposed dams in a telephone conversation.

Page 52

the Navasota River: Dr. Calhoun's statement is in *Senate Hearings*.

Engineers and economics: Haveman's study, "The Postwar Corps of Engineers Program in Ten Southern States: An Evaluation of Economic Efficiency," is in Melvin Greenhut and Tate Whitman, eds., *Essays in Southern Economic Development* (Durham: University of North Carolina Press, 1964). In case you've spotted that $1,169 million is not 44.2 percent of $1.5 billion, the apparent discrepancy is because the first figure is money actually *spent* by 1962; the second is money *committed* by Congress, but not necessarily expended.

Page 53

low-flow augmentation: The data here are from testimony, in *House Hearings*, by Dr. Wolman. Further information on the Potomac plans was sent to me by Theodore Edison.

Page 54

Lake Erie: Representative Horton's suggestion and Representative Brown's suggestion at the end of the chapter are from *House Hearings*.

Marine Resources Act: This is Public Law 89–454 (1966). One of its stated goals is "increased utilization of marine resources," otherwise unspecified.

V: YOU GO THROUGH SEDRO WOOLLEY

Page 55

Sedro Woolley: I don't know where the name came from, but fellow journalist Steve Murdock, who knows more about Western labor history than anyone else, tells me that the lumber town of Sedro Woolley was the scene of a great battle between the authorities and IWW lumbermen who were organizing in the area. It's still, as we'll see, a lumber town.

Page 56

the lakes: The 1968 World Almanac lists the largest lake within the boundaries of each of the fifty states. Thirty-three of the fifty lakes listed are man-made. In Washington it's Franklin D. Roosevelt Lake, behind Grand Coulee Dam on what used to be the Columbia and Kettle rivers.

"the fish still swim": The most important steelhead artery is the flow down the Suiattle River into the Sauk, and down the Sauk into the Skagit. The Sauk flows into the Skagit *below* Gorge Dam. It is this artery, however, which is in serious danger from the Kennecott mine described later in the chapter.

the comfort vs. preservation balance: The point doesn't, of course, apply only to dams. Referring to depredations by lumbermen, Dasmann, in *The Destruction of California* (cited in second note for p. 18), writes that "even the most ardent conservationist uses wood and paper."

Page 57

The Wilderness Act: Officially Public Law 88–577, 88th Congress, S. 4, September 3, 1964. The first version of the bill was introduced in the Senate by Hubert Humphrey of Minnesota in 1957, and in the House by John Saylor of Pennsylvania in the same year. Senators Clinton P. Anderson of New Mexico, Henry M. Jackson of Washington, Frank Church of Idaho and Lee Metcalf of Montana played important parts in its passage. P. L. 88–607, enacted later, says in effect that land administered by the Bureau of Land Management, in addition to the lands named in the Wilderness Act itself, can be made wilderness areas.

wilderness areas: Write to The Wilderness Society, 729 15th St. N.W., Washington, D.C. 20005, for a list of all present and contemplated wilderness areas.

Page 58

ecology: Representative Melvin Price of Illinois, in his remarks urging passage of the bill, stressed its ecological importance, particularly with regard to rare and endangered species of plants and animals.

The three are the Chiricahua Wild Area (in Coronado National Forest, Arizona), the only known habitat of the Chiricahua squirrel; the Marble Mountain Wilderness Area (in Klamath National Forest, California), which includes stands of the rare Brewer's spruce; and the Kalmiopsis Wild Area (in Siskiyou National Forest, Oregon), where there are several rare plants and trees. Of course other wilderness areas *have* ecological importance—

possibly they all have—but the point is that this isn't a value reflected in anybody's language. The proposed San Rafael Wilderness Area near Santa Barbara, California, is of crucial ecological importance (it's part of Los Padres National Forest) because it includes the last remaining habitat for the extremely scarce California condor, of which only 51 remain at last count (*The Sunday Ramparts,* October 23 and November 6, 1966; *The Oakland* [California] *Tribune,* June 21, 1967).

John Buchanan: This talk was inserted in *The Congressional Record* (for January 16, 1967) by, of all people, Wayne Aspinall, chairman of the House Committee on Interior and Insular Affairs. By the time you've finished the book, this won't surprise you.

Pages 58–59

the mayor of Sedro Woolley: Mr. Pearson's remarks were before a hearing conducted by the Subcommittee on Parks and Recreation of the Senate Committee on Interior and Insular Affairs, April 24–25, 1967. The hearing was on S. 1321, a bill to set up the North Cascades National Park, a nearby national recreation area, and a wilderness area in the Cascades. Mayor Pearson also testified that the park alone would "withdraw [a] billion to three billion board feet of usable timber from the Forest Service sustained yield program"—but other witnesses said that the park, as proposed in the bill, would have no effect whatever on the lumber industry.

A 505,000-acre North Cascades National Park was created when President Johnson signed the appropriate bill on October 2, 1968. An additional 600,000 acres were included in two adjacent "recreation areas" and a wilderness area. See *The New York Times,* October 3, 1968, and *The San Francisco Chronicle,* September 20, 1968.

Page 59

myths: "Overmature timber" is, of course, a semantic invention by lumbermen. The Olin ad is quoted from *The Olympic Park Associates Newsletter,* Summer, 1967 (the *Newsletter* is *not* where Olin placed the ad).

"You can't stockpile animals": The editorial from *Fishing and Hunting News* is from the February 18, 1967, issue.

Ecologist Ian McTaggart Cowan of British Columbia ("Management, Response and Variety," in Darling and Milton) writes, not incidentally: "Fire has become anathema to the manager of forest areas who consciously or unconsciously harbors as his objective the ideal of a uniform stand of well-shaped trees unmarked by fire, disease, insects, deformity or senility. But fire has been the great reinitiator of forest areas, the creator of a variety of cover type on the large scale, while insects, disease and senility have instigated diversity of habitat on the smaller scale."

state forestry agencies: For a detailed explanation of how one state agency—California's—has pretty much failed to protect anything but the lumber industry, see David M. Wilson, "Trees, Earth, Water, and Ecological Upheaval: Logging Practices and Watershed Protection in

California," *California Law Review,* Vol. 54:1117, 1966. The state's fish and game commissioners, and her fishermen, have come into some conflict with the lumbermen about the whole thing; see Walt Radke's "Sports Afield" column, *The San Francisco Examiner,* May 31, 1967.

Roger Allin's boss: The man's name is George B. Hartzog, Jr. See Harold Gilliam, "Parks Are for People to Have Fun In," *The San Francisco Sunday Examiner and Chronicle,* October 15, 1967.

Page 60

Everglades: Superintendent Allin did not say whether he favors the proposal to turn an unused part of the park into a wilderness area, a plan which would still leave a lot of Everglades for other park uses.

"with my car in sight": One self-characterized "backpack snob," Tom Lyon of Logan, Utah, wrote (*Ramparts,* May, 1967) in criticism of my articles that "there is such a thing as quality recreation, which he [meaning me] could find out, maybe, by leaving his car (perfect expression of the technological arrogance he decries) behind next time."

In the first place, if Mr. Lyon wants (and can afford) to wander around Mount Baker National Forest on foot in February, he's welcome. In the second place, a car is hardly an expression of technological arrogance; it, and its cousin the airplane, can make it possible for a city boy to get out where the "quality recreation" is. That's a meaningless phrase, anyway: to some of us, listening to Dizzy Gillespie in an unhealthily smoky bar, simultaneously drinking harmful alcoholic liquids, is also "quality recreation."

But the real point is: Okay, so I could have left the car behind. But could I take my mother, too? She's never seen the Cascades, and she's eighty-one. I'm only saying that—in the excellent phrase of the hippie movement—she should be able to do her thing and Mr. Lyon should be able to do his. See third note for p. 188.

Lassen Park: The quotation and the item about the steam plant are from a Wilderness Society bulletin dated September 22, 1966. Their bulletin of November 21, 1966, seeking improvements in a proposed Washakie Wilderness Area in Wyoming, is in notable contrast, with its concern for fossil protection and elk habitat, among other things. Incidentally, John Buchanan (see p. 58) was at the Washakie Wilderness hearing (Riverton, Wyoming, December 8, 1966), where his statement didn't mention that he's a lumber industry representative, but where he did attack the whole wilderness concept on the basis that it's one kind of recreation to be measured against other kinds. The Wilderness Society became a "willful [*sic*] minority of less than 3%"—and their cause became "single-use preservation." The idea that leaving land alone might have any other purpose than to be looked at or camped in is not mentioned. This is, of course, typical of the propagandist anti-wilderness approach; see Chapter X for other examples.

Page 61

"This rather clever version": William F. Lenihan, general counsel for Outdoors Unlimited (Yakima, Washington) and executive vice president of the Pacific Northwest Ski Instruc-

tors Association, was testifying at the Senate hearing described in the note for pp. 58–59.

Page 61
". . . and have lumber besides": Raymond Dasmann (mentioned above) describes the case of the Monterey pine. Only a few natural groves of this tree survive–all in California–but it has been transplanted to Australia, South Africa and other countries, where it is grown in plantations for its excellent softwood timber. It is one of the most widespread timber trees in the world–and its original ecological habitats still exist, although only in relatively small areas.

Page 62
the work of the Forest Service: At least they do their damnedest. Dasmann points out that "it is not possible today to say whether or not the national forests are being properly managed," and in the fourth chapter of *The Destruction of California* explains why.

Pages 62–63
Wilderness Act amendments: It's all in *The Congressional Record.*

Pages 64–69
Kennecott: Information not otherwise identified is from *The Wild Cascades,* regular publication of the North Cascades Conservation Council, and/or from the Council's files. It was Rod Pegues of the Sierra Club who first told me about the proposed Kennecott pit. I'm grateful to him and to M. Brock Evans, Clark H. Jones and Patrick D. Goldsworthy for help on this subject.

Page 64
mining law: For a short, clear explanation of patented and unpatented claims, see Adam Hochschild, "Teapot Dome 1967?" in *Ramparts,* May, 1967. In fact, see it anyway, as a supplement to this book. It tells a Colorado story I don't have room for.

Page 65
"to be seen from the moon": The Sierra Club used the phrase in a newspaper advertisement during 1967.

Page 65
Kennecott's plans: Mr. Michaelson revealed some of these plans, and said what he's quoted as saying here and later, at a meeting with conservation leaders in San Francisco on January 30, 1967.

Page 66
a man-made lake: Kennecott has snowed a few people with this one. State Representative Henry Backstrom of Arlington, for one, is for the mine, he says, because "in three to four years, they'll leave us with roads into the area and a man-made lake" (Associated Press story in *The Ellensburg* [Wash.] *Record,* August 7, 1967). You can't "leave roads into" a wilderness area, and Kennecott says they'll be there mining for as long as thirty years; possibly Mr. Backstrom doesn't know these things. He also says the mine will boost the local economy. It won't; it will employ a maximum of 200 people, pay no taxes on the Federal land, and ruin any possibility for growth in

tourism—and it will drive out fishermen by driving out fish.

"natural talus piles": "Talus," in geology, is the sloping pile of rock fragments at the foot of a cliff.

the boys overseas: "Spokesmen for the company . . . say copper mining is necessary for national strategic metal stockpiles and the Vietnam War effort." Stephen Ponder of the Associated Press, in the *Longview* [Wash.] *News,* July 27, 1967.

Pages 67–68

Cal Dunnell: The quotation is from Allan May's story in *The Everett* [Wash.] *Western Sun,* August 8, 1967.

Page 69

Kennecott's income: The figures are from *Moody's Industrials.*

the Milliken quotes: The Kennecott president's words are from his letter of June 12, 1967, to Clark H. Jones, president of the Federation of Western Outdoor Clubs.

Page 70

the man in Teaneck: Whyte is quoted in James Nathan Miller's "Conservation Is Everybody's Battle," originally from *National Civic Review,* July, 1964, reprinted in *The Reader's Digest,* August, 1964. Whyte could have picked a better place than Teaneck, many of whose citizens can easily spend a vacation in Wyoming.

National Parks on television: The Eichhorn quote is from his paper, "The Special Role of National Parks," in Darling and Milton.

Page 70

Frome: The quotation is from his "The Politics of Conservation" in *Holiday,* February, 1967.

Page 71

helping each other: "Too often conservation conferences end up in a two-step frustration pattern something as follows: First, individual speakers present logical and impassioned pleas for this or that species or problem, after which it is suggested that 'we all must work together' even when it is quite obvious that species-oriented or problem-oriented missions are often in basic conflict with one another" (Eugene P. Odum, address to a symposium on Estuarine Ecology of Coastal Waters of North Carolina, University of North Carolina, Raleigh, May 12, 1966).

Bormann: From *Senate Hearings.*

INTERLUDE: GOODBY, RUBY TUESDAY

Page 73

the Florida wardens: The story of the Audubon egret wardens is told by Loris and Margery Milne in *The Balance of Nature* (cited in note for p. 17).

Page 74

letting nature take its course: "Just think," Lewis Mumford once said to a symposium, "only 5,000 years ago there was no North Sea—there was a land bridge between Britain and the Continent. If we think of that we see that even the most stable environment is involved in the flux of history" (spontaneous remarks in Darling and Milton).

But we do make changes we don't think of. A. Starker Leopold, at the same symposium, argued that by having regular shooting hours—which are "learned" and then "taught" by ducks—we "may be creating [through selection of the quicker learners] a new strain of mallard that tends to conform to mass behavior patterns and is less prone to make mistaken individual judgments" ("Adaptability of Animals to Habitat Change," in Darling and Milton).

Save the Jack Tar: If you think public regulation of esthetics comes anywhere near being a simple problem, or if you're sure you know how you feel about it, read Richard F. Babcock's delightful and stimulating "Billboards, Glass Houses, and the Law" in *Harper's,* April, 1966.

the Selway: Michael McCloskey, the energetic conservation director of the Sierra Club, took one look at this passage in its original magazine form and immediately phoned to assure me that there is, indeed, a unique ecological importance to the Magruder Corridor on the upper Selway. So don't say I didn't say so.

Page 75

elephants and the Capitol: The New York Times, January 29, 1967.

more on ecosystems: Just to insult more people, let me note that I have a 64-page booklet, "Concepts of Conservation," published by the Conservation Foundation and labeled "A guide to discussion of some fundamental problems." Nowhere does it mention ecology or genetic information.

Great Basin National Park: See a report prepared by Richard C. Sill of the University of Nevada for university president Charles Armstrong, dated April 18, 1966. Excerpts from the report are a part of the record of *Senate Hearings.*

Dasmann: The book is cited in the second note for p. 18.

grass: No, not that kind of grass. Dr. Allen's remarks are from his paper, "The Preservation of Endangered Habitats and Vertebrates of North America," in Darling and Milton, and Dr. Leopold's in the next paragraph were spontaneous, also recorded in Darling and Milton.

Page 76

chaparral: Also from Dr. Allen (see above). Besides the thousand acres in the United States, there's still a little chaparral in Mexico where the same animals live. The Mexican Government is buying up some of that to save it, too.

government money: Raymond Dasmann, "Preserving Open Spaces in Urban Areas," in *Call of the Vanishing Wild* (cited in fourth note for p. 24).

Page 77

redwoods: On the Sierra Club proposal, see their *Bulletin,* November, 1966, and their brochure, "The Case for Redwood Creek." They also issued a series of fact sheets; Number 2 is dated August, 1966. I've omitted the Redwood Creek-vs.-Mill Creek controversy described in the original *Ramparts* articles because events have bypassed it; it has now been decided that the park will be on Redwood Creek but on only part of the proposed area, with some other redwood land thrown in.

Secretary Udall's remarks are from an Associated Press story in *The Portland Oregonian,* August 19, 1966.

Page 78

the Park approved by Congress: As approved by Congress, the Park totals 58,000 acres. The Secretary of the Interior can buy an additional, unspecified 2,400 acres.

Bull Creek: The story is told by David M. Wilson, "Trees, Earth, Water, and Ecological Upheaval: Logging Practices and Watershed Protection in California," *California Law Review,* Vol. 54:1117, 1966, and in *The Sierra Club Bulletin,* January, 1960.

Page 79

kidding yourself: Dr. Ian Mc-Taggart Cowan, in "Management, Response and Variety" in Darling and Milton, puts it simply: "The only tenable approach to the maintenance of the largest part of the biota is the management of ecotypes rather than species."

Pages 79–80

resources: Sanford S. Farness, "Resources Planning *versus* Regional Planning," in Darling and Milton.

Page 79

aurochs: The attempt to recreate the aurochs is described by Cain, "Biotype and Habitat," in Darling and Milton. The quotation is from the same paper.

Adirondack Forest Preserve: 2.4 million acres in the Adirondacks, 200,000 acres in the Catskills. See " 'Forever Wild,' " an editorial in *The New York Times,* June 7, 1967.

Page 80

knowledge and conscience: Ian McHarg's spontaneous comments are in Darling and Milton. The definition of the "ecological conscience" is by Dr. Cowan in the paper cited above. The term originated with Aldo Leopold's *Sand County Almanac* (New York: Oxford University Press, 1949), which you ought to read. Everybody else ought to too.

VI: EVERYBODY SHOULD BREAK AN ANKLE

Page 81

Georgia-Pacific: *The New York Times,* January 13, 1967, and Raymond Dasmann, *The Destruction of California* (cited in second note for p. 18).

Page 82

PG&E executives: In the *Progress* for February, 1967, for instance (which, not incidentally, is Vol. XLIV, No. 2), it's "Art" Kezer of Red Bluff, California. In his case it's the Recreation and Parks Commission (it's never the Public Utilities Commission; that farce takes place only on the state level), the 20–30 Club, the advisory board of "a school system work-experience program," "many other civic and charitable activities" and "various youth projects." He's thirty-seven.

"Dig we must!": See the advertising column, *The New York Times,* June 7, and Con Ed's full-page ad in *The New York Times,* October 3, 1967. It's interesting, incidentally, that in June Con Ed was responsible for half the excavations in Man-

hattan, but in October for only one-third. The nickname "Con Ed" is itself, of course, a public relations creation.

Page 83

nuclear plants: The best roundup of objections I've seen was privately mimeographed by Dr. J. B. Neilands of 185 Hill Road, Berkeley, in February, 1963, and is titled "A Consumer-Oriented Survey of the Possible Consequences of the Nuclear Power Program in North-Central California." I listed some objections in "Outrage on Bodega Head," *The Nation,* June 22, 1963.

In the address cited in the third note for page 26, Dr. LaMont Cole said: "The fuel for present reactors has to be rejuvenated periodically. This yields long-lived and biologically hazardous isotopes such as strontium-90 and cesium-137 that should be stored where they cannot contaminate the environment for at least 1,000 years; but a fair proportion of the storage tanks employed so far are leaking after only about 20 years [see pages 115–116]. This process also releases krypton-85 into the atmosphere to add to the radiation exposure of the earth's biota including man, and I don't think that anyone knows a practicable way to prevent this." Fusion reactors, which everyone talks about but no one knows how to make, "will produce new contaminants, among others tritium (H_3), which becomes a constituent of water, in this case long-lived radioactive water, which will contaminate all environments and living things."

The utility companies, on the other hand, tend to push nuclear power in general; see for example *PG&E Progress* for July, 1967. There's more on this in Chapter VII.

Indian Point: In retelling this story I have generally followed Wesley Marx, *The Frail Ocean* (cited in third note for p. 22), and from that book took both the Ottinger quotation and the quotation from Marx himself.

Page 84

once-suppressed pictures: I was shown the photos in the Manhattan office of the Scenic Hudson Preservation Conference.

Page 85

Benson Lossing: The book is *The Hudson, from the Wilderness to the Sea, Illustrated by Three Hundred and Six Engravings on Wood, from Drawings by the Author, and a frontispiece on Steel.* Virtue and Yorston published it in 1866. See *The New Yorker,* January 7, 1967.

the view from Breakneck Ridge: The original, much shorter *Ramparts* version of this Storm King section evoked a response from Charles E. Hoppin of Consolidated Edison Company, which was published in full in *Ramparts,* June, 1967. I won't reprint it here because I had an article I like, on another subject, in that issue, and I'd just as soon you'd look it up. Mostly, though, Mr. Hoppin said I should have looked at Storm King from another point of view (I had, but it wasn't clear in the magazine version); that various of Con Ed's paid experts don't think the plant will hurt fish; and that the plant will use only 4 percent of the water that flows by. The latter is a great example of taking your mind off your broken ankle by telling you how healthy your ears are. The fish are dealt with in the text to a greater extent than they were in the *Ramparts* version.

It is true, however, that the Storm King project wouldn't change the view from Breakneck Ridge too much, except maybe to wreck its scale. Mr. Hoppin also objected to my comments about the project's reservoir, but I won't go into that because the whole section is rewritten.

puniness: Said Con Ed Senior Vice President Waring at one of the Federal Power Commission hearings: Storm King, described by every other witness on both sides as a place of at least unusual beauty, is "simply a piece of acreage." (Project No. 2338, official stenographer's report of hearings, page 8,431.)

On page 7,505, Herbert S. Conover demonstrated—lest you think that by "Engineers" is meant "engineers"—that a landscape architect can be an Engineer too. Asked whether he had "ever in your experience found an area which you decided was so beautiful that you didn't think that you could improve it?" Mr. Conover (of Uhl, Hall and Rich) replied, "Personally I think practically anything can be improved." The best argument for atheism I know is that Mr. Conover was not struck dead on the spot.

Page 86

Cornwall's park: See the testimony, in the hearings cited above, of Gordon Cameron, supervisor of the town of Cornwall, particularly the portion beginning on page 6,015; that of Village Mayor Michael Donohue, beginning on 6,407; and that of Mayor Joseph Mullin of Newburgh, beginning on 6,811.

It's interesting to compare Mr. Conover's description of the Storm King project itself, which, he said, "will attract many visitors from New York" (p. 10,966). Earlier, he said, "They would come from New York City—anywhere—all around that area" (p. 10,947). Does Cornwall know about this?

Bodega Head: See my "Outrage on Bodega Head" in *The Nation*, cited above.

Page 87

taking credit: The telephone company is great at this on those rare occasions when a state regulatory commission forces them to make a refund. They'll fight it for six months, lose, and then mail you a notice saying, "Hey! Our costs went down, and *naturally* we've *decided* to pass the savings along to you."

word magic: See the full-page ad cited in second note for p. 82, and consistent usage by company spokesmen throughout the second set of FPC hearings.

historical importance: The U.S. Court of Appeals has specifically found (note for p. 88) that "the Storm King project [the court didn't call it "Cornwall"] is to be located in an area of . . . major historical importance."

the state's position: The committee's report was quoted by Nassau County Executive Eugene H. Nickerson in *Senate Hearings*.

Pages 87–88

Con Ed's experts: See second and third notes for p. 85. They also claim that the Storm King area is not all that good for spawning, and that the figure is much lower than the claimed 85 percent. Just little enough is actually known, in fact, that probably no real percentage can be fixed; but the argument is just as good if you simply say "some."

Page 88

eggs and larvae: McBroom's testimony, and a couple of other details in this section, are from Maxwell C. Wheat, Jr., "Precedent on the Hudson," in *The Sierra Club Bulletin,* March, 1966.

historic decision: Scenic Hudson Preservation Conference v. Federal Power Commission, 354 F. 2d 608 (2d Cir. 1965), Cert. denied, 384 U.S. 941 (1966). Just in case you want to look it up.

Page 89

Lurkis: A former chief engineer of New York City's Bureau of Gas and Electricity, Lurkis had advocated jet turbines, fueled by natural gas, of the type that kept Holyoke, Massachusetts, alight during the Northeast power blackout. Con Ed later advertised (second note for p. 82) that "jet engines on aircraft . . . are objectionable because of air pollution and noise," but jet engines on aircraft aren't fueled by natural gas; Lurkis had specifically testified that there would be no pollution. There is no record of the FPC's having gone to Holyoke to check on noise.

Engineers' sneers: Electrical World, December 12, 1966.

High Mountain Sheep: Actually it's Udall v. Federal Power Commission, 87 S. Ct. 1712 (1967). High Mountain Sheep is the name of the spot where they were going to build the dam; it's on the Oregon-Idaho border. See Harold Gilliam, "Udall, the FPC and High Mountain Sheep," *The San Francisco Sunday Examiner and Chronicle,* November 26, 1967.

Page 90

Con Ed ad: This is quoted from the ad cited in second note for p. 82. On June 7, 1967, *The New York Times* announced the retention by Con Ed of Lippincott and Margulies, "consultants in design, marketing and communications," to study "how we look to the public." If I had proper Madison Avenue *chutzpah* myself, I'd make something out of the fact that this was right after my *Ramparts* articles appeared.

Pages 90–91

the tailrace: These details and those on subsequent pages are from the second set of FPC hearings; exhibit numbers in the notes to follow are from the hearing record, and page numbers are from the stenographer's transcript. A "tailrace," by the way, is simply a channel through which water flows; in this case it's the intake/outflow for the "hidden" tunnel.

The question whether the project is "on the mountain" came up in the testimony of Gilmore Clarke (p. 11,699). See also the Sierra Club brief, August, 1967, p. 131.

Page 91

6,000 feet: Exhibit 281-A in FPC hearings.

shoreline and hole: Uncontested testimony of Dr. Charles W. Eliot II, pp. 4,852–3. The quotation is from the testimony.

depth and height of gouge: Exhibits 282 and 283 in FPC hearings; Dr. Eliot at pp. 4,858–9. A rock wall would rise another 20 feet high (Exhibits 283, 475, 476).

camouflage: Testimony of Gilmore Clarke, p. 4,669.

Page 91

recreational plan: Exhibits 241 and 282-A in FPC hearings. The description is by Herbert S. Conover (see third note for p. 85), pp. 4,659–60. The quotation describing observation terraces is from the company's description of Exhibit 241. The quotation about planting is from Clarke (p. 11,657) as is the admission (same page) that it won't work unless oysters are in season.

Pages 92–93

Cornwall's park again: As these notes are being prepared, the President's Commission on Riots and Civil Disorders (the Kerner Commission) has just issued its extensive report, giving, as the primary cause of urban racial disorders, white racism. The point is too sharp to ignore, especially in view of Father Hogan's inane testimony, mentioned later in the text.

Details of the park are again from Mr. Conover's testimony (p. 4,662). Dr. Eliot's following remarks are from pp. 4,870–1. "Rip-rap" means broken stone thrown together loosely to make a wall, a bulkhead or a foundation, usually in water; sometimes chunks of concrete are used, but at Storm King it would of course be pieces of Storm King.

Pages 93–94

the reservoir: The first description is by James M. Mullarkey (p. 4,433). Dr. Eliot's comments are from pp. 4,871–3, and make use of Exhibits 312 and 313. The crack about rattlesnakes is Mr. Conover's (p. 4,664). Information about disguises and where they won't work is from Mr. Clarke (pp. 11,722–3). The quotation about unsafeness is from Mr. Conover (p. 4,664). The information about 15 high points is from cartographer Richard Edes Harrison (pp. 7,168–76). The incredible statement about lakes is Mr. Clarke's (p. 11,720). See also Wheat, "Precedent on the Hudson," cited above.

Page 94

the overlook: Again, the description is by Mr. Conover (p. 4,665). On geographical criticism, see the Sierra Club's reply brief, September 5, 1967.

Page 95

cost figures: The $162 million is from Wheat, but that was more than two years ago, before we started hearing about invisible fireplaces, hidden tunnels, and scenic overlooks for mud piles. The $44.5 million is from the testimony of E. Barrett Shew, reported in *Electrical World*, December 12, 1966.

more figures: The $79 million is from Exhibit 257, introduced by Mr. Fisk, and from the testimony of the

Rev. William T. Hogan, pp. 4,690–1. Mr. Waring's figure is on p. 14,522. Father Hogan's $56 million is on p. 4,691.

social implications: Father Hogan's testimony, from which brief passages are quoted, is on pp. 4,699–4,701.

Pages 96–97

still more figures: For a long time in the hearing, everybody seemed to have settled on 22 cents a year as the "right" figure for the savings by that Harlem family—assuming Con Ed's cost figures to be correct. See for instance pp. 8,097–8,100. Other figures were later thrown in. Since Con Ed figured its differential over a twenty-year period, "per year" seemed an easy way. But economist Reynold Sachs gave a flat figure of $1.50 (p. 15,301). Not $1.50 a year. Just $1.50, period.

Page 97

another economist: This is Professor Sachs; the quotation is from p. 15,311. The quotation a little farther on is from p. 15,313.

the FPC staff: If the High Mountain Sheep decision (p. 89) drives Engineers out of their minds, Representative Ottinger (p. 84) can get them climbing the walls. He has a bill that would, in effect, give the Secretary of the Interior a veto over the FPC on horrors like Storm King if they would, in his judgment, interfere with fish, wildlife, scenic values, etc.

Pages 98–99

detergents: This section is taken mostly from a 1966 presentation by

Senator Nelson. *The West Bend* [Wisconsin] *News* covered the Milwaukee River pollution in 1965, with pictures. The quotation about eggs and larvae is from Senator Nelson.

Page 99

auto makers and safety standards: Smog standards, too. S. Smith Griswold, who heads the Los Angeles Air Pollution District, said in 1965 that the smog-control measures then being taken by auto manufacturers (to meet California law) had been known to the industry for ten years but ignored because of "arrogance and apathy." "Control of air pollution," he said, "does not make cars easier to sell; it does not make them cheaper to produce; and it does not reduce comebacks on the warranty. To people interested in profits, expenditures for the development and production of exhaust controls are liabilities." Quoted in C. W. Griffin, Jr., "America's Airborne Garbage," *Saturday Review*, May 22, 1965.

the detergent changeover: Effects and/or non-biodegradable detergents remain. During the summer of 1967, my wife and I stood on a California beach near Davenport, in Santa Cruz County, and watched the gentle summer waves delicately deposit detergent foam on the golden sands.

Not incidentally, *Advertising Age* for July 29, 1968, announced that a large industrial firm would begin a series of full-page print ads dealing with major social problems. The firm is Monsanto, and the subject of the first ad was water pollution.

catch-22: I can't believe that you

haven't already read it, but anyway: Joseph Heller, *Catch-22* (New York: Simon and Schuster, 1961; Dell Publishing Co., 1962, for the paperback). The catch-22 quoted is not, of course, the *only* catch-22.

"true conservation": Mr. Train's satirical statement was in an address to the Governor's Conference on Natural Beauty in Boston on May 23, 1966.

"child labor": The Train quotation is from an address to the American Forestry Association at Jackson Lake Lodge, Grand Teton National Park, Wyoming, on September 6, 1965. Mr. Train is president of the Conservation Foundation.

Page 100

the Yankee atomic plant: Dr. Goodwin's statement is in *Senate Hearings*.

pollution hearings: *House Hearings*.

Savannah and St. Croix: On the Savannah, see p. 50 and note for page 50. On the St. Croix, see Alfred D. Stedman, "St. Croix: Who Owns a River?" in *The Nation*, December 21, 1964. It has since gone to court, where the river lost: Save the St. Croix, Inc. v. State of Minnesota, Department of Conservation and Northern States Power Company (memorandum opinion, 2nd Judicial Dist. Court).

Pages 100–101

Adirondack Forest: These details came to me from Stewart M. Ogilvy of the Sierra Club's Atlantic Chapter.

VII: THE EFFLUENT SOCIETY

Page 103

eutrophia and algae: See Odum's *Ecology*, cited in Foreword, and Gladwin Hill, "The Great and Dirty Lakes," *Saturday Review*, October 23, 1965.

Pages 103–104

BOD in Lake Erie: "Last summer [1964], 2,600 square miles of Lake Erie, over one-quarter of the entire lake, were almost without oxygen and unable to support life because of algae and plant growth, fed by pollution from cities and industries." Senator Gaylord Nelson addressing the National Wildlife Federation in Washington, D.C., March 5, 1965. Algae and plants *are* "life," of course, but you get what he means.

Page 105

John Dingell: Mr. Dingell is one of those people who *do* give a damn. See p. 46.

Page 105

Detroit sewage: Gladwin Hill, in *Saturday Review*, mentioned above.

Astrodome: The Astrodome, according to *Facts on File*, carried a price tag of $31.5 million the day it was opened. There have been some costly improvements since.

Pages 105–106

steelmakers: Cleveland's three major steel companies, in response to prodding by the Ohio Water Pollution Control Board, have agreed to quit discharging pickling acid into the Cuyahoga River (and thus into Lake Erie) by 1969. See Louis B. Seltzer's optimistically titled "Cleveland: Saving Lake Erie," *Saturday Review*, October 23, 1965.

Page 107

dumping in the ocean: On the general subject of pollution and the ocean, see Wesley Marx, *The Frail Ocean* (cited in third note for p. 22). Pollution also comes *from* the ocean in a sense, as the accident to the oil tanker *Torrey Canyon* in 1967 made clear. President Johnson in May of 1967 ordered an urgent government study of ways to prevent future pollution of, and subsequently by, the ocean due to oil spillage (*The San Francisco Chronicle,* May 27, 1967). A California water official told the *House Hearings* that he had to stop the United States Navy from dumping garbage and oil into California bays.

Page 108

the fourteenth-century Londoner: See C. W. Griffin, Jr., "America's Airborne Garbage," *Saturday Review,* May 22, 1965.

Page 109

garbage: On New York City, see William Vogt, "Population Patterns and Movements," in Darling and Milton, and *The Wall Street Journal,* October 18, 1961. On foreign cities, William O'Brien's story in *The San Francisco Sunday Examiner and Chronicle,* May 21, 1967.

Pages 109–110

San Francisco garbage: Russ Cone in *The San Francisco Examiner,* April 15, 1967; Harold Gilliam, "The City's Absurd Crisis in Garbage," *The San Francisco Sunday Examiner and Chronicle,* April 30, 1967; *The San Francisco Chronicle,* June 15, 1967.

Page 110

incinerators: On the problems involved in using incinerators, see R. M. E. Diamant, "Refuse Burning for District Heating," *Air Conditioning, Heating and Ventilating,* August, 1968.

Wesley Marx on beaches: The Frail Ocean, mentioned above.

Pages 110–112

pesticides: Although I seem to have collected a small library on DDT (which Senator Nelson is trying to control in Congress, without a lot of success), I am omitting any detailed study of it from this book because it seems to have been pretty well covered elsewhere. The best single source I've seen, however, is not generally available; it's the transcript of Carol A. Yannacone v. H. Lee Dennison, the Suffolk County Mosquito Control Commission and the County of Suffolk. This is a New York suit to stop Suffolk County from spraying DDT, and the record contains a roundup of almost everything that anybody knows about it. The National Audubon Society is backing the suit (Roland Clement of the Society sent me the transcript), and if you live around there *you* ought to back *them.*

Otherwise, since I seem to be recommending Wesley Marx (above) in this chapter, he's also good on DDT.

The quotation from Dr. Ayres is from *Senate Hearings.* For Rachel Carson, see her *Silent Spring* (cited in second note for p. 26).

Page 111

the Mississippi fish: 5,000,000 dead in the Mississippi, 2,000,000 dead at Con Ed's Indian Point: 1963 was a bad year for fish all around.

more pesticides: Memphis calculates that it would cost $80 million to provide adequate treatment for the *sixty million gallons* of raw sewage which it dumps into the Mississippi *every day*. They have no plans for spending it. Irving Dilliard, "St. Louis: One City's Contribution," *Saturday Review*, October 23, 1965.

Page 112

the wrong insecticide: The Argyle story is from John W. Tukey and John L. Buckley, "Problems of Pollution," in *Call of the Vanishing Wild* (cited in fourth note for p. 24).

dieldrin: The Lake Michigan item is from *The San Francisco Sunday Examiner and Chronicle*, December 3, 1967.

Pages 112–113

still more pesticides: California examples are from a roundup in *The San Francisco Sunday Examiner and Chronicle*, October 15, 1967, by George Dusheck.

Johnson on water: The quotation, which dates from Mr. Johnson's days as Senator and Majority Leader, is from his introduction to Senator Robert Kerr's *Land, Wood, and Water* (cited in note for p. 40).

Page 113

Los Angeles "air": Among its other effects, Los Angeles smog—and specifically ozone, which is produced by the action of sunlight on automobile exhaust components—affects athletic performance. The San Marino High School cross-country track team was studied and found, after other factors had been checked, to perform relatively poorly on high-smog days (*Journal of the American Medical Association*, June, 1967, reported in *The New York Times*, June 7, 1967).

sulfur waste: The figure of $300 million is from Edmund K. Faltermeyer, "We Can Afford Clean Air," *Fortune*, November, 1965.

blaming the automobile: It's hard to find an independent automotive engineer, but John Bond, who owns *Road and Track*, is one, and he agrees, as frequent comment in his monthly column makes clear. He also reports on every new development in steam or electric cars; he tends to favor steam, and I'm becoming convinced.

rush-hour drivers: Mr. Griffin's comments are from his *Saturday Review* article cited above.

And I have to note that the Bay Area Rapid Transit System is designed to bring affluent, white suburban types into downtown San Francisco, not to provide poor people with a way to get to where the jobs are, and thus fails one of the primary tests of an urban-area transit system.

Page 114

desalinization: The White-Boulding exchange is in Darling and Milton. Incidentally, seaweed *is* delicious. Especially with beans.

Page 115

the San Joaquin River: I'm grateful to Regional Director William B. Schreeder of the Federal Water Pollution Control Administration for the FWPCA publication, "Effects of the San Joaquin Master Drain on

Water Quality of the San Francisco Bay and Delta," and for the information that California has postponed its part in this operation. The Federal Bureau of Reclamation is going ahead with a piece of it. I'm sorry there isn't space to describe the project—and a number of ecological problems it creates—more fully. Representative Jerome Waldie of California is eloquent on the subject, especially about dumping the polluted water into the Sacramento-San Joaquin delta, which is in his district. See *The San Francisco Chronicle,* May 20, 1967.

salt and alkali flats: See F. Raymond Fosberg, "Restoration of Lost and Degraded Habitats," in Darling and Milton.

Page 116

West Pakistan: The information about West Pakistan is from the same Dr. Fosberg, but from *Senate Hearings.*

radioactive wastes: Congressman Miller's remarks, and his later dialogue with Dr. Hibbard, are from *House Hearings.*

Page 117

thermal regulation: It's *The Frail Ocean* again (second note for p. 22).

Pages 117–118

sewage: Corrosive gases from a sewage treatment plant at Sunnyvale, California, caused damage to an FAA radar facility that served San Francisco Airport, making for some danger to incoming flights. *The San Francisco Chronicle,* September 12, 1968.

Page 118

hepatitis: And tuberculosis, polio, diphtheria, typhoid, and a host of others. See Robert and Leona Train Rienow, "Last Chance for the Nation's Waterways," *Saturday Review,* May 22, 1965. The oyster bootleggers are from the same issue: Ralph McGill, "Atlanta: The Waiting Game."

septic tank seepage: See a paper by James Spear, delivered in September, 1968, at an exposition sponsored by the American Society of Plumbing Engineers. The paper is abstracted in *Air Conditioning, Heating and Ventilating,* a trade journal, in its August, 1968, issue.

Europe: On the Netherlands, J. J. Hopmans, "The Importance of the River Rhine for the Water Economy of the Netherlands," Rhine-Seminar, United Nations Economic Commission for Europe, Geneva, 1963. On France, Report of Sen. M. Maurice Lalloy to the French Senate, No. 155, Paris, 1964.

Page 118

the United States: Dr. Darnell's report is in *Senate Hearings.*

TVA: Norman E. Isaacs (Louisville: Law or License?" in *Saturday Review,* May 22, 1965) details strip-mine rapine, but notes that "TVA has established four Appalachian demonstration sites to prove that reclamation, if not real restoration, can be done in mountain areas." Of course strip mining goes on; see ahead, p. 123.

Page 120

Manhattan rents: From Dr. Ayres (mentioned in note for pages 110–112).

Manhattan air: Charles G. Bennett, "New York: Too Little, Too Late?" in *Saturday Review*, May 22, 1965.

Pages 120–121

Houston: Oveta Culp Hobby, "Houston: The Race Is On," *Saturday Review*, May 22, 1965.

Page 121

"advisory panel": *House Hearings*.

Page 122

nitrous oxides: It should be noted that lowering hydrocarbon emissions in auto exhaust causes nitrous oxide emissions to increase.

Mr. Logan: You remember Olin Mathieson. See p. 59 and first note for that page.

Pages 121–122

industry and ecology: Dr. Cain's remark is in *Senate Hearings*.

Page 123

Appalachia: Paul Good's extremely important article, in *The Nation* for September 4, 1967, is called "Kentucky's Coal Beds of Sedition."

Pages 123–124

Pittsburgh: Ted O. Thackrey, "Pittsburgh: How One City Did It," *Saturday Review*, May 22, 1965.

Page 124

nailing the polluters: James A. Crutchfield, "Water, Washington and Welfare," in *University of Washington Alumnus Magazine*, April, 1967.

North Carolina: Jonathan Daniels, "Raleigh: A Long Look Ahead," *Saturday Review*, May 22, 1965.

Page 125

copper refining: *The San Francisco Chronicle*, September 19, 1967 (from The Associated Press).

Whittier Narrows: The process seems to have been cooked up first at Penn State, according to John Lear, "What Brought It On?" in *Saturday Review*, October 23, 1965.

Pages 125–126

reclamation: "We do recover newsprint," said Congressman Vivian, ". . . but when we do the ink from the newsprint is generally sluiced off chemically and dumped into the stream. Newsprint ink, I might add, is considered to be a very difficult pollutant to handle."

Ruhr Valley: The Ruhrverban is described by Lear in the article mentioned just above.

Page 126

filling the Bay: *The San Francisco Chronicle*, May 20, 1967.

compost in Berkeley: Harold Gilliam, "The City's Absurd Crisis in Garbage," mentioned above.

electric cars: George Dusheck described the Bureau of Mines test in *The San Francisco Sunday Examiner and Chronicle*, February 26, 1967. The Rowan-Ghia possibility in the next paragraph is from John Bond's column in *Road and Track*, October, 1967. The same column, in the issue of August, 1968, reports on a meeting of engineers and California legislators at which the concern about power requirements was voiced. A Rowan-Ghia car was shown at the New York Auto Show in the Spring of 1968, and later in Los Angeles, but not in ready-to-sell shape.

Page 127

steam cars: The CHP testing program is described in the Bond column for August, 1968, cited immediately above. The Chevelle test, involving Belser Developments, Inc., is reported in *The San Francisco Chronicle* for August 9, 1968. Belser, incidentally, built a steam airplane in 1933 which flew successfully.

Mr. Bond's column in November, 1968, describes use of liquid natural gas as an auto fuel and describes some current applications. Both hydrocarbon and nitrous oxide emission is very low, and Bond says that LNG "looks as good as steam for the future."

Department of Natural Resources: Wallace Stegner, "Myths of the Western Dam," *Saturday Review*, October 23, 1965.

Page 128

Senate hearing: Senate Hearings. The same exchange is quoted by Wesley Marx in *The Frail Ocean*, but this time I used it first.

VIII: I GOTTA HAVE MY ROAD

Page 129

roads in National Parks: The quotation from former Secretary of the Interior Ickes is from *The Living Wilderness*, September, 1935.

Page 132

Gatlinburg: The "living memory" is that of Walter A. Damtoft ("What Now for the Wilderness?" in *The National Observer*, January 9, 1967). There's a description of present-day Gatlingburg in "America the Beautiful–Heritage or Honky-Tonk?" in *Changing Times*, November, 1962. There hasn't been any important change since then.

Page 133

the agreement: On the entire legal question, see an analysis by Robert W. Jasperson, general counsel of the Conservation Law Society of America, reprinted in *The Living Wilderness* (see beginning of notes).

Pages 134–135

U.S. 441: On relieving congestion, see the editorial proposals of *The Knoxville Journal*, June 9, 1966.

Page 136

Yosemite: See *Cry California*, Spring, 1967.

park visitors: Fosberg's figure is from his paper, "Restoration of Lost and Degraded Habitats," in Darling and Milton; Damtoft's from *The National Observer*, cited above. The higher figure is for visitors to "Park Service areas outside Washington, D.C." That would include wildlife refuges, national monuments, etc., which probably accounts for the difference. Damtoft also gives 6,400,-000 visits to the Great Smoky Mountains National Park for 1966. The other figures in the next paragraph are also his.

Yellowstone: From Peter Farb, "National Parks: Noisy Crowded

Crisis," in *Call of the Vanishing Wild* (cited in fourth note for p. 24). Farb also writes: "Each fall coyotes leave the high country of Yellowstone for valleys where they are hunted by sheepmen and cattlemen—who get a subsidy for this from the same Department of the Interior that protects these animals during the summer!"

Page 137

all those national forests: There is a map, and an excellent one, in Michael Frome's *Strangers in High Places: The Story of the Great Smoky Mountains* (New York: Doubleday & Company, Inc., 1966). It's reproduced in *The Living Wilderness*.

Page 137

protection from disturbance: The importance of such protection—as opposed to management strictly for recreational purposes—is shown in another context by Dr. Durward Allen, "The Preservation of Endangered Habitats and Vertebrates of North America," in Darling and Milton: "The widespread introduction of nonendemic fishes to streams and lakes of western states is a notable example [of ruining ecosystems by introducing alien forms]. The effects of such 'management,' plus watershed damage and alterations in the nature of waters through damming and diversions, have wrought major changes in aquatic life. From these causes, Miller records the extinction of eight species of fish in the Southwest and considers 31 others to be in jeopardy. These 39 species, he points out, represent nearly 40 per cent of the

known native fishes of western states." "Miller" is Robert R. Miller ("Is Our Native Underwater Life Worth Saving?" *National Parks*, 1963).

See also Dr. Stanley A. Cain, "Biotype and Habitat," in Darling and Milton, on the fragility of ecosystems. Noel D. Eichhorn, in "The Special Role of National Parks" in Darling and Milton, points out that "in places in Great Smoky Mountains National Park the Appalachian Trail has been worn more than six feet wide and more than one foot deep."

for and against the road: The comments of Dr. Bennett and Mr. Smith, and the second quotation from Mr. Hartzog in the next paragraph, are from Damtoft in *The National Observer*, cited above. Mr. Hartzog's quotation about cars is from Harold Gilliam, "The City's Absurd Crisis in Garbage," *The San Francisco Sunday Examiner and Chronicle*, April 30, 1967.

changing national park philosophy: Farb (mentioned above).

the Leopold Committee: Quoted in Fosberg (mentioned above).

Page 139

Park Service principles: Quoted in *The Living Wilderness*.

Yosemite and the California parks: Both figures are from *Cry California*, Spring, 1967.

Wilderness Society statement: Printed in full in *The Living Wilderness*.

Pages 140–141

Udall: Most of the review of Mr. Udall's up-and-down career on these pages is taken from Michael Frome, "The Politics of Conservation," *Holiday*, February, 1967.

Page 140

mineral exploration: The discussion of mineral exploration in national parks, etc., is from a story by William Steif in *The Washington Daily News*, April 12, 1966.

Page 141

wilderness in the Smokies: The two proposals are described in detail, with maps, in *The Living Wilderness*. It also reprints the statement of the Ecological Society of America, which is quoted later and from which much of the material in the next few paragraphs is taken.

National Park Service document: "National Park Service Wilderness Management Criteria," issued as part of the Service's notice of public hearings on the proposed wilderness area in the Smokies.

Page 143

"this new and foreign input": Compare the quotation from Dr. Allen in the "protection from disturbance" note for p. 137.

fence lines in the Great Swamp: Mrs. James Hand showed them to me.

Indian Gap Road: Frome, *Strangers in High Places*, cited above.

Page 144

the record developed: The Great Smokies wilderness hearings were on June 13 (at Gatlinburg) and 15 (at Bryson City), 1966. Representative Taylor testified in Bryson City: "Wilderness should be created for

people's sake, not for birds or animals or trees"—an acceptable politician's way of saying, "I gotta have my road." See Damtoft, article cited above.

IX: DIZZYLAND, U.S.A., INCLUDING ALASKA

Page 145

Mike's ditch: We journalists normally sneer at *The Reader's Digest*, but reporter William Schulz did an outstanding job on Mike's ditch in the June, 1967 issue, which was called to my attention by a *Ramparts* reader. My account is taken from the article, "Mike Kirwan's Big Ditch," which includes a great deal more information than I have provided about the details, and the overall foolishness, of the Lake Erie-Ohio River Canal, and incidentally about several other Engineers' boondoggles.

the role of the Engineers: The Corps of Engineers has been trying to build this silly canal since 1850 or so (the idea first came up under George Washington), the principal idea being cheap transportation for the Ohio industrialists then, as it is today. In 1961 Congress appropriated a quarter of a million dollars for the Corps to study the project's feasibility, which was described as "like having a five-year-old child determine the 'feasibility' of buying an ice cream cone." The Engineers, says Schulz (see note above), "hired a private economist to estimate barge rates that would be practicable for the waterway—then blithely slashed his figures 25 to 35 percent." The consulting firm of Arthur D.

Little, Inc., was called in (for $75,-000) and said the canal wouldn't help the Ohio area much; the Engineers threw the study out. When the Engineers finally reported, to nobody's surprise, that the canal was "feasible," Vigorito said, "Costs are systematically underestimated, benefits fantastically exaggerated. . . . The favorable cost-benefit ratio [see Chapter IV] is obtained through the use of a 3⅛% interest rate. There is absolutely no way the government can borrow money that cheaply, and the Corps knows it."

Railroad economists found that the Corps' estimates had omitted such expenses as the relocation of bridges, the building of access roads, and the construction of loading terminals; had underestimated other costs drastically; and had included things like "recreation benefits" that were totally unsupportable. Undoubtedly some of these charges may be slanted the other way—the railroads are naturally against the canal, and may even have had something to do with the appearance of Schulz's article for all I know (a lot of pro-railroad stuff seems to turn up in the *Digest*)—but the whole project is so typical of the Engineers, and of their relationship to Congressmen like Kirwan, that it scarcely matters.

Page 146
the canal goes on: Probably the only factor operating against it is Kirwan's age. Most Congressmen know the project is a dog; should Kirwan die, the canal may die with him, if work has not progressed too far. This is obviously too drastic a solution for general application.

John Bell Williams: Mr. Williams is no longer in Congress.

Mississippi's share: See Robert Haveman, "The Postwar Corps of Engineers Program in Ten Southern States" in *Essays in Southern Economic Development,* cited in note for p. 52.

California: Samuel E. Wood and Daryl Lembke, "The Federal Threats to the California Landscape," *Cry California,* Spring, 1967.

Kentucky: See Paul Good, "Kentucky's Coal Beds of Sedition," in *The Nation,* September 4, 1967. I have never understood why journalists all over the United States are not more concerned with Kentucky. Bourbon comes from Kentucky.

Page 147
Benicia: The San Francisco Chronicle, May 22, 1967.

tule elk: It's also called the dwarf wapiti. Both examples—Merced County and Owens Valley—are from Ian McTaggart Cowan, "Management, Response and Variety," in Darling and Milton. I'm sorry there isn't room for the story of how Los Angeles got its water rights in Owens Valley; it's a classic story of Engineers, local politicians and developers, pliant Congressmen and an occasional killing, either financial or human.

Stratified Primitive Area: The hearing, in November, 1966, is reported by Damtoft ("What Now for the Wilderness?" in *The National Observer,* January 9, 1967).

Mrs. Ingram and the lumbermen: See p. 58, for instance.

Pages 147–148

dinosaur tracks: *Footprints*, May, 1966.

Page 148

northwestern California: David M. Wilson, "Trees, Earth, Water, and Ecological Upheaval," in *California Law Review*, Vol. 54:1117, 1966.

Isle Royale: Wilderness Society bulletin, January 12, 1967. On fire in Isle Royale, see Cain's observation in first note for p. 40. This passage on the Houghton hearing is not intended to suggest that there ought not to be local hearings on wilderness proposals.

the Federal courts: See, for example, Namekagon Hydro Company *v.* Federal Power Commission, 216 F. 2d 509 (7th Cir. 1954).

Pages 148–149

Cowan: In the paper cited above.

Page 149

Riverton hearing: From Damtoft, cited above.

Gettysburg and Mount Rushmore: These examples are from *Changing Times* ("America the Beautiful—Heritage or Honky-Tonk," November, 1962). Yellowstone is described both there and by Farb ("National Parks: Noisy, Crowded Crisis" in *Call of the Vanishing Wild,* cited in fourth note for p. 24).

northern Wisconsin: Senator Nelson's "legislative memo" to constituents, May 23, 1966.

Page 150

North Cascades Park facts: From "Last Chance for a Northern Cas-

cades National Park," prepared by (and available from) The North Cascades Conservation Council, The Mountaineers, The Sierra Club, and The Federation of Western Outdoor Clubs.

Central and Warinanco Parks: From James Nathan Miller. The item about Westchester County builders is from the same source. So is the quotation from the Prudential man.

Page 151

Hatteras and Hearst: From an address by Roger Allin to the Audubon Society of the Everglades, West Palm Beach, Florida, April 5, 1966.

for and against: In Ralls County, Missouri, the Engineers are constructing Cannon Dam (named for former Representative Clarence Cannon) in order, says a local weekly, "to bring electric power, water, recreation and conservation to this area" (there is already water in the Salt River—it has supported generations of farmers—and of course dams don't conserve anything). The people in the county are up in arms, and have militantly organized—not to stop the dam or to force ecological questions to be considered, but to get the Engineers to pay more, and more equitably, for the land. *Monroe County* [Missouri] *Appeal,* March 30, 1967.

second home colonies: Dennis Durden, "Use of Empty Areas," in Darling and Milton.

what they ought to be against: Robert Haveman, whose study of the cost-benefit methods of the Corps of Engineers was so devastating (see his essay, mentioned above), also demonstrates—using the Southern states as his example—how complex the whole question of costs and benefits can be. Flood control projects, for example, are "of relatively little benefit to the cause of Southern growth," because while production, land values and income may go up, "it appears rather doubtful that the increase in income will be sufficient to bring it into equality with the farmer's potential income off the farm." They also keep the small farmer on the land "while farm productivity is not significantly increased," and thus reduce the economic value of the entire region by keeping the argiculture inefficient. Flood control does move people out of flooded reservoir areas, of course, but it also takes the land out of agriculture entirely.

Flood control projects also tend to protect existing wealth, rather than providing stimuli to new capital accumulation, which is what relatively backward areas like the South need. The local people think it's all good, because for the moment it may provide jobs and because it makes a few small farms safer to work. But in the long run it may hurt an area more than it helps it.

The data about New York fishermen are from *House Hearings*. The St. Lawrence example is from Pierre Danserau, "Ecological Impact and Human Ecology," in Darling and Milton.

Page 152

Rampart Dam: In the main this section follows Paul Brooks in "The Plot to Drown Alaska," *The Atlantic Monthly*, May, 1965. The mention of climate was suggested by Theo-

dore M. Edison in a private communication.

As a writer, I found Brooks's opening sentences irresistible: "As any small boy knows, the presence of running water is a compelling reason to build a dam. Most boys when they grow up turn to other things, but a select few go on to join the U.S. Army Corps of Engineers."

Alaskans: Some white Alaskans don't consider the native Indians to' be "Alaskans" in the same sense, of course, but racism is a lousy excuse for a dam.

Page 153

Arthur D. Little, Inc.: See second note for p. 145 above. These fellows have a bad habit of making realistic surveys and telling the truth, although—being essentially Engineers —they normally only answer the questions they are asked. They're an ideal antidote to the Corps of Engineers' constant figure-juggling, however.

Page 154

ignoring Interior: Representative Ralph Rivers didn't ignore at least the Secretary of the Interior. "I should think," he said, "that Stewart has a few punches coming." After the wildlife report, George Sundborg, administrative assistant to former Senator Gruening, asked, "What can we expect of a Department whose Secretary seems to conceive of his mission as dealing primarily, if not exclusively, with parks and recreation?" One is tempted to introduce Mr. Sundborg to a couple of lovers of the Grand Canyon, and listen to them all talk about Mr. Udall.

plenty of other places: Brooks lists Wood Canyon on the Copper River, the Yukon-Taiya project near Skagway, and "most immediately practical of all," Devil's Canyon on the upper Susitna River between Anchorage and Fairbanks.

the D&R report: The report was by the Development and Resources Corporation.

Page 155

give the money to Alaskans: This will be taken as an ironic suggestion. It's not; it's perfectly serious. Spread the gift over the same number of years as spending on Rampart Dam would be spread, and it makes far more sense. Besides, it will avoid, at least temporarily, the unpleasant fact that "a shot in the arm for the economy" usually means a few people getting rich, the middle-class types gaining a few bucks, and a whole lot of people getting nothing at all.

Point Reyes and Mr. Chase: The *San Francisco Chronicle*, August 12, 1967.

Quinault Valley: *Olympic Park Associates Newsletter*, Summer, 1967.

Cape May Point: From Wesley Marx, *The Frail Ocean* (cited in third note for p. 22). *The San Francisco Sunday Examiner and Chronicle* describes (April 30, 1967) the fate of an $85-million bond issue in California, passed in 1964 to finance purchase of park lands. By 1967, with some of the money still unappropriated and only $25 million actually spent, officials figured California was already out $10 million due to rising costs. The newspaper

said that "procrastination by the Division of Beaches and Parks, red tape-plagued supervision by state finance directors [ironically, former *Chronicle* reporter Hale Champion was finance director during almost all of the period in question], and manipulation by land owners and real estate operators had driven up costs of the property involved tenfold in some cases."

Page 156

Senator Nelson's bill: Writers tend to get hipped on their subjects, but I suspect that Nelson's may be one of the most important bills ever introduced in an elected legislature. Naturally nobody's ever heard of it. If it should ever pass, of course, what passes may not be the same bill.

X: THE MASSIVE FUND-
RAISERS

Page 159

Hualapai reservation: Also spelled Hualapai.

Bridge Canyon Dam: Los Angeles' proposal is reported in *The San Francisco Chronicle*, May 6, 1967. The Engineers, by the way, have taken to referring to Bridge Canyon Dam as "Hualapai Dam," presumably because it doesn't sound so much as though it's being built in a canyon.

Page 160

Central Arizona Project: A massive, federally aided project to divert water from the lower Colorado and the Gila in order to irrigate desert land in central Arizona. *The San*

Francisco Chronicle for August 2, 1968, reports agreement on its final authorization in Congress. See text, page 172.

evaporation: In fact, if you add in Lake Havasu behind Parker Dam, there is almost enough water wasted by evaporation alone—and easily enough water if you include percolation—to replenish the annual loss in Arizona's ground-water table. See pp. 171–172.

Lake Powell percolation: Wallace Stegner, "Myths of the Western Dam," *Saturday Review,* October 23, 1965.

Page 161

the Santa Ynez: Raymond Dasmann, *The Destruction of California,* cited in second note for p. 18.

Pages 161–162

flat alluvial plains: There are in the United States about 2,000 irrigation "dams" which are already "useless impoundments of silt, sand and gravel" (Dr. LaMont Cole in his AAAS speech, cited in third note for p. 26).

Page 162

a hundred years: I confirmed the Sierra Club's claim that the siltation behind the dams and the probable timetable were worked out by geologists in the U.S. Geological Survey, which—like the National Park Service and the Bureau of Reclamation —is in the Department of the Interior. I also confirmed that the Geological Survey people were told by Interior to shut up about their findings. I asked Assistant Secretary Cain about it—gambling on my personal feeling that as an outstanding

ecologist he doesn't like the dams —and he neither confirmed nor denied it. He did say that in any organization where there is internal disagreement, particularly in government, the usual course is to fight it out inside the department, settle on a position, and maintain an unbroken front to the outside world. Apparently, in this case, it would mean keeping some of the most important facts from the public.

Page 164

hydroelectric dams: See Stegner, article cited above.

Page 165

Boulding: Spontaneous remarks recorded in Darling and Milton.

Nicholson: Spontaneous remarks recorded in Darling and Milton.

The Household Gazette: It's dated June, 1967. "This area" is, of course, the area near Bryn Mawr, Pennsylvania, which is some distance from the Grand Canyon, though very near Philadelphia.

Page 166

revealing the shoreline: An anti-dam newspaper advertisement by the Sierra Club asked whether we ought to flood the Sistine Chapel so tourists could get nearer the ceiling. It would be an apt analogy only if Michelangelo's best work were on the walls, down near the floor.

For an intensely personal impression of the meaning of the Engineers' proposal by a man who actually *walked* through the Grand Canyon, see Colin Fletcher, *The*

Man Who Walked Through Time (New York: Alfred A. Knopf, 1968).

Page 167

Commissioner Dominy: From Stegner article mentioned above. So is the quotation that follows. The Commissioner's remarks make my reference to Chartres, and Dr. Boulding's religious explanations, seem a little less farfetched.

Page 168

Morris Udall and the Sierra Club: The Sunday Ramparts, January 1–14, 1967. The Assistant Secretary was Joseph Barr. I wrote the story. The tax exemption was allegedly lifted because of a $10,000 Sierra Club newspaper ad against the dams. The Central Arizona Project Association, a private, tax-exempt group, had admitted, at the time, to spending $74,065.02 to get Congress to authorize the dams. The state of Arizona, of course, has used actual tax money for that purpose.

Page 169

how many dams?: The outgoing Secretary of the Interior—Congressman Udall's brother—has so far been unable to make up his mind whether he's for two dams, one dam or no dam. Or rather, he *has* made up his mind—several times.

California dreamin': Director of Water Resources William Gianelli is quoted, and Governor Reagan's position is reported, in *The San Francisco Chronicle,* May 27, 1967.

Pages 169–170

Governors Love and others: The San Francisco Chronicle, May 6, 1967.

Page 171

Bear and White: The dialogue is recorded in Darling and Milton.

$500 million a year: The facts about Arizona's water and its agriculture are from Bill Werley, "Phoenix; Drought Underground," *Saturday Review,* October 23, 1965.

Page 172

automobiles in the Northwest: The only organization willing to pay such freight charges is the United States Government, either directly or by subsidizing airlines. Boeing is in Seattle.

Senator Jackson's proviso: The San Francisco Chronicle, August 2, 1968.

at our expense: The Metropolitan Water District of Southern California sells water for less than it pays for it, and the difference is made up in real estate taxes (Crutchfield).

Page 173

Florida: See Chapter III generally. On canal C-111, p. 41. On the shrimp industry, the paper "C-111," described at the beginning of the notes. The work being done on tracing the cycle of the Tortugas shrimp was described to me by Bill Odum and Nancy Maynard at the University of Miami Marine Institute, and I was shown the agricultural development of Florida, in person and on maps, by a number of concerned individuals in the area. Additional details about the shrimp industry are in Roger Allin (note for p. 44).

economics of the Everglades: Roger Allin, address to the Audubon

Society of the Everglades, West Palm Beach, Florida, April 5, 1966.

Page 174

Representative Bennett: The statement is in *Senate Hearings*.

estuaries: Wesley Marx, *The Frail Ocean*, cited in third note for p. 22.

Norwood: From *Senate Hearings*.

Page 175

oysters: William Vogt, "Population Patterns and Movements," in Darling and Nelson.

pollution costs: Edmund K. Faltermeyer, "We Can Afford Clean Air," *Fortune*, November, 1965.

XI: THE RUBBER JETPORT

Page 176

the Secretary's book: Stewart Udall, *The Quiet Crisis* (New York: Holt, Rinehart and Winston, 1963). Even in the Rocky Mountains there have been important changes "since the Indians first came," but let's not quibble.

Page 177

water retention basin: Even in drought years, water is always visible from the entire 500-foot length of that boardwalk we were standing on. A North Jersey Conservation Foundation fact sheet, dated January, 1967, quotes a December, 1966, statement by Robert A. Roe, who heads the schizophrenically named New Jersey Department of Conservation and Economic Development: "Aside from any other reason, Great Swamp must be kept in its wild state so it can provide waters vital to the flow of the Passaic River which rises there. . . . Paving

the swamp would not only reduce the Passaic, but would destroy recharging of underground water supplies drawn from wells in the area."

Page 178

the jetport threat: Another local organization, the Jersey Jetport Association, came into being at about this time and joined the fight. It still exists.

Page 179

the Dodge Wilderness Area: See ahead, page 186. There have been several proposals for designation of a wilderness area in the Pine Barrens farther south (see John McPhee, "The Pine Barrens," *The New Yorker*, November 25 and December 2, 1967), but none of the Barrens is Interior Department or Forest Service land.

Refuge Director Tom McAndrew: McAndrew has since been replaced by George W. Gavutis, Jr.

a hub and felly factory: A felly is the rim, or part of the rim, of a spoked wheel. It's learning about things like fellies and rip-rap and four kinds of club moss that makes journalism such a rewarding profession.

Page 181

Governor Hughes: In 1962 Hughes commended the Great Swamp Committee's project "to secure lands in the Great Swamp of Morris County for preservation as open space and wildlife habitat." At the refuge dedication in 1964, he took credit for "some part in the achievement," and said, "I have not altered my conviction that the location of a jetport in the Great Swamp would be unwise. And . . . I have no doubt about the soundness of my decision to resist the encroachments upon this magnificent natural tract" (fact sheet of North Jersey Conservation Foundation, mentioned above). The doubts appeared in time for Ronald Sullivan to report them in *The New York Times* for December 23, 1966. "I do have regrets that I took this pledge," Hughes said. "I think I did it hurriedly."

William Vogt: "Population Patterns and Movements," in Darling and Milton.

Page 182

stretching the jetport: So far as I know, the proposed acquisition by Port Authority Engineers of several thousand phantom acres, to be squeezed somehow into the landscape, was first described in a letter to the Authority, dated January 20, 1967, from William Bartlett of Riverdale, New York.

Page 183

part if not all: You can't tell from the Port Authority map exactly where the "boundaries" of Green Village are.

Pages 183–184

Senator Javits and Mr. Bakke: *The New York Times,* December 22, 1966.

Page 185

Theodore Edison: The hearings were on February 17, 1967; Mr. Edison's statement was submitted in writing. Lest I sound too much as though I have my own subsidy from the Association of American Railroads, let me hurry to get in my opinion that a lot of the "defeat" of the railroads is the railroads' own fault.

Page 186

the new wilderness area: Officially called the Great Swamp National Wildlife Refuge Wilderness, it came into being on September 30, 1968, and is described in detail in *The New York Times,* October 3, 1968. The larger acreage follows a proposal, and some effort, by The Wilderness Society.

avoiding the Great Swamp: No amount of *chutzpah* will help me here; my first *Ramparts* article came out two weeks too late for me to take credit, and anyway I didn't mention the Great Swamp until the following month.

. . . by March, 1967: The items in this paragraph are from *The Hunterdon County Democrat* [Flemington, New Jersey], March 23, 1967, except for the Somerset County freeholders. That's from *The Plainfield* [New Jersey] *Courier-News,* April 4, 1967 (but it happened in March). The Readington Township Committee also passed a resolution against a jetport in the Great Swamp, and Somerset's resolution was meant to include it.

the Trenton conference: *The Plainfield Courier-News,* April 1, 1967, and *The Hunterdon Review* [Whitehouse Station, New Jersey], April 4, 1967.

Page 187

"the press pointed out . . .": This and the Associated Press story that follows are from *The Plainfield Courier-News,* April 5, 1967, which

ran the AP story under a front-page banner: SOLBERG SEEN JETPORT CHOICE.

Page 188

a day later: *The Plainfield Courier-News,* April 6, 1967, again on the front page.

the people of Hunterdon: According to the same news story cited just above, there are 63,000 people in Hunterdon County. The 1960 census gives 77,500 for Somerset, but it gives only 54,000 for Hunterdon. If Hunterdon has gone up 17 percent since 1960, Somerset probably has too. And megalopolis may be on its way, jetport or no.

H. Mat Adams: *The Plainfield Courier-News,* April 5, 1967. There is, incidentally, a state park at Round Valley-Spruce Run. Robert Roe, who now has Mr. Adams' old job, is using it for a pilot program on making recreational areas more accessible to older citizens and the handicapped—with, for instance, boat ramps for people in wheelchairs (*Footprints,* February, 1967). See Chapter V.

Page 189

Hughes-Boyd: *The New York Times,* June 7, 1967. On the Pine Barrens and why ecologists would be unhappy, see McPhee in *The New Yorker,* cited in second note for p. 179.

changing the patterns: The Engineers never considered it, but an anti-jetport group, the Hunterdon-Somerset Jetport Association, did. *The Hunterdon Review,* April 4, 1967.

Public Service: This information was provided by Theodore Edison.

Solberg again: See *The New York Times,* August 19, 1968.

Page 190

airports in the ocean: *The San Francisco Sunday Examiner and Chronicle,* September 10, 1967. I don't know how Wesley Marx missed this one.

supervisors: See p. 110.

the 707s: *The New York Times,* June 7, 1967. As of that date Boeing had delivered a thousand jet airliners of various types, including 436 707s. The 1,000 planes cost somebody $5,519 billion.

Page 191

the SST: The section that follows is taken from Karl Ruppenthal, "The Supersonic Transport: Billion-Dollar Dilemma," *The Nation,* May 22, 1967, and two long stories—one by George Dusheck and one by George Lardner, Jr.—in *The San Francisco Sunday Examiner and Chronicle,* June 18, 1967. Ruppenthal wrote two more articles in subsequent issues of *The Nation* (May 29 and June 19), including some of the same information and much more.

The Concorde *and speed:* It has turned out that, because they're to be built of aluminum, both the *Concorde* and a Soviet SST, the TU-144, are stuck at 1,450 m.p.h. Faster speeds and the resultant friction make it too hot for aluminum. Boeing's SST, using titanium, is supposed to be able to do 1,800 m.p.h. Except that *it* has turned out to be too heavy (25 tons too heavy), and the "swing wing" design with which Boeing beat Lockheed will now, it appears, be abandoned, since Boeing is out of government money for the moment. See *The New York Times,* September 14, 1968, and *The Economist* [London], September 21, 1968.

Page 192

bigger jetport: It has been suggested in the San Francisco Bay Area that San Francisco and Oakland both extend their runways into the Bay until they meet—thus achieving an SST airport and another Bay crossing in one fell Engineers' swoop.

Page 194

the restless condors: The Oakland [California] *Tribune,* June 21, 1967.

sparsely populated land areas: I remember that back in the 1950s the Atomic Energy Commission used to brush off people who complained about fallout from Nevada atomic tests by replying that all the fallout was over sparsely populated areas. Apparently your importance, or your rights, or both, increase when you huddle more closely together.

the determined Engineers: In Great Britain, *The New Scientist* editorializes (March 30, 1967): ". . . the determination to get the *Concorde* aloft whether or not its noise is humanly tolerable is . . . the outcome of technological progress outstripping society's capacity to judge what is best for it." I disagree. Except for those involved in the project, everyone who knows anything about the SST has the capacity to judge that it's a dog, and most have done so. The problem is that only a few people give a damn either way—and the ones on the other side have the money, the or-

ganization and the single-mindedness. They will get rich, and they sincerely don't care what happens to the rest of us, to the environment or to the future; and those few who do care talk themselves out of it when their own profits are involved.

Page 195

Everglades jetport: Private communication in November, 1968, from Les Line, editor of *Audubon.*

XII: KILL A BABY THIS WEEK

Page 197

Tikopia: Originally described by Dr. Raymond Firth in *Tikopia Ritual and Belief* (Boston: Beacon Press, 1967), the population control methods of the Tikopians are retold by Robert and Leona Train Rienow in *Moment in the Sun,* cited in third note for p. 24. Whether the patriarch's authority works "because" he controls the land or he controls the land "because" he has the authority is one of those anthropologists' questions at which a physicist would smile.

"we do not kill our babies as directly": Except, of course, in Vietnam and Algeria and places like that.

10,000 a day: Quoted by the Reinows (mentioned above) as a 1965 United Nations figure. It appears to be the estimate still in use; it also appears in the *Encyclopaedia Britannica Yearbook* for 1967. In articles prepared for a magazine section in *The Daily Californian* for April 2, 1968 (that's the campus newspaper of the University of California at Berkeley), biochemist Dr.

Nick Hetzer uses a figure of 3,000,-000 starvations a year, and population expert Dr. Paul Ehrlich uses 3,500,000. The latter figure is just about 10,000 a day.

Page 198

"greenhouse effect": See p. 28.

you're a weed: The simile is from Wallace Stegner, "What Ever Happened to the Great Outdoors?" in *Saturday Review*, May 22, 1965.

more than two children: The mind of anyone with three or more children tends to reject this. I know, because I'm guilty too: I have four. The youngest two are both good-looking and brilliant, and I not only love them very much but am convinced that the world will be a better place for their existence. Of course I wouldn't trade them (even on the most coldly rational grounds) for two babies doomed anyway to ignorance and disease and bare subsistence in Paraguay or Kurdistan.

But there is another question about comparing my fifth child—who does not exist and whose birth I can prevent—with the life of one such child who will be born anyway. The basic question is as simple as that, and is not less true because I understood it relatively late. If a good many of us don't understand it sooner, then *our* children, or theirs, are *equally* doomed to ignorance and disease and bare subsistence.

Even two children are too many to keep the population of the United States from expanding, at least for a while—because there are more mothers than there have ever been before. But you start somewhere.

"We must love one another," wrote W. H. Auden, "or die." It's still true, but now we also have to be careful about it or die anyway.

Page 199

Moment in the Sun: Cited in third note for p. 24.

Stegner quotation: From *Saturday Review* article cited above.

three lifetimes: The noted film maker, Felix Greene, and I were radio commentators on the same station fifteen years ago or so. He used this method of measuring historic time once; I thought it made much more sense than counting in decades or centuries, and it has stuck with me ever since.

Page 200

you can't predict, but: All from Philip M. Hauser, "The Population Explosion—U.S.A.," in *Population Bulletin*, August, 1960. The piece was originally a paper given at a national conference on "A New Look at the Population Crisis," in Dallas, May 19, 1960.

the 1967 birth rate: The *San Francisco Sunday Examiner and Chronicle*, March 3, 1968.

your end of the boat: Dr. Ehrlich is quoted in *The San Francisco Sunday Examiner and Chronicle*, November 26, 1967.

Pages 200–201

Waggoner quotation: From spontaneous remarks recorded in Darling and Milton. Raymond Dasmann said very much the same thing about "land affluence" in the same conversation.

Page 201

pills and IUDs: On some of the problems of "persuasion and education," see Dr. LaMont Cole's AAAS talk (cited in third note for p. 26). It's worth remembering that in 1968 we found ourselves unable to feed the starving in Biafra–for political reasons.

paving over the plants: On the diminishing oxygen supply, see Cole (third note for p. 26). That note itself includes Dr. Cole's statement about potassium and phosphorus, and p. 26 explains the nitrogen cycle. On tritium in the ground water, W. J. Frank, "Characteristics of Nuclear Explosives," in the Atomic Energy Commission's *Engineering with Nuclear Explosions* (1964).

Page 203

Ian Nairn: Reprinted in *The San Francisco Sunday Examiner and Chronicle*, September 10, 1967.

a favor for the world: Stegner in *Saturday Review*, mentioned above.

Page 204

black faces in national parks: Raymond Dasmann, "Preserving Open Spaces in Urban Areas," in *Call of the Vanishing Wild*.

stress on vacation: The discussion is in Darling and Milton.

Page 205

citing the figure: ". . . the size of a city, we say, is beyond control, so the best we can do is to adapt political institutions to the facts. I am reminded of Rousseau's comment on Grotius, that his invariable mode of reasoning was always to establish right from fact. One might employ a more logical method, Rousseau remarked, but not one more favorable to tyrants." Robert A. Dahl, "The City in the Future of Democracy," *American Political Science Review*, December, 1967.

Morris County: See the beginning of these notes.

Pages 205–207

Farness: From "Resources Planning *versus* Regional Planning" in Darling and Milton.

XIII: WHO NEEDS INTERSTATE 20?

Page 208

Wisconsin: Senator Gaylord Nelson, "If We Are to Save America," *Better Camping*, April, 1966.

California bond issue: See *The San Francisco Sunday Examiner and Chronicle*, April 30, 1967 (third note for p. 155).

Huntington, Sacramento and East Concord: All from Senator Nelson (note just above).

Page 209

Mendham Township: Footprints, April, 1966.

Century City: The San Francisco Examiner, May 28, 1967. You might compare this true engineering-mentality story from *The San Francisco Chronicle*, July 21, 1967: "The [state highway] commission had just received a staff report revealing that $10 million is spent annually on freeway landscaping and maintenance–including $1.5 million for watering. It was that $1.5 million for watering oleanders, etc., that startled [commissioner Vernon J.] Cristina the most. 'Some of the most fantastic things in the world are being done with plastics these days,' he said—noting that plastic flowers or other forms wouldn't require watering." I regret to report that Mr. Cristina is a *northern* Californian.

the Heinzmans: Marian Sorensen, "Conservation—What You Can Do," in *Call of the Vanishing Wild* (cited in fourth note for p. 24).

Page 211

Mrs. Tatton: *The Hunterdon Review*, April 4, 1967. For the Trenton conference, see p. 186.

the California Water Plan: See *The San Francisco Chronicle*, May 20 and 22, 1967.

"quick clay": See *Water Control News*, published by Commerce Clearing House, and—on the same geological phenomenon applied to San Francisco Bay—the *Chronicle* for May 8, 1967.

Page 212

water shortage: It should be noted that water-use regulation far more stringent than any ever applied in Los Angeles has not driven many people out of New York City. And at the moment Palm Springs, California, uses 1,000,000 gallons of water a year on the greens of its golf course.

Page 213

David Rockefeller: *The San Francisco Examiner*, February 24, 1967.

Santa Fe and the Bay: *The San Francisco Chronicle*, March 12, 1968. A group of conservationists has taken the state of California to court in an attempt to stop another Bay fill project, involving some tidelands adjoining San Mateo County, the Leslie Salt Company, and the state's rights to the land. The state is fighting on the side of the Bay fillers (private communication from the Alameda Conservation Association, March, 1968).

Bay Area population capacity: Wesley Marx, *The Frail Ocean*, cited in third note for p. 22.

a comprehensive plan: The BCDC has come up with its plan, and nobody likes it but Engineers and profiteers (it passed 13–10). It provides that developers may fill parts of the Bay if they improve the shoreline and give "new public access." It allows fill for "Bay-oriented commercial recreation and water-related public assembly"—and gives as examples "restaurants, specialty shops and hotels." The legislature of California now has the ball. *The San Francisco Chronicle*, September 20 and 21, 1968.

Okamoto and Liskamm: *The San Francisco Chronicle*, February 23, 1967, anticipated the report—correctly.

Page 214

NAWAPA: *Water Control News*, published by Commerce Clearing House.

the sea-level canal: Cole's AAAS speech (third note, p. 26). I have deliberately omitted such troublesome but important questions as the rights of the people of Panama.

Pages 215–216

Raynes: From *House Hearings.* Re General Motors and the engine, see first note for p. 99, on auto exhaust systems. State Senator Nicholas Petris of Oakland, California, has introduced a bill to make ownership of two vehicles, both powered by internal combustion engines, illegal after a set future date, and he is considering introduction of precisely the bill I used as an example (except for a later deadline), although I didn't know it when the passage was written. There are, of course, exceptions to the industry pattern. California's kelp industry, on its own initiative, voluntarily pays increased fees to the state's fish and game department, from which the industry leases the kelp forests, in return for which the department strictly enforces harvesting regulations (Wesley Marx, *The Frail Ocean,* cited in third note for p. 22).

Pages 216–217

the interstate highway system: Figures are from the Bureau of Public Roads pamphlet, "America's Lifeline: Federal Aid for Highways," which ought to lead to a joke about being in deep water and strangling on your lifeline. The Rhode Island comparison is from Sidney Z. Searles, "Bulldozers at Your Door," *National Civic Review,* July, 1963, and *Reader's Digest,* September, 1963. On oxygen production, see p. 201.

Page 217

highway law: The legal discussion is from Roger Tippy, "Review of Route Selections for the Federal Aid Highway Systems," *University of Montana Law Review,* Vol. 27, No. 2.

Page 218

the eviction: The New York Times, May 17, 1967.

Atlanta: See *The New York Times,* January 29, 1967, which also mentions Philadelphia. On New Orleans, see *The San Francisco Sunday Examiner and Chronicle,* August 27, 1967. Lawrence Halprin—interviewed in *Science and Technology,* November, 1967—was asked to look at the New Orleans waterfront site and to testify in a hearing there. "I went down," he said. "I looked at it. And it was worse than I thought it was going to be. I came back and I said: No matter what happens, if putting it on the waterfront is the only solution, then don't build it." "Not at all?" asked Halprin's interviewer. Replied Halprin: "That's not a thought an engineer accepts easily, is it?"

Pages 218–219

San Francisco: Harold Gilliam, "Stupidity of Single Purpose Planning," *The San Francisco Sunday Examiner and Chronicle,* September 10, 1967.

Pages 219–220

progress in Manhattan: Mr. Palmer is quoted in *The San Francisco Sunday Examiner and Chronicle,* November 26, 1967. If I ever write another book, I'm going to get a single typewriter key that produces the full name of my hometown Sunday paper, complete with underlining.

Page 220

air rights: C. W. Griffin, Jr., "America's Airborne Garbage," *Saturday Review,* May 22, 1965.

rapid transit systems: Mayor Alfonso J. Cervantes of St. Louis is a transit-system fan and notes with some rue that "our transit system represents an investment of $25 million, yet a new area expressway is a public investment of at least $750 million or 30 times as much" (*The San Francisco Sunday Examiner and Chronicle,* April 16, 1967). Gilliam (mentioned above) is for Golden Gate Bridge buses, but there's a serious question whether Marin County commuters would use them unless forced to as suggested in the text. The Moses-Williamson study was reported in *House Hearings* by Henry W. Riecken of the Social Science Research Council.

XIV: CHILDREN OF SUN AND GRASS

Page 222

Freeman: The Secretary's statements are from a San Francisco press conference, covered by Charles Howe for *The San Francisco Chronicle,* February 23, 1967. Putting industries on arable land while world population grows is, of course, as irresponsible as putting them on filled-in estuaries, but there is marginal land even in farm-belt areas, and Secretary Freeman's suggestion is still valid with that qualification.

discouraging California immigration: Raymond F. Dasmann, "Man in North America," in Darling and Milton.

Page 223

the ecologists' failing: Boulding, spontaneous remarks; in Darling and Milton.

Page 224

the asphalt desert: Robert A. Dahl, "The City in the Future of Democracy," *American Political Science Review,* December, 1967.

Gallup poll: Details are in an American Institution of Public Opinion release, April 24, 1966. Of course the poll may, in part, reflect the fear of whites in some cities that blacks are "taking over."

experimental city: For Dr. Spilhaus' suggestion, see *Senate Hearings.* On its planning stage, *The San Francisco Sunday Examiner and Chronicle,* August 6, 1967.

Page 225

planning abroad: Theodore Osmundson, "Lessons in Urban Planning from Europe," *The San Francisco Sunday Examiner and Chronicle,* July 30, 1967.

Pages 225–226

Cosmopolitas: Harold Gilliam's column, *The San Francisco Sunday Examiner and Chronicle,* August 6, 1967.

Page 226

the right size for a library: Dahl (see note above). The article cites a number of works by Otis Dudley Duncan.

cooperative museums and base-ball teams: Wilbur R. Thompson, *A Preface to Urban Economics* (Baltimore: Johns Hopkins Press, 1965). On this whole general subject, see also Paul and Percival Goodman, *Communitas* (Chicago: University of Chicago Press, 1947), and Jane Jacobs, *The Death and Life of Great American Cities* (New York: Random House, Inc., 1961).

Pages 227–228

Columbia, Maryland: The Rouse letter is in *Senate Hearings*.

Page 228

the Nile basin: Alan Moorehead, *The Blue Nile* (New York: Harper and Row, 1962). Cole told the AAAS (third note, p. 26) that since the 1902 dam at Aswan was built, Nile basin soils have deteriorated through salinization (see p. 116), and that the new Aswan High Dam "may well prove to be the ultimate disaster for Egypt."

butterflies: Russell Train, "Challenge to Youth," an address to the National Youth Conference on Natural Beauty and Conservation, Washington, D.C., June 29, 1966.

Pages 228–229

zoning: Eugene P. Odum, review of *Waste Management and Control*, a report to the Federal Council for Sciences and Technology by the Committee on Pollution, Athelstan Spilhaus, chairman (which is Publication 1400, National Academy of Sciences, National Research Council). Review published in *Scientist and Citizen*, November–December, 1966. See also Odum (address at University of North Carolina, cited in first note for p. 71).

Page 229

landscape zoning: John Buckley's statement is from *House Hearings*, and Raynes' is from *Senate Hearings*. The concept would have to be applied, at least for some time to come, to preserve farmlands (such as those now covered by urban sprawl near San Jose, California, or those long since buried under Detroit) as well as estuaries and other valuable areas. See Donald A. Williams and Peter Farb, "Our Farmlands Are Shrinking," *Coronet*, May, 1957 (which was, you'll note, some time ago).

Page 230

Dasmann: Paper presented to the 11th Pacific Science Congress, University of Tokyo, 1966.

Stegner: From "What Ever Happened to the Great Outdoors?" in *Saturday Review*, May 22, 1965.

Pages 230–231

the environmental way of thinking: Associate Professor Richard Sill, a University of Nevada physicist, has put together the fact that fluorescent light puts out a considerable energy in the ultraviolet range and the fact that some humans can "see" ultraviolet light: "I tested a girl in the optics laboratory the other day who can go down to 3,100 Angstrom units. This girl had perpetual headaches. Evidence suggests that as we deal with the younger and younger age group, we are dealing with a larger and larger percentage of those whose crystalline lenses will pass ultraviolet light. I ask, then, what happens when we get to the place of building elementary schools lighted, if you will, totally with fluorescent lights?" From *Senate Hearings*.

Page 231

Huxley: From his introduction to Lorenz, *King Solomon's Ring*, cited in first note for p. 22. Huxley is referring to Lorenz' pioneer discoveries, which Lorenz himself says took place in the Altenberg district of Austria in "an island of utter wildness," an "oasis of virgin nature," which was "protected against civilization and agriculture."

the sea elephant: Marx, *The Frail Ocean*, cited in third note for p. 22.

Cantlon: In *Senate Hearings*.

Page 232

Odum: Address at University of North Carolina (first note, p. 71).

INDEX OF NAMES

[Subject index will be found on page 292]

INDEX OF SUBJECTS